D1565124

DRAMATIC
ENCOUNTERS

DRAMATIC ENCOUNTERS

The Jewish Presence
in
Twentieth-Century American Drama,
Poetry, and Humor
and the
Black-Jewish Literary Relationship

LOUIS HARAP

*Published in cooperation with the
American Jewish Archives*

FOREWORD BY JACOB RADER MARCUS

Contributions in Ethnic Studies, Number 20

GREENWOOD PRESS
New York • Westport, Connecticut • London

Library of Congress Cataloging-in-Publication Data

Harap, Louis.
  Dramatic encounters.

  (Contributions in ethnic studies, ISSN 0196-7088 ;
no. 20)
  "Published in cooperation with the American Jewish
Archives."
  Bibliography: p.
  Includes index.
  1. Jews in literature—United States. 2. American
literature—20th century—History and criticism.
3. American drama—Jewish authors—History and
criticism. 4. American fiction—Afro-American
authors—History and criticism. 5. Jewish wit
and humor—History and criticism. 6. Afro-Americans—
Relations with Jews. 7. United States—Race relations.
I. American Jewish Archives. II. Title. III. Series.
PS173.J4H294 1987   810'.9'35203924   86-29401
ISBN 0-313-25388-9 (lib. bdg. : alk. paper)

Library of Congress Catalog Card Number: 86-29401
ISBN: 0-313-25388-9
ISSN: 0196-7088

First published in 1987

Greenwood Press, Inc.
88 Post Road West
Westport, Connecticut 06881

Printed in the United States of America

The paper used in this book complies with the
Permanent Paper Standard issued by the National
Information Standards Organization (Z39.48-1984).

10 9 8 7 6 5 4 3 2 1

Contents

Series Foreword

The Contributions in Ethnic Studies series focuses on the problems that arise when people with different cultures and goals come together and interact productively or tragically. The modes of adjustment or conflict are various, but usually one group dominates or attempts to dominate the other. Eventually some accommodation is reached: the process is likely to be long and, for the weaker group, painful. No one scholarly discipline monopolizes the research necessary to comprehend these intergroup relations. The emerging analysis, consequently, is of interest to historians, social scientists, psychologists, psychiatrists, and scholars in communication studies.

For centuries Jews everywhere have been the victims of prejudice and discrimination while preserving many of the main tenets of their culture and religious beliefs. In these three volumes the treatment of Jews in fiction, serious journals, drama, and poetry by Jewish and non-Jewish authors in the United States during the twentieth century is vividly portrayed. In each case, a concise, arresting, critical summary of the story, plot, or theme follows the salient biographical details concerning the writer himself or herself. The reader thus either can nostalgically recall a book or character he once read or knew, or else he can be stimulated to pursue for the first time a literary experience by dipping or plunging into the publications of a popular or scarcely known writer.

We have in these pages an opportunity to view the impact of changes within American society upon the depiction of Jewish characters and indeed of anti-Semitism among gentile, Black and Jewish authors. In the earlier part of the period conditions in the slums of East Side New York City, for example, impelled many Jews to join the forces supporting unions and the American version of socialism. Then the rise of Nazi ideology in the 1930s and later the depictions of the Holocaust caused Jews and non-Jews alike to appraise anew their own Jewish stereotypes. In addition, as readers we are challenged by a philosophical and social issue that still confronts Jews as well as other minority ethnic groups: should or how can we choose between the now less popular melting-pot objective for these groups, or have we really come to tolerate or favor cultural pluralism?

Louis Harap emphasizes quite rightly what he calls the problems of acculturation and assimilation of Jews as described in the literature and by the writers of the period, particularly when he examines differences between older and younger generations of Jews and also when he analyzes alienation generally in our society. The fiction and other literary creations, therefore, have never been wholly fictitious; perhaps more than scholarly tomes they depict the struggles and the satisfactions of Jews as well as unfriendly and friendly appraisals by other Americans. Simultaneously, moreover, they influence the views of a very large public. We are thus offered a most compelling documentation of the significant interaction between literature and what we too easily call reality: accurately or not, literature both reflects and affects us, or at least some of us.

Leonard W. Doob

Foreword

There are minds which insist on literature as pure artifice, and there are minds which see in literature a reflection not only of literary tradition but also of history and sociology. Louis Harap belongs—has long belonged —to this latter company. Literary merit is not the sole value he seeks when he confronts a work of the imagination. He looks for social value as well. It is important to discern and appreciate in him an accomplished social analyst of literary effort, a scholar who tends to concentrate unfailingly on the (not always so clearly discernible) nexus between a work of literature and the social or psychosocial context in which it was composed.

Dr. Harap is not a literary critic or literary theorist. He is an historian and draws on literature for his work as an historian. He is, more emphatically, a social historian, an historian devoted to the study of social reality with literary expression as a major instrument for his research.

Now to say this is not to suggest the lack in Dr. Harap's work of a *Tendenz* or ideological preference. His work does evince bias and offers a left-of-center perspective—but he is certainly not to be thought of as an ideologue in his judgments. It is Dr. Harap's sensitivity to social experience, not any ideological commitment he may have, that gives his thought a large interest for those concerned, as I am, to find in American-Jewish literary expression some index to how Jews have found their way through the labyrinths of American life.

What Dr. Harap offers in these three new volumes are erudite, forthright, incisive discussions of fiction and other works, discussions which are consistently "socioliterary"—that is, art-for-the-sake-of-art, the purely esthetic, is never his goal or preoccupation. No, it is something else, awareness of the socioeconomic and psychic context, which governs his understanding of the stories and novels he examines so intelligently.

I think worth noting also Dr. Harap's readiness to consider women writers and women characters a major factor in the web of literary expression documenting American-Jewish life. It is impressive to see him calling our attention to Clara Yavner in Abraham Cahan's 1905 novel *The White Terror and the Red*; Clara, he observes, "is among the distinctly new figures . . . in all American fiction" and is "of special interest because she anticipates the new place of the Jewish woman in radical fiction of the first decades of the century—the courageous, effective, able Jewish woman labor organizer and socialist." Dr. Harap notes with approval James Oppenheim's incorporation into his 1911 novel *The Nine-Tenths* of a "recognition that the waistmakers' strike in 1911 had brought forward perhaps for the first time in the United States the 'New Woman,' the active and heroic participant in labor struggles and the struggle for a better world." The illumination of Jewish women by non-Jewish writers is not overlooked. He takes into account, for instance, Albert Edwards (*né* Arthur Bullard), who in 1913 published *Comrade Yetta*, a novel about Jewish radicalism, and speculated about Jewish "single-mindedness and consistency of purpose" in contrast to "Anglo-Saxon . . . compromise and confused issues."

In general, it may be said, Dr. Harap is fully and commendably alive to the documentary potential, the documentary implications, of fiction by non-Jewish writers. He is as much interested in Judeophobic writers like Frank Norris, Owen Wister, Edith Wharton, Jack London, and David Graham Phillips as he is in more sympathetic fictionists like Mark Twain, William Dean Howells, O. Henry, Thomas Nelson Page, and Dorothy Canfield Fisher. He understands that, "to achieve a comprehensive picture of the status of the Jew in our literature . . . it is not enough to study how the Jewish writer regarded his own Jewishness." He wants us also to "look at the way . . . non-Jewish writers depicted the Jew and met the challenge of anti-Semitism." As Dr. Harap points out, "the responses varied widely."

Readers may rely on Dr. Harap for formidable learning, and also, it is a pleasure to add, for a most accessible expository style. It is an honor to help bring these volumes to print; they will in time to come, I am confident, be recognized for the classics they are.

Jacob Rader Marcus
American Jewish Archives
Hebrew Union College–Jewish Institute of Religion
Cincinnati, Ohio

Preface

This book surveys the special literary relations of Blacks and Jews and the Jew in humor, poetry, and drama in twentieth-century American literature. Nearly half the volume is devoted to drama. This book is the third of a series of three. The first, *Creative Awakening*, and the second, *In the Mainstream*, cover the Jew as character and author in the voluminous genre, fiction. In spanning the century from 1900 to the present, the series is necessarily highly selective because the sheer mass and variety of primary material are too great to include within the compass of a three-volume series. There will, of course, be differences of opinion about authors and tendencies selected for treatment of our multi-faceted literature. I should, however, point out that my earlier work, *The Image of the Jew in American Literature: From Early Republic to Mass Immigration* (1974), which deals with a similar range of genres up to 1900, and the present three-volume study together form the most comprehensive and inclusive treatment in English of the Jew in American literature from the mid-eighteenth century to the present.

Acknowledgments

After publication of *The Image of the Jew in American Literature: From Early Republic to Mass Immigration* (1974), I turned to reading and writing on other, though related, topics. Toward the end of the Preface to that volume I had written, "We leave the proliferation of literature by and about Jews in our century to other, younger hands." But the respite proved brief. I was strongly encouraged by the late Oscar Cohen, by then retired program director of the Anti-Defamation League, to continue my research on Jews in American literature from the cut-off date of the earlier volume, 1900, to the present. I soon found myself committed to the second part of a comprehensive study of the Jew in American literature from the days of the early Republic to our own time. I am indebted to Oscar Cohen for his stimulus to continue on this project and for his many kindnesses.

My thanks also are due to several libraries and their helpful personnel: New York Public Library and its Library of the Performing Arts, the Bobst Library of New York University, the Harvard University Library, and the Hebrew Union College–Jewish Institute of Religion Library in New York City. The dedicated staff of the Southwest Regional Library of the Vermont State Library system responded most helpfully to my numerous requests for books on interlibrary loan, thus enabling me to work in my mountain home.

I wish to thank Jacob Sherman, of Rutland, Vermont, who devotedly typewrote the manuscript at various stages so accurately and helped with other kindnesses relating to the preparation of the manuscript together with his wife Madeline, as also did a Jewish group in Rutland. My thanks are also due to Joan Wright, who typewrote the final draft for the press.

Morris U. Schappes kindly loaned me his valuable files on several current authors. Professor Ellen F. Schiff, of North Adams (Mass.) Community College, read the material on drama and made helpful suggestions.

Most particularly I wish to thank Dr. Annette Rubinstein for her careful, critical scrutiny of the entire manuscript, for her editorial suggestions, and for her copy-editing at several stages of the writing. We did not always agree, but she was ever sensitively aware of the distinction between difference of interpretation and indefensible error on my part. My debt to her is very great.

However, full responsibility for the entire work, mistakes and all, is of course mine alone.

1

Special Black-Jewish Literary Relations

On the night of August 15, 1868, a masked mob of Ku Klux Klansmen broke into the drygoods store of S. A. Bierfield, a Russian Jew, in Franklin, Tennessee, and fatally shot both Bierfield and his Black clerk, Lawrence Bowman. The reason given by the lynchers was a false charge of Bierfield's implication in a murder a few days earlier. But as the *New York Times* reported about a week later, the real reason for the lynching was that Bierfield was "an intelligent advocate of the present reconstruction policy of Congress and a friend to the freedmen of his neighborhood, among whom—he being a merchant—he commanded quite a trade, and perhaps found it expedient to keep one from among their number in his employ."[1] A Nashville newspaper account stated that Bierfield was "an active and prominent Republican, having considerable influence with the colored people.... Our informant says that was his only crime."[2]

This event is an indication of the special relationship that has existed between Jews and Blacks in the United States. Historical as well as current reasons give the two groups similar motives for advocating social justice, civil rights, and equality. Both have a history of persecution and oppression during the Christian era, the Jews in part because they were considered collectively responsible for the crucifixion of Jesus, the Blacks as something repellent and inferior to whites. One need only recall Iago's fulminations against Othello in vicious envy of the Black general, which seeks relief in Iago's animalistic metaphors for his Blackness at a time when Blacks were enslaved in the New World.

In the United States there is a vast difference. A history of slavery introduces deep qualitative differences between the treatment of the two peoples. Yet they have a community of interests. While Jews have suffered discrimination from the beginning of their life in this country, they nevertheless enjoyed most of the rights of citizens and have even assymptotically approached equality. Yet, the Blacks, to our own day, notwithstanding some lifting of barriers, still have far to go to achieve equal status. At the same time, under the favorable situation of American Jews, they still sense the need for alliance with Blacks because they are well aware of the fragility of their status. Recurrent outcroppings of anti-Semitism at home and abroad and continuing availability of Jews as scapegoats, as demagogic diversions from social ills, are omnipresent. The interests of both peoples are therefore served by alliance on issues of civil and human rights.

For most of our country's history many, if not most, Jews (we have no figures) have followed their fellow white citizens in their attitude toward Blacks. Yet in the past few decades Black candidates for public office have generally received a higher percentage of their vote from Jews than from any other non-Jewish white group. And throughout American history there were also many individual Jews who perceived the common ground of Jews and Blacks and acted accordingly. A few outstanding examples: A New York merchant Moses Judah was elected in 1806 as a member of the Standing Committee of the Manumission Society of New York, whose functions were to protect free Blacks from being enslaved and to facilitate manumission.[3] The brothers Joseph and Isaac Friedman in the 1850s helped the Black slave Peter Still buy his freedom in the face of local hostility;[4] August Bondi and Theodore Wiener fought with John Brown in the Kansas Border War in 1856;[5] the abolitionist rabbi, Dr. David Einhorn, was forced to flee from Baltimore in 1861 under threat from a proslavery mob;[6] Ernestine Rose was a prominent abolitionist and early woman's rights leader.[7]

It is estimated that there were more than 6,000 Jews in the Union Army, many of whom served as high officers and many with great distinction—although it is true that from 1,200 to 1,500 Jews fought in the Confederate Army.[8] In our own century Jews have been active in the freedom movement: for instance, among the founders of the National Association for the Advancement of Colored People were Jews like the social worker Henry Markovitz, Rabbi Stephen S. Wise, and Lillian D. Wald, while Professor Joel E. Springarn, of Columbia, was for a quarter of a century one of the leaders.[9] Inevitably, awareness of their own people's history of persecution and the persistence of anti-Semitism enhanced the sensitivity of these men and women and many other Jews in American history to the situation of the Blacks.

If this "natural" affinity of Blacks and Jews is questioned, both peoples may be reminded by their association in the primitive American mind. In his documented study of "Blacks and Jews in American Folklore," Nathan Hurvitz shows that the derogatory connotations of the adjective "black" were early associated with Jews, as in a 1733 verse, "Farewell, Mr. Jew;/ How I hate your tawney face:/I'll have no more to do/With any of your race."[10] The demeaning application of "boy" to mature Black men has its partial counterpart in "Jewboy."[11] Blacks and Jews were usually joined as twin targets by nativistic, anti-democratic demagogic movements like the Ku Klux Klan and the various pro-Fascist agitations in the 1930s, as well as by post–World War II neo-Nazi propagandists. Often an anti-Semitic non-Jew, when he wishes to pass "favorable" judgment on a Jew, calls him "white," thus lifting him into the "superior" category. In the 1930s, a graffito proclaimed that "A nigger is a Jew turned inside out."[12] Hurvitz cites many contemporary jokes invidiously associating Jews and Blacks. He concludes that "it is likely that blacks and Jews are coupled together in the folklore and humor of white Christian Americans more than any other minority, ethnic or 'racial' groups."[13] The close association of Blacks and Jews, organizationally and as individuals, for common action in human rights and civil rights struggles in our century is one response to their common problem, although the oppression is incalculably more severe for American Blacks than for American Jews.

But Jews are "white" after all and are by no means entirely immune from the racism that is endemic in the United States. Before the civil rights issue came to the forefront of popular attention and awakened activism among both Blacks and whites, large numbers of Jews shared the prevailing white prejudices against Blacks. Although both minority peoples were associated in the Christian mind as inferior, the temptation was strong for each one to share the majority's prejudices against the other. The Jews, as whites, could look down upon the Blacks; the Blacks could exploit widespread anti-Semitism to gain a sense of superiority over Jews. Yet the Blacks' immersion in the Old Testament was so deep that they identified their own condition with that of the ancient Hebrews; they manifested this in their religious expression as well as in their folk songs and spirit of resistance to oppression. The implied identification of Black slavery with Hebrews enslaved by the Egyptians and with the liberation of the Jews from that slavery under Moses' leadership is particularly striking. Ralph Ellison remarked on "The preference of the slaves in re-creating themselves, in good part, out of the images and myths of the Old Testament Jews."[14] Yet, such profound identification did not prevent many Blacks from joining white Christians in echoing the centuries-old anti-Semitic attack on Jews as killers of Christ. Richard Wright recalled that as a boy in his Southern town he first knew a Jew as the storekeeper with his strange language. "All of us black people who lived in the neighborhood hated Jews," he adds, "not because they exploited us, but because we had been taught at home and in Sunday school that Jews were 'Christ killers.' With the Jews thus singled out for us, we made them fair game for ridicule." The children taunted the Jews with folk jingles like "Bloody Christ Killers/What won't Jews do?" There were many "folk ditties," he wrote, "many of them, some mean, others filthy, all of them cruel." So deep was this attitude among Black children, he said, that "it was not merely prejudice, it was a part of our cultural heritage."[15] He further related in *American Hunger* (1977) how in Chicago the understanding attitude of Jewish employers made him recall with shame his childhood baiting of Jews. Black folk attitudes simultaneously adopted the ancient Hebrews as their model and joined their white Christian enslavers in baiting modern Jews.

Something of the complexity of the Black attitude toward the Jews was indicated in an essay by James Baldwin in 1948. He calls the relationship "ambivalent." Though the devout Black does not question that "the Jews killed Christ," he nevertheless thinks of himself as a Jew awaiting a Moses to lead him from the land of bondage. Although he sees salvation through the New Testament, it is the Old Testament to which he appeals for reassurance of ultimate freedom and vindication. But at the same time the economic exploitation of Blacks in the ghetto, "in accordance with the American business tradition of exploiting Negroes," causes the Jew to be "identified with oppression and hatred for it." Baldwin says that no Jew is trusted, that all Jews are held in contempt. Yet Baldwin observes that at the same time the Black expects of the Jew, because of his historical experience, "an understanding" which "none but the most naive and visionary Negro has ever expected of the American Gentile." But most Jews fail the test, he says, in order to gain their own safety by adopting conventional white attitudes. In this way "the American white Gentile" has divided potential allies and remains dominant. While granting the possibility of valid personal friendships between individual Jews and Blacks, Baldwin despairs of the likelihood of these tensions being resolved and of cooperation being achieved between Blacks and Jews because of the dual specter of Jewish exploitation and vocational competition. Finally, he says, Black hatred "must have a symbol. Georgia has the Negro and Harlem has the Jew."[16]

This duality, or ambiguity, or ambivalence, the internal contradictions within the complex of relations between Blacks and Jews, has in the course of the years since the 1930s found its expression in the writing of both Blacks and Jews. These contradictions were present in the writings of both groups, but differently at different periods, depending upon the shape of left and liberal sentiment and the forms taken by the civil rights movement. In the proletarian 1930s and 1940s and the radical 1960s Jewish and Black writers were generally positively oriented toward each other and sensing their common goals. The culmination of this union was probably the "Mississippi Summer" of 1964. Over one-half of the young people who braved the hazards of participating in the movement for Black voter registration were Jewish, and Andrew Goodman and Michael Schwerner were murdered together with the Black, James Chaney. The registration drive was followed by the Black Power movement. Changes on both sides altered their relations. These stages in their relationship were reflected with an obvious fidelity in important literary expressions of both groups.

Blacks had not figured significantly in major American literature until Faulkner. There were some exceptions: the blatant stereotypes in some of

Poe's fiction, especially *Narrative of A. Gordon Pym*, and the positive figures of Pip in *Moby Dick* and Jim in *Huckleberry Finn*. Perhaps the first major twentieth-century treatment of a Jewish-Black relationship was Richard Wright's *Native Son* (1940). This novel includes centrally an articulated attitude of the author to the Jewish lawyer, Boris Max. The tormented, frustrated, oppressive existence of the young Black, Bigger Thomas, and his inchoate confusions and longings are depicted through the story of his accidental killing of the rich white, Mary Dalton, and the murder of his own Black lover Bessie, the hunt for his capture, and his trial. In an introductory essay to the novel written two decades later, the author explained that Bigger was the distilled essence of a succession of actual "Biggers" whom Wright had observed. Bigger exemplified the total frustration of their striving for self-fulfillment. The multiple oppressions—economic, social, cultural—forced "Bigger" to respond with violence and an impulsive, almost blind, striking back. During the course of Max's long defense speech at Bigger's trial, which was largely Wright's analysis of the murder, Max makes a central point. "He murdered Mary Dalton accidentally," said Max, "without thinking, without plans, without conscious motive. But after he murdered, he accepted the crime. And that's the most important thing. It was the first full act of his life; it was the most meaningful, exciting and stirring thing that had ever happened to him. He accepted it because it made him free, gave him the possibility of choice, of action, the opportunity to act and to feel that his actions carried weight."[17] Max's address at the trial in defense of Bigger is Wright's own view of Bigger's situation and his understanding of its desperate possibilities. Indeed, Wright's warning in his "How Bigger Was Born" that "the lispings, the whispers, the mutters" that he heard in the Black community "someday, under one stimulus or another, will surely grow into open revolt unless the conditions which produced Bigger Thomases are changed,"[18] were realized in the risings in many cities during the later 1960s and the 1970s.

That Boris Max, Bigger's defense attorney, is a Jew as well as a Communist was altogether probable as is shown by many trials with Black defendants. Wright was a Communist while writing the novel, but left the party in 1942. Jewish participation in these trials was highly significant in any consideration of Black-Jewish relations, Wright was fully aware. He knew that many Jews had joined with Blacks to overcome oppression, even though he was under no illusion as to the flawed understanding of many Jewish, as well as non-Jewish, Communists of the Black situation, and of the degree to which many shared deep-seated white stereotyped attitudes and behavior toward Blacks. But the relationship of Max and Bigger is an expression of the positive side of the ambivalence. Wright is careful to include an offshoot of the anti-Semitism of the period in the false identification of Jews and Communists. When the Dalton cook Peggy is interrogated by Dalton's private detective Britten, he asks about Bigger, "When he talks, does he wave his hands around a lot like he's been around a lot of Jews? ... You see, Peggy, I'm trying to find out if he's been around Communists."[19] To Bigger's assertion that he refuses to reenact for the police the events around the murder because police "hate black folks," Max replies, "They hate others too. ... They hate trade unions. They hate folks who try to organize. ... They hate me because I'm trying to help you. They're writing me letters calling me a 'dirty Jew.' "[20] Wright is here saying that just as the racist doesn't see the individual Black (the "invisible man") but only his stereotyped notion of one, so the anti-Semite—frequently also the same person—does not see any given Jew but only "Jews" as conceived by the stereotype. Even though the ensuing problems for the Blacks in this country are incalculably more serious than those confronting Jews, the fact that the two groups confront similar, if unequal, anti-human manifestations does provide the basis for a common purpose in combatting them. Despite the many differences that he developed with the Communists, Wright would not, I think, have denied that Communists were among the few organized whites, at times even at the cutting edge of white alliance with Blacks against oppression, even if one considers that this aid at times amounted to exploitation for propaganda purposes. And among these Communists were many Jews, of whom Max is a superior example.

Another Black writer during this period who responded to various forms of anti-Semitism was Langston Hughes. In a poem entitled "Un-American Investigators," Hughes contemptuously exposes the committee's exploitation of their "investigations" to indulge in a thinly veiled appeal to anti-Semitism. While this poem is not among Hughes' best poetry, his attitude toward both McCarthyism and those who exploited it for racist purposes is obvious.[21] More complicated Black-Jewish relations are involved in the black novelist Willard Motley's *We Fished All Night* (1951), which deals mainly with white business life in Chicago and contains only one minor Black character. This story, spanning the late 1930s and late 1940s in Chicago, was inspired by *Studs Lonigan* and *USA*, though it did not reach their level of reality. It has several Jewish characters. One of these, Aaron Levin, is pathologically hypersensitive; his condition is aggravated by the fact that his mother was a Gentile prostitute. The author's condemnation of anti-Semitism is apparent, as is his awareness of the limitations in both peoples. Aaron has a frustrated love life and finally refuses to join the Communist party, of which his father was a member, because he lacks the confidence in his ability to resist intimidation. He even tries Catholicism for a while but then drifts back to Judaism. Finally, while he is under treatment for a breakdown, a "truth" drug brings out the hatred of Jews because it is so hard to be a Jew, but Aaron finally says, in tears, "No, that isn't so. ... My poor suffering people. I have failed my whole race. I don't want to be a Jew. What chance has a Jew in the world? What chance has a Negro? What doesn't Dave feel his Negro-ness? Why does he think he's just a human being like everybody else? Who's he kidding?"[22]

Those Black writers who began to write during the significant Black-Jewish alliance for civil rights mirrored this understanding in their depiction of Jews. Among these Lorraine Hansberry, who died of cancer in 1965 at the age of thirty-four, was outstanding. In notes written in 1962, she asserted her agreement with the Israeli prosecution of Adolf Eichmann as a "deliberate and carefully balanced *reminder* of what was done—and by *whom*."[23] Then came her almost inevitable recall of the link between the Jewish and Black peoples.

Confusion on the matter [she wrote] should be alien to oppressed peoples everywhere in the world—including American Negroes; something will in fact be achieved if Black men and women everywhere begin to lose their universal tendency to think racially as regards the oppression of people.... For me there is a strong and powerful current of Justice in the fact: a representative figure of Nazism [i.e., Eichmann] tried on *Jewish* soil. Under *Jewish* justice. By *Jewish* judges. I am moved by the thought of it. It is about time.[24]

Lorraine Hansberry combined ethnic particularism and universalism in just proportion so that they completed rather than contradicted each other. On another occasion, she criticizes Norman Mailer's use of the term "Negro" in the "The White Negro," name of his notion of the Hipster. She observed something similar in Seymour Krim's identification of the small sampling of Blacks he met in Harlem in his search for the exotic, with "Harlem" as a whole: "Seymour Krim does not understand," she said, "that when he left the most lowly of barflies in Harlem they re-engaged in chitchat concerning the most traditional of *very* exotic notions about the Jewish people which, steeped though these may be in the curious quality of brother envy, are as grim and unworthy as they are any place else in America."[25] Her passionate condemnation of prejudiced stereotypes of Jews, or indeed of *any* ethnic or national group, is unmistakable.

After Hansberry's immense Broadway success with *Raisin in the Sun* in 1958, which concerned resistance to restricted housing for Blacks, her next produced play, *The Sign in Sidney Brustein's Window* (1964), addressed itself to the sociopolitical confusions of disillusioned radicals in the Greenwich Village of the late 1950s. It ends in the renewal of commitment by the Jewish protagonist, Sidney Brustein, married to a non-Jewish failed actress. He proposes to start a newspaper in the Village to "become an insurgent again." As Wright did in *Native Son*, Hansberry projected a Jew for her spokesman, and Sidney invokes his ancient Hebrew forbears to express his active resistance to the evils of his day.

In the ancient times [says Sidney] the good men among my ancestors, when they heard of evil, strapped a sword to their loins and strode into the desert; and when they found it, they cut it down—or were cut down and bloodied the earth with their purifying death. But how does one confront these thousand nameless vapors that are the evil of our time? Could a sword pierce it?... Wrath has become a poisoned gastric juice in the intestine. One does not *smite* evil any more,... one takes a pill.... Oh, but to take up the sword of the Maccabbeans again![26]

Even if one discounts the rhetorical flourish in such statements, it remains true that the complex and subtle problems of modern hyperorganized life and the workings of an intricate economy with its impersonality and de-humanization make it hard to locate some of its "evils." But the unjust situation of the Blacks is easy enough to locate though exceedingly hard to uproot, economically and psychologically. This question is introduced as a subtheme in the play through Sidney's friend, the Black ex-Communist Alton, who is in love with Sidney's sister-in-law Gloria, a call girl in Florida. Alton wishes to marry her but does not know her profession. When he learns the truth, he rejects Gloria, although he admits a white man might be able to forgive. He tells Sidney that his mother, a domestic, would bring home odds and ends of food and articles given her by her employers. One day his father swept this "booty" off the table, exclaiming that he could no longer accept the "white man's leavings." Alton adds, of Gloria, "I don't want white man's leavings.... Not now. *Not ever.*"[27] Thus, while projecting in small the Black situation, and without mitigating militancy, Hansberry has framed it within the need for a commitment to tackling the ills of the whole society.

Another highly gifted Black woman writer, Paule Marshall, was born in Brooklyn in 1929 of Barbadian immigrant parents. After graduating with distinction from Brooklyn College, she wrote poetry, was a journalist re-porting on the West Indies and Brazil, and a librarian. In 1959 she published her first fiction work, *Brown Girl, Brownstone*, an account of Selina, a Black girl growing up in Brooklyn. Marshall's style and temperament are different from Hansberry's. Her writing lacks Hansberry's rhetorical flair; it is spare and direct with a wry turn. But her approach is somewhat similar. Like Hansberry she combines uncompromising militancy with a sense of universality across racial barriers. Selina the college student talks with her Black boyfriend Clive, who discusses "this tired race theme" with her. He warns her against refusing to participate in activities with whites. Otherwise, he says, "you are only a Negro, some flat, one-dimensional, bas-relief figure ... you rule out your humanity and... your complexity as a human being. ... At some point you have to break through to the larger ring which en-compasses us all—our humanity... caught with all men within the common ring." Whatever whites may expect in their relations with Blacks, he goes on, they must be confronted "always with the full and awesome weight of our humanity, until they begin to see us and not some unreal image they've superimposed."[28]

As with Wright and Hansberry, Marshall's central character has a special relation to Jews. The studious Selina is told by one of her fellow students that she should have gone to Bergen High School, which is "full of Jewish kids and every one of them is a brain." Selina's own experience with a Jewish student is significant. Quick rapport is established with Rachel Fine, the president of the college dance club, who has invited Selina to join the club. Clive tells Selina that Rachel is "probably some Prog from the Village Hootenany set who just loves Negroes." But the girls become genuine friends and even confide about each other's love lives. After a dance recital at which Selina has successfully danced a solo, the mother of a fellow dancer, at an after-performance party, deeply affronts her. The woman said she reminded her of her "girl" (servant)—and thus "reminded her that she was a nigger after all."[29] But her relationship with Rachel is unimpaired, and Selina calls on Rachel for help in getting transportation to the West Indies through a relative of hers in the tourist business. The interracial friendship is unemphasized in the novel and is the only one in the story.

If anyone suspects Marshall of "philo-Semitism," an uncritical admiration, one will be disabused by "Brooklyn," one of four novellas in her second book *Soul Clap Hands and Sing* (1961). In this story Max Berman, a professor of French who had been a Communist in the 1930s, had withdrawn after the Soviet party purges of the period, and had been fired from an upstate New York community college during a purge of radicals. In the 1950s he is once more teaching in the area. He lives alone after having been divorced twice. In his class there is a silent Black girl who seems lonely. He begins to think that she could revive some life in him. "He felt a fleeting discomfort—and irritation: discomfort at the thought that although he had been sinned against as a Jew he still shared in the sin against her and still suffered from the same vague guilt";[30] he had himself been diverted from a desired career by the Jewish quota in medical school. When he first asks her to share a weekend at his country place, she rejects him. Weeks later, she accepts his offer, spends a platonic day, and at the end makes him feel her contempt: "her smile was like a knife she pressed to his throat," and she explains that she decided to come to tell him: "You let me know how you—and most of the people like you—see me."[31] The story exemplifies more than Black-white relations, for it exposes specifically ambiguities of Black-Jewish relations.

It is apparent that Marshall's childhood and education in Brooklyn gave her firsthand knowledge of Jews. In her third novel, *The Chosen Place, The Timeless People* (1969) she offers one of the fullest perspectives of Jewish-Black relations given by any Black fiction writer. Written during the five years from 1963 to 1968 and running to nearly five hundred pages, this is one of the major novels by a Black American. It is an intensive study of the underdeveloped "Bourne Island" (Barbados?) in the West Indies and richly portrays the life from everyday to carnival, as well as the frustration of attempts to improve the lot of its people. The protagonists of these efforts are the vital, English-educated, perceptive Black woman Merle and the Jewish anthropologist, Saul Aaron, director of an American foundation project set up to plan the development of the island. Saul is a radical whose interest in anthropology was not as a theory but as a means to help under-developed peoples. Alone among the whites on his project, he had refused to distance himself from the island people, and didn't, as Merle's wise old Aunt Leesy had said, "put on no lot of airs like some of them who come here call themselves trying to help."[32] One day Saul joins the workers in the field cutting cane; exhausted, he is reminded of his mother's story of the persecution his Sephardic ancestors suffered from the Inquisition, which came "to stand . . . for the entire two-thousand-year history of exile and trial including the worst Nazi horror." This embodied for him "all that any other people had had to endure. It became the means by which he understood the suffering of others."[33]

Quick rapport is established between Merle and Saul, based on their mutual recognition of their common concern for the welfare of the island, itself grounded in their socialist attitude toward humanity. "Sometimes," Merle tells Saul, "you come close to being what we call . . . real people. . . . Perhaps it's because you're a Jew and that's given you a deeper understand-ing. After all, your people have caught hell longer than mine." Perhaps recalling some bad experiences, she adds, "I doubt it," for Merle had known Jews in London; a few were close friends and "most of them were as bad as the English and had no use for black people."[34] But on his own evidence it is true that Saul's Jewish identity has contributed to his sensitivity to Blacks. So we are confronted once again with the ambiguity in Black-Jewish relations, although this novel, like the writing of Wright and Hansberry, is concerned to bring out the positive side of this ambivalence. It is revealed with perhaps unprecedented fullness in everyday detail as well as social perspective in Marshall's novel through the relationship of Merle and Saul. Marshall's unusual novelistic talents exhibit their scope not only in this, the central relationship of the story, but also in the vivid variety of character-izations of many island people and of the other American visitors.

Over and over, as in the writing of Marshall, Hansberry, and Wright, the Jewish character in Black literature of the period has a special relation to the Blacks. This testifies to the special relationship in social actuality. It is again exemplified in John Oliver Killens' *And Then They Heard the Thunder* (1963). The Jewish lieutenant, Robert Samuels, is executive officer of a Black Quartermaster company during World War II to which the central Black character, Saunders Solomon, is assigned. Samuels is a New York liberal, perhaps a leftist, and he makes a genuine, if at times bumbling attempt to understand the Black soldiers and to alleviate the outrageous injustices they suffered in the army. Solomon is an educated, militant Black, continuously skeptical of Samuels' steadfastness and effectiveness in behalf of the Black soldiers. Samuels several times fails severe tests. But the relationship of Samuels with Solomon and the other Black soldiers is far different from theirs with other officers. The author several times shows how Jews and Blacks are coupled in the minds of the prejudiced, and in a letter to the Black press, Solomon writes that his officers are "mostly solid Negro-haters, and ... [their commanding officer] *has* to give Hitler credit for his handling of the Jews."[35] Solomon's doubts about the genuineness of Samuels' devotion to the Black cause are finally overcome in Australia when Samuels joins his Black soldiers during a shootout with white American soldiers who have subjected Blacks to intolerable indignities. "You're a colored man tonight, old buddy," Solomon tells Samuels. "You have naturally earned your spurs. I'm going to vote you into the club."[36] It is significant that a militant Black writer like Killens should have chosen to depict a Jew as an unconditional ally.

Under a different set of circumstances this special relationship is also presented by John A. Williams in his *The Man Who Cried I Am* (1967). Two Black writers, Harry Ames and a younger aspirant, Max Reddick, are helped in their careers and are given literary advice by Bernard Zutkin, an established and influential Jewish critic. Zutkin's "criticism seemed to have roots in the struggles taking place within the society."[37] Ames is denied a writing fellowship to which he is clearly entitled and which the judges have unanimously assigned him when the director of the institution vetoes the selection. Zutkin then tries unsuccessfully to get the matter reconsidered. Zutkin also redirects Reddick from journalism to fiction. Max "was grateful that Zutkin had taken him to task for not writing novels." The author himself comments on the mutual interest of Blacks and Jews which led them to an alliance: "Anti-Semitism was in the American air, Zutkin knew, and to avoid recurrence of what had happened in Germany, the Jew needed allies. There was the Negro who himself needed allies."[38]

Before the 1960s this special relation between literary Blacks and Jews persisted despite marked anti-Semitism in the Black community. This problem had first become serious following the great migration of Blacks to the cities of the North after World War I. Jews then came into potentially hostile relations with Blacks on a large scale as merchant versus customer, landlord or rent collector versus tenant, housewife versus domestic. Blacks always were in the disadvantageous position in these relationships and were exploited by some Jews. To make matters worse, Jewish storekeepers, like all others, tended to conform to prevailing discrimination in employment against Blacks, so that Blacks found themselves trading in shops where they were denied employment. In many cities the migrating Blacks moved into formerly Jewish neighborhoods, and some Jewish landlords and merchants retained their holdings. Added to these circumstances was the general increase in anti-Semitism and the specific spread of Nazi influence.

As the Great Depression wore on in the 1930s, anti-Semitism in the Black community was sufficiently overt and widespread to call forth considerable discussion in the Black press. Especially egregious was the "Bronx Slave Market," street corners where domestics who were deeply exploited would assemble to be hired. Because the Bronx was a dense Jewish area, this ugly "slave market" was especially associated with Jews. Black journalists and sociologists studied and commented on these sources of anti-Semitism and exposed exploitation where it occurred.

But the Black press roundly condemned Nazi persecution of the Jews at the same time that it maintained that the Black in the United States was hardly better off than the Jew in Nazi Germany. A representative editorial in the Black paper, the *Philadelphia Tribune*, on July 5, 1934, said: "The persecution of the Jews in Germany by the Nazi government is deplorable, stupid and outrageous. The persecution of colored Americans by Americans is cruel, relentless, and spirit-breaking."[39] The Nazis were also widely compared to the Ku Klux Klan at home by the Black press, which also observed that the general white press was hypocritical: while it was indignant and concerned at the treatment of German Jews, it ignored the oppression of Blacks right here at home.

Some Black leaders and writers discussed Hitler's treatment of the Jews. For instance, Chandler Owen, a Black writer on labor who deplored Black anti-Semitism, wrote critically in 1941 that it was common to hear Blacks say, "Well, Hitler did one good thing: he put those Jews in their place."[40] In those years Black leaders like W.E.B. Du Bois and Adam Clayton Powell, Jr., deplored anti-Semitism among Blacks. In a study of the problem two Jewish scholars wrote in 1969,

By the early 1940s black writers, while articulating widely divergent opinions about Jews, were virtually all agreed that Negro anti-Semitism was definitely on the rise ... the confrontations between first and second generation American Jews and multitudes of transplanted Southern Negroes in Northern cities gave rise to the expression of more criticism of Jews by blacks than that heard at any time before or since, including the late '60s.[41]

General neglect of both the problem of the Blacks and of the material in the Black press in the 1930s may explain why the question did not receive attention from the general white press before World War II. After World War II, however, Black complaints against whites generally and Jews in particular were forced into wide public notice by postwar Black militance and the articulation of grievances by the emerging Black writers whose books and essays were widely read.

Several aspects of this attitude are illustrated in Claude Brown's auto-biographical novel, *Manchild in the Promised Land* (1965). When Claude is hurt by a bus, he thinks he is "bound to get a lot of money—we had a Jewish lawyer from way downtown."[42] When Claude is told by his friend Reno that he won't work for "Goldberg," he asks, "Who's Goldberg?" Reno explains: Goldberg "runs the garment center"; "Goldberg ain't gon ever get up off any money. Goldberg's just as bad as Mr. Charlie. He's got all the money in the world, Sonny, believe it or not. Look across the street. He owns the liquor store, he owns the bar, he owns the restaurant across there, the grocery store. He owns all the liquor stores in Harlem, 'cause that's where all the nigger's money goes, and he gon get all that." And Reno concludes that he'll "steal me some money from Goldberg, not . . . beg for it. . . . That cat's got all the money in the world, and what he'll give you is carfare back downtown for another day's slavery." Another young friend of Claude's tells about being asked by "Goldberg," "do you know where I might find some nice honest colored girl who could come in and help my wife clean up the house?" The "girl" who had just left "was about sixty years old." When Claude was a "boy" working in the garment center, "Goldberg" didn't distinguish the younger militant Blacks from the older compliant ones. The author says that this "new nigger was something that nobody understood and that nobody was ready for." Later Claude works for jewelers who live in a Jewish section of Brooklyn, and he reflects that they think the Emmett Till lynching is "terrible," but "I knew that if I went out to the Flatbush section of Brooklyn or Brighton Beach, where all those cats lived, they'd probably lynch the landlord if he rented me an apartment. This was the relationship between the Jew and descendents of Ham." Even though Claude is fairly treated, he quits his job. The upshot was not a feeling of "animosity," he says, but only a feeling that neither understood the other; he was asking more of them than he could expect, just because "You've been close to me. My mother been buying the pigtails and neckbones from you. . . . She's been paying you the rent, she's been pawning stuff to you . . . so if anyone should give us some kind of understanding, you should."[43] But this was expecting too much, he believes. When he meets a Black Muslim, who insists that Blacks must "revolt" and "get Harlem out of Goldberg's pockets" by totally boycotting 125th Street as a shopping center and buying up 145th Street, the author is obviously out of sympathy with this viewpoint, but he fears its effectiveness. To the litany of justified complaints about poor pay, poor food, exploitation of Blacks by Jews, the Christians among his listeners assent, adding "Yeah! Yeah! Them goddam Jews killed my Jesus, too!"[44]

As might be expected, Jewish ownership of small business in Harlem is exaggerated. A Black writer not animated by prejudice, Richard Wright, is more circumspect than the speakers Brown reports in alluding to such a phenomenon. In 1940 Wright wrote that "Almost all business in the Black

Belt was owned by Jews, Italians, and Greeks." I am not aware of any figures about non-Jewish white-owned Harlem business before the 1960s. The sociologist Herbert J. Gans reports results of a survey by a 1968 New York Mayor's Task Force on the ethnicity of business owners in Harlem. It showed that *Jews* owned about 40 percent of all stores in Harlem. All *white-owned* stores added up to about 47 percent. Thus, 53 percent were owned by Blacks or other non-whites. But the actual capital invested by non-whites was only 10 percent of the total.[45] Significantly, the Kerner Commission in the same year showed that Jews formed 39 percent of store-owners. This situation may have changed quantitatively since 1942, but not qualitatively in these respects. In 1941, I had written,

friction between the two groups . . . has hindered mutual understanding. In Harlem, for instance, it happens that many of the storekeepers are Jewish. Negro resentment at high prices has been directed at them as Jews. To a certain extent such Jewish merchants have followed the Jim Crow policy in employment—hardly a peculiarly "Jewish" practice. Jews are also employers of Negroes as domestic workers at low wages. . . . Unjustified blame for high rents in Harlem was placed on Jewish rent-collectors, who were only agents of the landlord.[46]

One is reminded of similar situations in Europe—seventeenth-century Poland or mid-nineteenth-century Germany—where Jewish rent collectors were blamed for peasant hardships.

Although such sources of friction persist and still trouble the two communities, a qualitatively new situation began to emerge in the 1960s. The initial phase of the civil rights movement, during which Blacks, Jews, and other whites cooperated closely, gave way to the "Black Power" movement. Militant young Blacks moved to take over exclusive leadership of the movement. The raising of Black consciousness resulted in removing whites, among them many Jews, from leading positions in such organizations as the Congress of Racial Equality (CORE) and the Student Non-Violent Coordinating Committee (SNCC) after Stokely Carmichael's call for "Black Power." This was enunciated during the Selma March led by Dr. Martin Luther King, Jr. Especially among Black intellectuals there was a determination to take over leadership of liberation and to allow whites—many of them Jews—to participate, if at all, only in a subordinate function. Contributions by Jews to the civil rights movement were minimized, and many whites, both Jews and non-Jews, who had faithfully served the movement, were brushed aside. Blacks were determined to lead their own movement. A wave of intense nationalist feeling swept the Black community, articulated by its intellectuals. The result among Blacks was a deepening of self-confidence and pride in their Blackness ("Black is Beautiful").

The civil rights struggle had made progress in abolishing segregation in public places, in the beginning to gain voting rights for Blacks in the South, as well as outlawing discrimination in employment. Measures were proposed to correct segregation in education as well as discrimination in the professions and industry. Busing of elementary and secondary pupils intended to overcome segregation in schools and "affirmative action" programs to override ingrained baseless conviction of white superiority by accelerating admission to college and the professions and to jobs in industry hitherto closed to Blacks, the movement began to affect all Americans directly. Many Jews in particular were disturbed because they themselves had risen only recently by their own efforts; preferential treatment in hiring and admissions to the professions and college and graduate school threatened, as they thought, the "meritocratic" system by which they had climbed out of the working class. Until the late 1960s, when this source of tension was exacerbated, Jewish and Black organizations had in fact engaged in a large measure of united action for their common goals. But when the Black civil rights struggle began to affect Jews in education and professions like law, teaching, and medicine by intensifying competition, this unity was broken. Under the "meritocratic" argument the "quotas" against Jews for several centuries had been overcome by sheer ability, and the same should also be applied to upwardly mobile Blacks. This position depended for its persuasiveness on ingrained habits of thinking about Black inferiority.

The result was a stimulus to the latent and quiescent anti-Semitic tendencies among Blacks, which traditionally existed, as we have suggested, in imitation of white Christian prejudice and in resentment against what has erroneously been perceived as *peculiarly* Jewish—and not *capitalist*—economic exploitation. Some Black intellectuals now openly expressed and published anti-Semitic statements, sometimes quite shockingly. A cumulative series of events also brought out anti-Black feeling among Jews as well as Black anti-Semitism. Jewish organizational support of whites' court challenges to affirmative action programs in medical schools and in some branches of industry deepened the mutual alienation, and Jews often behaved no differently from non-Jewish racists. Some joined protest movements against new housing projects open to Blacks. Some joined anti-busing groups and their non-Jewish activists; many resisted affirmative action programs which attempted to make Black equality of opportunity an actuality in a reasonable time. The issues were now quite complex, and it could not be denied that some Jews now would meet competition which might limit the educational or professional opportunities open to them. But was the proximate approach to equality of Black Americans as a whole to be delayed indefinitely because some white Americans, Jewish or non-Jewish, would be obliged to search harder for their opportunities?

The event which perhaps more greatly than any other exacerbated this alienation was the teachers' union strike of 1968 in New York City. Blacks in the Ocean Hill-Brownsville section of Brooklyn sought to achieve participation in their children's education through community control of

schools. Since such control also included the power to hire teachers, the
union felt threatened, and declared a strike. The majority of teachers were
Jews (about 59 percent in 1960), so that the strike took the form of a Black-
Jewish confrontation. Each side used prejudiced demagogy against the other;
ugly racist epithets were exchanged on the picket line. The teachers' union
committed inexcusable offenses against the interests of both groups by re-
producing and distributing throughout the city about a half-million copies
of a viciously anti-Semitic leaflet originally issued by a very small local
group of Blacks in about two thousand copies. The strike left a deep wound
in relations of the two groups. Other events in those years exacerbated the
situation. An anti-Semitic poem by a fifteen-year-old Black girl wished Jews
were dead and was "sick" of hearing of the Holocaust of the 6 million. It
was read on a radio program in New York during this period, and the
public airing of this shocking anti-Semitic verse generated much friction
between the two groups.[47]

That such bloodthirsty sentiments should be expressed by a teenager is
not surprising when one considers what several mature Black poets were
writing in those days. The gifted young Black poet Nikki Giovanni, in the
poem "The True Import of Present Dialogue, Black vs. Negro" challenged
Blacks to "poison" and "stab" Jews. And in another poem, "Love Dream,"
she writes that it is "impossible" to "love" Jews.[48]

Perhaps the most notorious example of this spate of anti-Semitic Black
poetry was that of LeRoi Jones (Amiri Baraka). Jones was a talented, leading
Black writer of the period in several forms—poetry, drama, criticism. He
was also a political and cultural organizer in the Black community of New-
ark. He wrote in "Black Art" a programmatic sketch of the militant's conception of Black "art," preaching every manner of violence against Jews.[49]
In the prose poem, "For Tom Postell, Dead Black Poet," Jones wrote that
he had "extermination blues" and figured out "the Hitler syndrome."[50] One
could go on, but we have cited enough. Fortunately this outpouring of anti-
Semitic bile did not last. By the end of the 1960s LeRoi Jones, now Amiri
Baraka, professed to have embraced Marxism and eschewed anti-Semitism
as an expression of his "reactionary" period. In his critical overview of
Baraka's work, Werner Stoller wrote in 1978, "Baraka now regrets and
renounces his own anti-Semitic phase and sees it as a 'reactionary thing,'
an aberration suggested by bourgeois Black nationalism.... Baraka's anti-
Semitism was also an intensely personal exorcism of his own past; and his
anti-Semitic references included his former wife and literary milieu in New
York."[51] One could cite other Black poets. Henry Dumas, who, we are told,
was shot to death by a white policeman in 1968, wrote "cuttin' down to
size," about two Blacks who go downtown ostensibly to buy suits; they
knife "the jew."[52]

The leading Black playwright, Ed Bullins, who makes occasional unflattering allusions to Jews, does not spare non-Jews or pretentious middle-

class Blacks either. While not friendly to Jews, his writing is not anti-Semitic. It is clear, however, that anti-Semitic feeling touched many Black intellectuals in the 1960s even though others, like Hansberry and Killens and Paule Marshall, exhibited no trace of it. Public evidence of Black anti-Semitism became less frequent as the 1970s wore on. However, the recently developed affinity of Blacks for the Third World, and for the Muslim Arabs especially, has led many Blacks to adopt an uncritical pro-Arab position vis-à-vis Israel, often with a strong overtone of anti-Semitism, which often is its concomitant.

For some time surveys have shown that the set of stereotyped beliefs which are symptoms of anti-Semitism are somewhat less prevalent among Blacks than whites. What, then, are the basic sources for the recent exacerbated expressions of anti-Semitism, especially among Black intellectuals? A substantial and illuminating analysis of one of some basic causes was made by Herbert J. Gans in "Negro-Jewish Conflict in New York City: A Sociological Evaluation" in the March 1969 issue of *Midstream*. The article was precipitated by the New York school strike, but Gans says that the strike was not a basic cause of the friction between the two groups. Gans shows one result of the fundamental "succession" process in ethnic economic and class development. As each immigrant group entered the country and expanded economically, it found a place in a productive economy— Central Europeans, Irish, Italians, Jews, others—and a greater or less possibility of upward mobility and movement into the middle class. They followed each other in succession in the slum areas of the cities. In New York the Irish and other non-Jews were followed by Jews at the turn of the century. When the Jews and the others moved out of the slums, their place was taken by Blacks and, increasingly, Hispanics. There was a crucial difference, however, for by the time these latter ethnic groups moved in, although their expectations had been raised by the civil rights and leftward movements, only a limited number of Blacks and Hispanics found it possible to rise in the economic and class scale. Meanwhile the condition of the uneducated or poorly educated mass remained static or even deteriorated. Not only did discrimination against them persist in industry, but the serious inferiority of their education often left them unprepared for the technological qualifications demanded by many jobs in a high technology society, even if these were opened to them. One result of the ensuing frustrations was the explosion of the Black ghettos across the country from Watts to Harlem. Another was the militancy of many Black intellectuals against the persistence of racism in education, housing, and employment, in education and the professions especially in which Jews were disproportionately represented. The opposition of the Jewish establishment to effective affirmative action and their championing of "meritocracy" reinforced the growing anti-Jewish sentiment among Blacks.

This situation had its reflection in literature as is amply illustrated by the

Black writing of the period and needs to be understood if we are to account for the virulence of the literary response of some Blacks. Jewish intellectuals and writers also expressed themselves with various degrees of understanding. Several Jewish journals held symposiums on the issue, and several collections of such articles were published: *Negro and Jewish Encounter in America* (1967), edited by Shlomo Katz, and *Black Anti-Semitism and Jewish Racism* (1969). The former had two Black contributors and twenty-five Jews, and the latter had four Black and seven Jewish contributors. One much-discussed essay was "My Negro Problem—And Ours" by Norman Podhoretz, first published in 1963 during his "radical" period—the essay that Hansberry characterized as "trash." He recounts his early intimidating experiences with neighborhood Black boys, and he confesses never to have overcome the fear and hatred he then felt. He now believes that all whites "are sick in their feeling about Negroes." There may be a partial truth in this assertion that the historical racist relation of whites to Blacks has not at bottom been extirpated, even among most of those allied in the freedom struggle. Podhoretz confesses that "today" he "does fear and envy and hate them still." His proposed solution is fatuous—complete "miscegnation" of whites and Blacks, he writes, "making color irrelevant, making it disappear as a fact of consciousness."[53] But even if such a mixture were to occur eventually, it could only be a *by-product* of a solution. For the problem is not *simply* a matter of color ("race") prejudice. Social and economic and class forces are at play as well, and they are in fact the basic ones.

But not all Blacks and Jews harbored prejudice against one another. One friendly, though astringent, exchange during the 1960s on the literary front was the civil exchange between Irving Howe and Ralph Ellison. Howe had written in his magazine *Dissent* an essay, "Black Boys and Native Sons" (1963) in which he examined what he regards as the conscious departure of both James Baldwin and Ralph Ellison from Richard Wright's model of the protest novel in *Native Son*. Ellison replied that he had never intended to be a literary follower of Wright. Baldwin had in his early years as a writer, continued Howe, resisted what he considered the constriction of the Black character if conceived only in terms of "protest." Howe comments that oppression is such an inescapable part of Black life and of the experience out of which Black novelists write that "protest" forces itself on him. Baldwin's work, especially the later novels, Howe suggests, can be judged only as "protest." Indeed, as Howe failed to note, the very title of Ellison's novel is a "protest." Ellison's *The Invisible Man* (1952) comes closer to Baldwin's prescription for a non-protest novel, says Howe. While fully aware of Ellison's "abundance of primary talent" and the richness of inventiveness and rendering of the varieties of Black life, Howe nevertheless regards the novel as "flawed." "To write simply about 'Negro experience' with the esthetic distance urged by critics of the fifties," says Howe, "is a moral and psychological impossibility, for flight and protest are inseparable from that experience, and even if less political than Wright and less prophetic than Baldwin, Ellison knows this quite as well as I do."[54] But Ellison saw in Howe's comments on his novel a reversion to "quite primitive modes of analysis." He held that Howe "sees (the Negro) not as a human being but an abstract embodiment of hell." Ellison charges that Howe seems unaware of the human fullness and variety in the lives of Blacks and implies that the Black writer is thus cut off from a vision of the universality of all humanity, the Black is incapable of seeing beyond his Blackness. He says that Howe denies the Black the right to be a literary artist in the fullest sense.[55] Howe protested that Ellison misrepresented his viewpoint. While Ellison is properly sensitive of his stature as an artist, I believe he tends to be overprotective of this status, which he feels he must defend against those who see nothing beyond social commitment in an artist. Yet in Ellison's own novel, after disillusionment, the Black protagonist realizes that he is an "invisible man," and at the end of his "hibernation" as an underground man, he reaches the inconclusive resolve—which seems to describe Ellison's own viewpoint. "There's a possibility," he thinks, "that even an invisible man has a socially responsible role to play."[56] Ellison seems to have little faith in the effectiveness of social activism for solving social problems, but still entertains the obligation of "social responsibility."

Howe did not deem it necessary to allude to his own Jewishness in his article, but Ellison calls attention to this. Ellison is explicit in disclaiming any "racial" motivation on either side, since this would have "missed the target." Ellison says he is among "many" Blacks who clearly distinguish "Jews" from "whites" because Jews have no responsibility for "the system of segregation." Ellison clearly has Jews of the mass immigration in mind here, those who began to come in large numbers beginning in the 1880s. But there were Jews in this country since 1654, and some were Southern slaveholders, though their number was small. Jews even fought for the Confederacy in the Civil War, and Judah P. Benjamin was its vice president. Ellison believes that Jews feel guilt concerning the Black condition because they perhaps "unconsciously," certainly "unrealistically," identify themselves with the "power structure," and Blacks would call this "passing for white." He believes the distinction between Jews and other "whites" must be maintained for the sake of historical accuracy and for their contributions in America to "dissent," "humor," and "ideas."[57] But I think Ellison overstates the case. Jews do indeed have little responsibility for the original sources of racism against Blacks in the United States. Yet despite the fact that Jews are disproportionately represented among those fighting to abolish racism, they are not nearly as clearly distinguishable from "whites" with respect to prejudice as those facts might imply. Even if they are not in control of "the power structure," they do share some responsibility for current racism.

Ellison's opposition to what he regards as Howe's constricted view "in blackface" of what Black writing should or "must" be becomes clearer if one studies an interview Ellison gave to *Harper's* in 1967. Ellison there suggested that Jewish writers had succeeded in becoming full-fledged American writers: they could project their own Jewish experience "as a metaphor for the whole" of America. But they first had to identify themselves as Americans, taking from the modern literary tradition whatever was usable for them as Jews who were thoroughly acculturated Americans. Ellison adds that this country is so diverse that no member of any one of its pluralistic groups can speak for *all* the other groups, and this is certainly true of the Black sector. He adds, "most Negro American writing today [1967]" is as "provincial" as Jewish writing in the 1930s in that both kinds of writing are so preoccupied with their differences from general society that they remain confined within these differences. The Jews "discovered," said Ellison, "that they possessed something precious to bring to the broader American culture on the lowest as well as the highest levels of human activity, and that it would have a creative impact far beyond the Jewish community ... that the Jewish American idiom would lend a whole new dimension to the American language." Thus far, Ellison affirms, the situation has not yet reached a comparable stage of full "American-ness" in most Black writing. One of the greatest obstacles to this realization, he says, is that Black living has been hitherto "described mainly in terms of our political, economic and social conditions as measured by outside norms, seldom in terms of our own sense of life or our *own* sense of values gained from our own unique American experience. Nobody bothered to ask Negroes how they felt about their own lives." In this way white America dictated Black writing. Thus Paul Lawrence Dunbar and Charles Waddell Chesnutt wrote "dialect humor" in the "minstrel tradition," and it was a "moribund" style of "literary decadence." The "most memorable character" in the "minstrel tradition," says Ellison, was Mark Twain's "Nigger Jim," and *Huckleberry Finn* is consequently "flawed." In the 1930s Black writers pursued the "proletarian" style. Instead of modeling themselves on other Black writers, says Ellison, aspiring Black writers should place themselves in the tradition of the greatest modern writers as Jewish American writers did; and they need additionally to write from *within* Black life in all its richness and, so to speak, indigenousness, best embodied in Black folklore, and to explore Black life in all its complexity.[58]

Ellison's insistence on the fullness of Black experience needs to be recalled when one deals with the treatment of Blacks—or any other ethnic group, for that matter—as a caution against falling into a stereotype. Norman Mailer's concept of the "White Negro" drew upon the quasi or actual criminality of some Blacks as his prototype of the "Hipster." This is a reduction to the stereotype. Basically the problem is the failure to see fictional characters as individuals rather than the stereotype. A satire of this literary practice can be found in Bruce Jay Friedman's successful play, *Scuba Duba* (1967). Set in the Riviera, the Jewish Harold Wonder's wife has run off with "a spade frogman... a goddammed scuba diver." Wonder is a pathetic *shlemiel* whose superficial pro-Black feelings are in fact exposed as fraudulent by the play. When his wife returns to him and the Black frogman and a friend come to visit, Wonder is furious, saying, "We're on my turf now, you sonofabitch. You're not at any Black Muslim convention.... I'm sorry I have to use the racial stuff. It gives me a slight edge, but I can assure you it's got nothing to do with my true feelings." The Blacks are represented in stereotypical terms, as sexually potent and physically imposing. If that were all, one might attribute the stereotyped conception to Friedman, but it is Wonder's stereotype that is being exposed, not the author's. The frogman and his friend sing before Wonder in order to conform to his stereotyped notion of the Black. "You've blown your cool, Mr. Wonder, and you far from a credit to your race."[59] This example shows that one always needs to keep in mind the distinction between the viewpoint of the author and that of his character. This is the case, for instance, in comments on Jewish stereotyping of Blacks by Stanley Schatt, who does not make clear that the stereotyped notion of the *shvartse*, the Black domestic, by Portnoy's mother is not shared by Philip Roth, but is rather a valid element in Roth's satire of middle-class Jewish life.[60]

There can be no mistaking the friendly attitude of Jay Neugeboren toward Blacks and their freedom struggle in the several volumes he wrote while still a radical, which preceded his later intensely religious *Orphan's Tale*. His collection of short stories, *Corky's Brother* (1969), includes several whose Jewish characters establish rapport with Blacks, in addition to several stories in which there are no ostensible Jewish participants but in which the author's understanding of the Black side of such conflicts is evident. "The Campaign of Hector Rodriguez" is a story told by the eponymous Puerto Rican student at a junior high school on New York's West Side. In a campaign for election to the student association leadership the Hispanic Catholic, Carlos, is one of the three "fusion" candidates; the other two are Sam, the Jew, and Louise, the Black Protestant girl, thus forming a common front of religions, colors, sexes, and races. The slate wins. The story exposes some of the hazards in the lives of minority young people in the city. In another story, "Elijah," a black boy of that name, a phenomenal runner, paces the track team runners of a Brooklyn Yeshiva as they train. Their coach is a Haganah veteran, and all become friendly with Elijah. At a track meet they induce Elijah to run in the anchor position for the Yeshiva team in the relay race. They win, but their team is disqualified because Elijah is not a student. Elijah's father is furious with his son for associating with Jews and with the coach. He assaults the rabbi in charge while Elijah runs away with the winning trophy. "Shalom, Elijah," shout the boys. "Shalom,

Jewboys!" Elijah replies as he runs off.[61] Although the stories are engaging, they are too pat and formulistic and not as strong as the titular novella of the collection.

Two novels by Neugeboren centering on the life of Blacks in professional sports are more successful. *Big Man* (1966) is a first-person narrative of Mack, a Black basketball star blacklisted for participating in fixing games by controlling the number of points scored. The basic theme of the novel is expressed by Rosen, a sports writer who loves sport and rejects the influence of commercialism when he tells Mack: "You are a symbol of the big-time corruption which corrodes our national fiber." The commercialism of sport makes an anti-educational medium of it by aborting the education of Black players, who are allowed to go through college without an actual educational training. Rosen campaigns through his sports writing to get Mack and other Blacks reinstated, arguing that they have been blacklisted long enough, and that in any case, those moneyed people who dominate the game "took the ballplaying away from them." When the Black ballplayers "were at college (or even before) they were given cars, money, girls, tutors, and tuition solely for their talents on the hardwood. They were told in no uncertain terms that they were neither amateurs nor students. And yet when they discovered this themselves, and did things no more 'corrupt' than coaches, alumni, businessmen, and educators—everybody suddenly became very righteous."[62]

It is apparent that Neugeboren is intimately knowledgeable about sports, loves them, and is deeply concerned about the situation of Blacks. He combines effectively these two commitments in his early fiction. They are conjoined with his personal experience as a Jew in a later novel, *Sam's Legacy* (1974). The central Jewish characters are Sam Berman and his father Ben. The central Black characters are the janitor, Tidewater Mason, who is Ben's closest friend; Flo, a Barnard graduate who heads a muscular dystrophy aid agency because her husband and two children died of the disease; and Stella, pretty and stricken with muscular dystrophy. These five are involved with two themes: love between white (Jewish) men, Ben and Sam, and Black women, Paula and Stella respectively, and the autobiographical narrative of Tidewater Mason as a batter and pitcher in Black professional baseball. This story of Tidewater's baseball career comes to Sam Berman as the legacy from his father's friendship with Mason. Mason is a better baseball player than Babe Ruth, a not improbable situation in those days of professional Black baseball. In the exposition of both themes, the Black-white Jewish relations can be called "liberated." While marriage is contemplated by the older couple, it does not happen because the dying Ben goes to San Francisco to join his brother, while the marriage of Sam and Stella is left in prospect. As for the second theme, the segregated, inhuman treatment of a Black professional baseball team with players said to be at least as good as any white, is recounted in the secret narrative that Tidewater has written. Sam is privileged to read it because his father believes it will transmit to his son the close friendship he himself had with Tidewater. The most striking technical feature of the novel is the sharp contrast between the colloquial, racy, informal style in which the author tells the story and the formal, dignified, elegant rhetorical style of Tidewater's narrative, which is a full-fledged story within the novel. The contrast is developed with some virtuosity. Much of the history of Black baseball leagues is informatively conveyed in Tidewater's account, and indeed a part of Neugeboren's main purpose is to expound Black-white relations in terms of sports from the perspective of Black liberation.

However, as the 1960s and 1970s wore on, gains won by the civil rights movement were seen as fragmentary. Black determination hardened and the special relations between Black and Jewish writers weakened and in some instances were even destroyed. Frustration at the halting movement toward Black liberation evoked in many Black writers intense nationalism; an awakened sense of pride in Blackness only too often expressed itself in anti-Semitism. These excesses aroused resentful insensitivity to the Black situation in some Jewish writers, who tended to concentrate on negative features of Black life in their writing.

With the worsening of Black-Jewish relations and the frightening rising incidence in crime and outcropping of overt anti-Semitism by some Blacks came a reflection of this mood in some Jewish writers. Treatment of Blacks in Saul Bellow's fiction in the 1970s and early 1980s is disturbing. In *Mr. Sammler's Planet* (1970) Bellow has Sammler observe a Black pickpocket at work on a Broadway bus. The description is vivid. The Black wore dark glasses, "a powerful Negro in a camel's-hair coat, dressed with extraordinary elegance . . . the face shared the effrontery of a big animal." After Sammler continued to see the same bus pickpocket at work some half-dozen times, he reports the crime to the police by phone, but they are indifferent, since to arrest him they must catch the thief in the act. Sammler describes the pickpocket as "Always gorgeously garbed . . . wore a single gold earring. . . . This handsome, this striking, arrogant black beast was seeking whom he might devour between Columbus Circle and Verdi Square."[63] Finally on one occasion the Black observes Sammler watching him take the wallet from an old man; he follows Sammler to his building, pushes Sammler into a corner of the lobby, and exposes himself, all without a word, compelling Sammler to look, then leaves. The figure of the pickpocket is the physically and sexually potent man, animal-like. He is given no voice in the entire narrative, which underlines his animality.

Since this is the sole Black in all of Bellow's work up to then (except for the fantastic Africans in *Henderson the Rain King*), one wonders why he chose to depict this sort of American Black. To be sure the figure of a Black pickpocket—or mugger, or thief—is only too common in our cities. And the passages involving the Black are, like most of Bellow's, splendidly written. In terms of the novel's thesis the pickpocket serves the function of an aspect of Sammler's (and Bellow's) revulsion from what Bellow considers the barbarity of the 1960s, of which the harsh, vulgar treatment of Sammler at his Columbia lecture by New Left students is another. In the perspective of the novel, the incidents involving both the New Left and the Black seem to be the beginning and end of Sammler's engagement with the larger phe-nomena suggested by both. Bellow may deny this with respect to Blacks, though not, I believe, to the New Left. But that is the way this impresses one. But how else can one explain that in a time when Blacks were straining to achieve equality, the sole American Black in Bellow's fiction is scarcely human? Sammler is living mentally and spiritually on another "planet" far from the values of the contemporary world, and his distaste for the violent, vulgar, and radical extremes of this flawed, existing planet *in extremis* amounts to his (and Bellow's) distancing from its problems.

In *The Dean's December* (1982) Bellow once again returns to Black criminality and the "underclass." He focuses on a Black pimp, Ebry, and his Black prostitute, who are charged with the murder of a white student from the dean's university. Dean Corde's nephew, Mason Zaehner, is a student radical, a close friend of Ebry's, and is working to exonerate him. But Mason is an extremist and aspires to be an "honorary black," as Bellow says; he is amoral and unscrupulous as was the student left depicted in *Sammler*.

This time Bellow also introduces three positive, countervailing Black char-acters, an ambassador, a reforming prison warden who is slandered by the politicians because he has successfully removed inefficiency and corruption from his prison administration, and an ex-criminal who runs a detoxification center in the Black slum. The two socially engaged Blacks do admirable work for the "underclass" in their individual efforts. Bellow admittedly has profound distrust of organized social activism in work for structural change in society.

Bellow is quite aware that he has left the problem in suspension, that his argument is "incomplete," as he says, because he "never did get around to explaining how we must resuscitate ourselves." That he does not have the answer is understandable—one can hardly expect that from a novel, and there are no easy answers in any case. The quantitatively small, though significant, achievements of the Black reformers in the novel are not to be scorned, but they are drops of water in a desert. Bellow grants that the desperate conditions of Blacks have "material causes" and can be helped by material measures and programs, but he gives short shift to these con-siderations. He promptly passes on because he believes there are other than "material" causes and it is in these unexplained and non-material causes that he is mainly interested. It is not so much, he writes, that we are "threat-ened" by the "inner city slum" as by the "slum of innermost being, of which the inner city was perhaps the material representation." Which really "represents" which, the "innermost being" or the "inner city" or vice versa? Toward the end of the novel Bellow declares, "I haven't begun to reach a conclusion."[64]

Malamud's fictional attitude is more complicated. In his early short story collections he had published two stories of Blacks and Jews, "Angel Levine" in *The Magic Barrel* (1958) and "Black Is My Favorite Color" in *Idiots First* (1963). These are followed by the novel, *The Tenants* (1971). Each story represents a stage in the rapidly developing Black Liberation movement. The first, represented by "Angel Levine," appears in the time when brotherly resolution of differences seemed possible to both. The second stage, represented by "Black Is My Favorite Color," signifies a more problematic, even frustrated period. Finally we get *The Tenants*, when the decades-old Black-Jewish coalition was breaking up and mutual hostility was developing in many quarters.

During this period what was psychologically inherent became overt. The situation can be somewhat clarified by a useful distinction Evelyn Gross Avery draws in *Rebels and Victims: The Fiction of Richard Wright and Bernard Malamud* (1979). Both Blacks and Jews, she holds, are "marginal"—though hardly to the same degree—and subjected to a "harsh environment, the scorn of fellow citizens, physical and psychological oppression." How can the Black or Jew respond, "internalize his frustration"? He can do so either as a victim "or become a rebel, striking out at others." As a victim he can passively accept the "predicament" or as a rebel he can respond with "violence" in order to survive. Avery knows, of course, that both types have appeared in literature in both groups. But in recent fiction the tendency has been for Blacks to be rebels and Jews to be victims. This distinction is largely borne out by the account we have given of Black-Jewish writing since Richard Wright. The widespread vogue of the Jew as *shlemiel*—the victim par excellence in postwar English fiction, not to mention the Yiddish literary tradition of the classical Yiddish writers—further confirms the general accuracy of this distinction. When Jews try to help Blacks, no matter how "well-intentioned" they may be, "aid engenders envy, shame, and hostility as well as gratitude." Genuine mutual confidence and rapport are extremely rare, if not impossible, because the chances for failure of understanding on both sides are high. The delicacy of the relationship is only too easily disturbed. "Jewish assistance, friendship, and sympathy only underscore black's impotency, the extent of their reliance on beneficent whites."[65] The relationship is too asymmetrical and one that very often may, and often does, offend the pride of Blacks.

In the Malamud stories the first stage is exemplified in "Angel Levine," in which the Jew Manischevitz perceives through his suffering that "there are Jews everywhere"; even Blacks are Jews. Manischevitz has lost his store by fire, and suffers many personal misfortunes. He is now desperate to save the life of his ailing wife. He remembers the visit of a Black who calls himself

"Angel Levine," whom he had incredulously dismissed. Now Manischevitz searches Harlem to find him in the hope of effecting a cure for his wife. At last he finds the Angel Levine carousing and begs him to come home to cure his wife. At Manischevitz's house the Angel Levine leaves, saying, "that's all been taken care of.... You best go in while I go off." As the Angel moves off, Manischevitz seems to hear wings whirring and something flying. When he arrives home, he sees his wife recovered. "A wonderful thing, Fanny," he says. "Believe me, there are Jews everywhere."[66] Malamud here is again using "Jew" as a metaphor for one who partakes of redemption through Job-like suffering, for Manischevitz has suffered a devastating series of misfortunes, and the Angel Levine is the agency for his redemption and hence is part of the "Jewish" scheme of things, irrespective of color or race. The possibility of brotherhood through suffering is still open at this stage.

Five years later, when "Black Is My Favorite Color" appeared in *Idiots First* (1963), the relationship had become more problematic and more difficult, if not impossible. A Jewish liquor store owner in Harlem, Nat Lime, comes to know a Black woman, Ornita Harris. They fall in love, and Nat asks her to marry him, but she refuses after three hoodlums Jew-bait and attack him one night when he is escorting her home. Her refusal is avoidance of the hardships she foresees in the mixed marriage. The predicament is too much for Ornita—potentiality for hurt on both sides is too great and immanent to allow marriage. For his part, Nat recalls his youthful friendship with a Black boy, Buster, whom he treated to candy and the movies. At last, without any provocation, Buster had hit him in the mouth. Why, Nat asked? "Because you are a Jew bastard."[67] When Nat's cleaning woman, called Charity Sweetness, eats her lunch, she retires to the bathroom. She refuses his invitation to eat with him because of ingrained custom in relation to whites. Even though external circumstances prevent Nat's marriage with Ornita, obliteration of the barrier between them is still desirable to Malamud himself.

But as the 1960s drew on and Black-Jewish antagonisms became overt, with the uninhibited anti-Semitism often expressed by some Blacks (especially some intellectuals and writers), overt racism by some Jews, and the mounting struggle for Black equal rights, Malamud was apparently overwhelmed. The result was *The Tenants* (1971), in which an aspiring Black writer's effort to get technical help in his writing from an established Jewish writer leads to their mutual destruction. On the way the Jew, Lesser, displaces the Black Spearmint in his Jewish girl's affections; Spearmint and his Black friends subject Lesser to anti-Semitic harassment, he destroys Lesser's years-old manuscript of an unfinished novel, and Lesser in retaliation breaks up Spearmint's typewriter. In the final climatic scene they encounter one another with the exchange "Bloodsuckin Jew Nigger hater," "Anti-Semitic Ape," and in an unreal scene they hack away at one another. "Lesser felt his jagged ax sink through bone and brain as the groaning Black's razor-sharp saber, in a single boiling stabbing slash, cut the white's balls from the rest of him. Each, thought the writer, feels the anguish of the other."[68]

Each writer feels the incompatibility between his aim in writing and the other's. Lesser the artist is concerned with craft, form; Spearmint is obsessed with lashing out in rebellion at the oppression of his people. The Jew is the victim of the Black's rebellion. As Spearmint's dissatisfaction with his writing rises, his antagonism for the artist, whom he regards as a misleader in art, becomes more intense, fueled also by Lesser's appropriation of Spearmint's Jewish mistress and what he regards as Lesser's attempt to sap his vitality in both writing and sex. Antagonism has turned to mortal enmity with razor and axe. The one revenges Lesser's succession to his mistress by destroying his sex; Lesser destroys Spearmint's power to write by smashing his brains. The outcome is one of mutual destruction with no possible solution. Malamud leaves the reader hopeless.

Malamud later told an interviewer that "He would be unhappy to have the book described simply as a story of black-white relations. He thinks of *The Tenants* as a sort of Prophetic warning against fanaticism." Then he added that "the book argues for the invention of choices to outwit tragedy." But it is precisely the *absence* of choices in the end that is troubling. No choices, but only inexorable destructive hostility emerge. Further, the "fanaticism," which obviously refers to Spearmint, is presented only in terms of sexual and anti-Semitic clichés. Evidence that there was some resentment against the story among Blacks can be seen in Addison Gayle, Jr.'s, review in the New York *Amsterdam News*. "Willie," he writes, "is a black man as seen through the eyes of a white man: crude, coarse, insulting—one whose dedication to the Black revolution is confused by his association with his white mistress."[69] If it is indeed true, as Malamud said, that we should not regard the novel as "simply a story of black-white relations," then it is pertinent to ask a question posed by a Jewish critic, Jerome Greenfield: "is it completely moral to exploit such an urgent and present problem as black anti-Semitism for fictional ends that have little direct bearing upon it? I wonder if it is moral for a writer to dilute and transform this problem, the way Malamud does, so that it becomes nothing more than a symbol of a much larger dislocation in the inherently tragic human condition . . . to transform it from the social issue that it is into an existential one about which nothing can be done."[70]

Whether one regards the novel as a study of Jewish-Black relations or, as Malamud says he would prefer, as a study in "fanaticism," the outcome is the same—an impasse. What is clear, however, is that the special relationship which had in previous decades prevailed in the literary relations of Blacks and Jews had been seriously impaired. In some cases the impairment may remain lasting. But the healing process has begun and some signs of return should appear in literature as they have in social life itself. The basic community of interests is too deep-seated not to reassert itself.

2

From Dialect Humor to Black Humor

The fictional and stage heritage of the Jewish image as the twentieth century opened was with few exceptions overwhelmingly that of the stereotype and the butt of ridicule. The last decades of the previous century had seen not only an exacerbated use of the stereotype in fiction but also the introduction of the "Hebrew comic," who takes his place alongside the Irish, German, and Black standard comic figures in entertainments. For instance, a hack play in 1904 supplies us with a professional description of "Hebrew makeup," the uniform of the Jewish character. He may not dress as an ordinary man of the time, but wears "a black and white vest, coat somewhat the worse for wear; large turned-down collar and red tie; light striped trousers, narrow at the bottom and short, showing the loud colored stockings; black wig and black whiskers; old derby hat in the back of the head and so large that it sets down over his ears."[1] Jews were assigned dialect bearing little or no resemblance to human speech. In the comic magazine *Puck* for 1901, one finds this "joke":

> Cohenstein: Mine frendt, vere are you from?
>
> Chinaman: From Hong Kong, China.
>
> Cohenstein: Mine frendt, take dot for a kevorter! I will lost monish, but I vant to get der China trade![2]

For several decades into the new century the Jewish place in the humor of the country was predominantly of this dialect sort. With the growth of a second generation there was a distinct movement in fiction away from the stereotype in the literary image of the Jew, which had predominated in the previous century. But the Jew remained the butt of ridicule in popular humor. This phenomenon was not, of course, unnoticed. Thus, the *Indi-*

anapolis News could write in 1901, "it is a curious thought, with the growing influence of Jews in theatrical matters, so little respect is paid on stage to the Jewish character of the Jewish tradition. It might be imagined that ... the frightful caricature of the Hebrew which has long served as the buffoon for the amusement of the unthinking would disappear, but there are no signs of any such change."[3] Change was indeed long in coming, for dialect comedians continued to be among the most popular in burlesque and vaudeville through the 1930s.

In fiction, however, comic Jews as *central* characters did not occur until Montagu Glass began to publish his Potash and Perlmutter stories in popular magazines in 1909, and to collect them into a book, *Potash and Perlmutter,* with over four hundred pages, in 1910. It is possible that the third- and fourth-generation Jews have never heard of these "funny" men, but they were vastly popular in their time, so popular that this book was followed the next year by *Abe and Mawruss* and *Partners Again* in 1922, and revived even as late as 1935. At first the two men were partners in the garment industry, but later stories had them selling autos and producing films. They did not speak in dialect but rather in outrageously ungrammatical English with Yiddishized word order. Often the incidents and episodes of their business dealings concern attempts at sharp practices that boomerang. The mood is relaxed and bland and purports to be amusing. Their business practices are pervaded by an atmosphere of petty dishonesty and sharp dealing, which are meant to invite indulgence. Sometimes these stories are mildly funny, but throughout, the reader (and the author) necessarily feel superior and condescending toward the patently harmless, well-intentioned joking pair. But in whatever situation they are, sharp practice seems second nature to them and somehow pertains to their Jewishness.

These stories were on the whole favorably received. The poet and socialist, James Oppenheim, greeted the first book in *The Bookman* with praise. Glass, he wrote, had "seized upon a section of life as yet not articulated through art." While he considered the character "dripping with faults; ... their mean-nesses, ... their money-lust and sharp practice," they yet "grow on us until we accept them as relatives—that is, we see their faults merged into a universal humanness." But he stresses that they represent only a small segment of the Jewish people.[4]

The stories were translated onto the stage in 1913 with great popular success for some years. An unsigned *New York Times* review (August 8, 1913) asserted categorically, "In no sense can it be regarded as offensive to the Jewish race." The unsigned review in the *Boston Herald* (September 30, 1913) commented that the play's "travesties of the Jewish character are thoroughly good-natured. There is nothing offensive in it." The *American Hebrew* (August 29, 1913) called the play "one of the most entertaining farces that has been seen on the New York stage for some time," but added that "some super-sensitive souls among us may resent the vulgarity which is the dominant note in the characters of the two partners." The plays do seem on the whole less objectionable than the fiction, but the overall effect of both is not only to promote stereotypic notions but also to cause Jews not to be taken seriously.

The danger of such plays can be illustrated from their effect on the anti-Semitic inclinations of Willa Cather, when she observed in connection with *Potash and Perlmutter* that the Jews were taking over New York City. In these matters the Jew cannot be regarded in the same light as the comic figures of the Yankee, the Irish, or the Germans at the time (the Blacks are a special, more severe case) as is sometimes suggested. Because hostility to Jews is so deeply imbedded in Western culture, the Jewish figure in humor finds himself in a different context from that of the other comic figures. So strong is the general predisposition to disapprove of Jews that the fact that the Potash and Perlmutter stories were written by a Jew, who had no wish to injure the Jews, is no defense against the stories' reinforcement of the stereotype. Freud has observed, "The jokes made about Jews by foreigners are for the most part brutal comic stories in which a joke is made unnecessary by the fact that Jews are regarded by foreigners as comic figures." At the same time, he goes on, "the Jewish jokes which emanate from Jews admit this too." But one difference is that the Jews also know "their good qualities" as well as "their real faults."[5]

Even this qualification has its limitations, for many Jews are insensitive to the hostile element in jokes about Jews as a manifestation of a lesser or greater degree of self-hatred. Peter Gay's remark about some German Jews in the latter years of the nineteenth century is relevant to some Jewish humor in our own century and country. "There were many Jews in Germany," he wrote, "... who chuckled at jokes directed against Jews and who indeed made many such jokes of their own." He reports that jokebooks published by a Jewish firm and addressed to Jews contained "often biting and always crude jokes [which] adopted anti-Jewish stereotypes without modification and without apologies: the ridicule of the Jew's blatant passion for profit, his indecent bargaining, his parvenu's self-importance and ignorance—all types familiar from anti-Semitic myth-making."[6]

While the situation was not quite so extreme in the United States, the insensitivity of some Jews in this regard has not altogether left us. Thus, *Isaac Asimov's Treasury of Humor* (1971) regards as "anti-Jewish" those jokes about Jews as "crass materialists of dubious ethical standards, reluctant to engage in sports or fisticuffs" *only* if they are "told in hostile fashion by someone clearly already non-Jewish in an accent such as no Jew ever spoke." In that case, he continues, "it well might" offend the Jew. He himself, he adds, tells such jokes "with relish," and he adds, "Why not?" There is, he says, "usually at least a little germ of truth in any stereotype; and if all groups are to live together in this world . . . let us know each other's weaknesses and laugh at them, instead of hating them." Asimov has missed

two aspects of the Jewish joke based on the stereotype, regardless of its
"little germ of truth."[7] First, as Gay noted above, they are often based on
"anti-Semitic myth-making." And second, such stereotypic jokes confirm
the stubborn anti-Jewish hostilities not far from the surface even of well-
intentioned non-Jews.

The stereotyped Jew-comic reaches some sort of apogee in the anti-Semitic
1920s with the play *Abie's Irish Rose* by Anne Nichols. This play had the
double advantage of exploiting the stereotypes of both the Irish and the
Jew, the Murphys and the Cohens, with a story of an intermarriage dis-
approved by parents on both sides and of the final reconciliation of the two
families through the birth of twins, one for each side. This play, first produced in 1922, was one of the most successful in American theater history.
It is shot through with caricatures of both peoples and uses the crudest
accents and dialect. There is continual reference to money, and the banter
runs like a series of vaudeville skits. The insensitivity of the entire proceeding
at the end of the play is clear when the Jewish and Irish fathers argue the
respective merits of their peoples:

> Pat: That's the trouble with your race; they won't give in; acknowledge when
> they're beaten!
>
> Sol: Give in, is it? That's the trouble with the Irish! Dod's the reason it took you
> so long to get free!
>
> Pat: Well at least we've always had a country—that's more than you can say.
>
> Sol: Ve god a country, too! Jerusalem is free! ve god it back!
>
> Pat: Now that you've got it, what are you going to do with it?
>
> Sol: Ve don'd really need it! Ve own all the other peoples![8]

As Gay observed of the German Jews, this last statement echoes "anti-
Semitic myth-making" about Jewish ownership of the world, and this remark is only the climax of a saccharine, painfully obvious exhibition of
blatant stereotypes. The *Boston Transcript* review (October 5, 1925) is
accurate enough: "this play is a painful burlesque on Jewish family life,
caricatures.... [It is] a dishonest exhibition for one seeking pure comedy
entitled to expect such ... only wit reeking with buffoonery and clowning."

During this entire period—and indeed, through the 1930s—the Jew-comic
continued to amuse vaudeville and cabaret audiences. For the most part no
ill-will was intended, but the Jew and the Yiddish language were subjected
to ridicule or, at best, condescension. Such comedy depended heavily on
dialect for effect. At the same time a number of talented Jewish song and
dance men and composers of popular music emerged in vaudeville and the
music theater, humorists who eschewed dialect and were ostensibly "American" but whose comic style contained elements of zany Yiddish humor as
practiced in the "Borscht circuit" in the Catskills. Many started their careers

as comedians in these Yiddish-speaking resorts and carried over some of their devices, without using explicit Jewish material, to the general public.

Also in the 1920s and 1930s some sophisticated Jewish writers achieved a reputation as humorous versifiers, writers like Franklin P. Adams, Dorothy Parker, Samuel Hoffenstein, and Arthur Guiterman. Their light verse contained little or no Jewish content and was totally in the current Anglo-Saxon tradition.

By the 1930s the vogue for the type of humor represented by *Potash and Perlmutter* and *Abie's Irish Rose* was largely spent though by no means completely gone. Jewish humor in book form in the 1930s was dominated by Milt Gross, Arthur Kober, and Leo Rosten (under the pseudonym Leonard Q. Ross). Although there were differences in their writing, all three relied in one way or another on dialect humor, if we include as "dialect" tortured and ungrammatical English as well as Yiddishisms and Yiddish-influenced word order. Each created a different frame for his exploitation of dialect or mangled English. For Milt Gross it was the mother trying to entice her baby into finishing the meal by telling her child fairy stories in outrageously transcribed dialect and scrambled English. Some examples of the speaker's unintended punning in Milt Gross' *Nize Baby* (1926): "magic want" (wand), "poison" (person), "welt" (wealth). Malapropism on top of dialect is also frequent: "preposition" (proposition), "conclusion from de brain" (concussion), "epson-minded" (absent-minded). Laughter at distortion of language is a persistent and invidious and basically primitive form of humor, since its suppressed premise is the superiority of the laugher. What I have called puns in dialect humor are, strictly speaking, more complicated than the straight pun, for added to the effect of the double meaning is the ignorant misuse of language. The pun is intended by the putative maker of it as a distortion of language whose misuse is known to the recipient but not to the speaker. Widespread opinion approves the use of Yiddish dialect and finds it genuinely humorous. "It is certainly assumed," wrote Max Eastman in *The Enjoyment of Laughter* (1936) "that when we smile at a misused language, what amuses us is the ignorance, or pretended ignorance, of the character using it. The fact is that distortions of our speech patterns are intrinsically funny when plausibly introduced, and the function of the ignorant individual is to introduce them plausibly."[9] Eastman then goes on to instance James Russell Lowell's Hosea Bigelow, Joel Chandler Harris' Uncle Remus, Finley Peter Dunne's Mr. Dooley, and the characters of Milt Gross and Arthur Kober. What Eastman does not take into account, as in so many discussions of this subject, is that the cases are different: between the Blacks and Jews on the one hand, and all the rest on the other hand. For in the cases of the Blacks and Jews the laughter tends willy-nilly to deepen prejudice that already exists in either latent or overt form, since it confirms the existing prejudice. Where there is no serious predisposition to prejudice, the laughter is directed against the individual using the distorted language, but in the cases of the Blacks and Jews there is a tendency to generalize the ridicule to embrace the group as a whole.

While the tortured language of Milt Gross signifies a closeness to immigrant origins, Arthur Kober's characters have risen to the petty bourgeoisie and are a more "Americanized" upwardly mobile Bronx family of mother, father, and eagerly marriageable daughter Bella. They are naive intellectually and socially, straining to achieve middle-class respectability and status. The humor lies not only in their patent social naiveté but also in the heavily Yiddish-influenced English transcribed with some phonetic accuracy. The humor is in part mild satire of social pretensions and in part ridicule of their speech. Although there is no apparent suggestion of malice or ill-will toward the characters, a sense of superiority on the part of the reader is unavoidable. There is some differentiation between the accented speech and Yiddish sentence structure of the parents and the accent-free but pretentiously correct speech of Bella with a number of Bronx locutions. The transcription of accent does not, in Kober, result in frequent punning effects as in Milt Gross. After the popularity of the stories originally published in *The New Yorker*, Kober collected the stories in *Thunder Over the Bronx* (1935). He continued to mine this lucrative vein with *Having Wonderful Time* (1937) about the travails of second-generation Bronx girls in search of husbands at a summer camp, and *My Dear Bella* (1941), more about the Gross family and Bella's tireless quest of a husband. *Having Wonderful Time* was made into a hit play on Broadway. But when it was translated into a movie in 1947, and into a popular musical in 1952, the names and milieu were changed from Jewish to non-Jewish in deference to the current sensitivity about the mention of the Jew in the mass media.

Hospitality for this type of story in Yiddish dialect or in mangled English was provided by the then current citadel of intellectual sophistication, *The New Yorker*. Leo Rosten (under the pseudonym Leonard Q. Ross) was also received into this magazine with his stories about a recent immigrant, Hyman Kaplan, and his efforts at acquiring the English language. These stories, which proved extremely popular, were first gathered into a collection, *The Education of H*Y*M*A*N K*A*P*L*A*N*, in 1937, followed in 1939 by *The Return of Hyman Kaplan* and then both revised, with additional material, in the *summa*, *O, Kaplan! My Kaplan!* in 1976. All these stories are located in the adult education class in English presided over by the ever-patient Anglo-Saxon Mr. Parkhill, attended by students with faltering English of over a half-dozen nationalities with Kaplan as the centerpiece. (Rosten himself had at one time taught such a class). Like Gross and Kober, Rosten wrote with the best of intentions and the kindliest feelings toward the objects of his verbal manipulation. In the preface to his 1976 volume Rosten defined humor as "the affectionate communication of insight." He expands on his conception: "Humor depends on characters. It unfolds from a fondness for those it portrays. Humor is not hostile. It is not superior to its players.

Unlike wit, it is not corrosive; unlike satire, it is not antiseptic; unlike slapstick, it is not ludicrous; unlike buffoonery, it is not banal. Humor is a compassionate account of human beings caught in the carnival and tragedy of living." We may accept this as at least an earnest of Rosten's benign intention; whether it is indeed true remains to be seen. At best this is an arbitrary constriction of the scope of humor. He goes on to argue specifically about the rendering of dialect that a "literal transcription"[10] involves the reader in a laborious deciphering process that is an obstacle to understanding and therefore "irritates" the reader.

Rosten labored long, he writes, to avoid this need for "decoding," and to form a dialect which would "create plausible deceptions," that is, rewards the reader by an instantaneous recognition of a risible double meaning.[11] For example, Mr. Parkhill assigns the class words to use in a sentence. "Pitcher" and "university" are the words assigned to Kaplan. He ruminates, "Is maybe pitcher for milk?... Is maybe pitcher on de vall? Also could be. Aha! So is two minnicks!"[12] On the second word, he offers, "Eleven yiss dey are married, so is time for de twelft univoisity." To use "department," he suggests, "An vhile ve are valkink, along somvun else pessink by, an' he by exident he's giving me a bump. So he says, 'Axcuse me,' no? But *sometimes*, an' dis is vat I minn, he says, 'Oh, I big depotment!' "[13] Such locutions can have the added feature of malapropism, as in the statement of another student that "Mary's little lamb had flees as white as snow."[14] While the word-play is the dominant mode of humor, the extreme social and intellectual naiveté of the good-natured Kaplan and his classmates is also a source of humor, as when Kaplan feels a proprietary right to espouse the interests of Columbus on discovering that his own birthday coincides with Columbus Day.

Perhaps one can get a handle on the real nature of dialect humor by recalling Freud's distinction between "innocent" and "tendentious" jokes. Whether they are one or the other depends on the hearers' reaction to them, Freud says. The innocent joke is enjoyed as "an end in itself"; a tendentious joke has some purpose, but only the latter "runs the risk of meeting with people who do not want to listen to them."[15] For instance, a purely verbal joke like a pun is innocent, but is this the case when the pun is unintended by the maker of it, but a device by a dialect writer? For instance, the phrase "of cuss" in Kober is not strictly a pun, since there is an actual English phrase, "of course," intended by the speaker. Is this an innocent joke? Certainly, like all three writers discussed here, Kober intended it to be such and would conform to Freud's definition. Many thousands of readers "wanted" to hear these jokes. (One wonders why Freud did not, except for two neutral passing references, make any effort to analyze dialect humor. Was it because he did not regard it as falling within the category of "jokes"? In one reference he notes that dialect "has an effect similar to joke-technique.")[16]

But is such dialect humor "innocent" if viewed from the standpoint of the Kaplans? To them, regarding their speech as funny entails a purpose, namely, to laugh *at* the speech foibles of immigrants. Tendentious jokes involve an act of condescending superiority, the suppressed premise of this humor. To what extent are these well-intentioned dialect stories different from the mocking oral dialect humor of stand-up Jewish comics or vaudevillians? Practicing in a less sensitive time, they made often cruel fun of the less acculturated and less language-assimilated Jews. The target is laughed at unsympathetically, and the ridicule is undeserved. Thus dialect humor is not in the end innocent, since it does have a purpose, which may be either friendly or unfriendly toward its target. This human object is unavoidably involved, no matter how innocent the joke-maker's intention.

Thus dialect humor is always at the least ambiguous in its relation to the speaker of imperfect English. This does not apply only to Yiddish speech, but to any distorted English. But not all ethnic humor of this sort is cruel or anti-social, depending on the status of the ethnic target and the intention of the joker and the context. A clear case of hostile ethnic humor occurred recently in a rash of so-called Polish jokes, which gained not only verbal but also written currency. It is difficult to understand why this should have happened, since the Poles of the United States are not generally subject to prejudice. On the other hand, the dialect humor of Finley Peter Dunn's Mr. Dooley was not inimical to the Irish—quite the contrary. But content is not the only determinant of whether any ethnic humor is hostile or not: the prevailing social attitude toward the group concerned is an important determining element as well. Thus anti-Semitism can convert any allusion to Jews into the "comic." For instance, it has been maintained that anti-Semitic feeling in *The Merchant of Venice* is so intrinsic to the play that Shylock can be, and has been, played as a comic villain by giving him an accent and Jewish mannerisms so that even the "Hath not a Jew eyes?" speech can be delivered so as to evoke laughter.

Because of this ambiguity of ethnic humor, during the Hitler period even the mention of the Jew in the mass media other than in a serious or neutral context tended to be avoided. Henry Popkin's factual article in *Commentary* in 1952 complained with ample documentation that " 'de-Semitization' is now a commonplace in the popular arts."[17] In paperback reprints, plays, movies, and television, characters who were Jewish in their original appearance were now rendered as non-Jews to avoid any allusion to the Jews. Popkin particularly lamented "the great retreat" during which "by 1935, most of the Jewish comedians had vanished from the screen," and the "disappearance" of the Jewish "dialect comedians."[18] Popkin adds that "only Sam Levinson has exhibited a fresh and personal flavor in his adaptations of Jewish stories and his discourses on Jewish life."[19] In these Levinson eschews talk about "the little Jew" and the dialect humor that usually accompanied it because, Levinson has said, they are "fundamentally anti-Semitic." To these comments of Popkin, Levinson promptly replied by granting that "in my own work I have deliberately expurgated dialect stories." He urged that Jewish dialect humor should stay "vanished" because "to mimic broken English is as painful to the immigrant as mimicking a limp is to the cripple." Further, he says, "there are even worse implications," that is, the response to such humor may bring out anti-Semitic ridicule. Levinson also observes that accented speech is not always hostile, and he instances Molly Goldberg's performance which, he says, "teaches love, kindness, honesty, respect for culture, and decency on a high level."[20] Like the work of Levinson himself, this material is sentimental and verges on the banal, but it cannot be said to be hostile in any sense.

One of the outstanding examples of benign humor with Yiddishized English word order in which the humor lies in the situation of gentle irony in the perceptions of a newly arrived teenage immigrant in Brooklyn from Poland, as he contrasts his new condition with that he has left behind in the anti-Semitic Poland of his native *shtetl*, is Yuri Suhl's *One Foot in America* (1950). The Yiddish dialogue is conveyed in straightforward English except for occasional lapses into Yiddishized word order to suggest immigrant speech: "You want to buy, buy. You don't want to, don't buy." The humor involved in the telling of young Shloimele's first meal at his American aunt's home with a large party of relatives immediately after disembarking begins with white rolls which quickly disappear from the table. "When I saw white rolls," says Shloimele to himself, "I decided immediately that my uncle was a rich man. For in Pedayetz only the rich could get white rolls." After the rolls were gone, pumpernickel appeared. "To me," he continued, "this was a terrific letdown, for in Pedayetz black bread was the bread of the poor: I was confused. Was my uncle rich or was he poor?" Later he learned that black bread was considered more healthful than white rolls. "I was now even more confused.... I decided to let Pedayetz and America fight it out between themselves while I went on catching up on white rolls."[21] The boy's education in American life is described through his boyish aspirations, his adventures at work, his boyish wooing of Beatrice, and numerous incidents in similar light, gently naive steps toward acculturation. This first novel was greeted favorably by the reviewers, who recognized the delightful, gentle humor. A few years later *Cowboy on a Wooden Horse* (1953) continued the adventures of young Sol Kenner and his development into an "American" boy without diminution of the freshness of its understated humor. Anzia Yezierska observed of Suhl's work, "The charm of something original, something perceived for the first time that made his first novel, *One Foot in America*, a delight to read, continues with surer craftsmanship in *Cowboy on a Wooden Horse*. ... Yuri Suhl's humor does not depend on dialect distortion of language or caricature of his people. His is a timeless humor and folk wit of compassion that deepen our acceptance of our fellowmen."[22] There is a touch of Sholem Aleichem's humane spirit in these novels of Yuri Suhl.

During the 1960s and 1970s dialect humor languished. Ethnic sensitivity was especially high during this period of radical revival, upsurge of the civil rights movement, and the recency of the Holocaust. Minimal immigration of Yiddish-speaking Jews and the almost total language acculturation of the second, third, and fourth generations tended to remove the Yiddish dialect from common attention and diminished familiarity with its currency. But the depressed economy and the ascent of ideological reaction to the presidency with Ronald Reagan in 1980 broke down restraints in such humor, and a spate of ethnic joke books flourished. The *New York Times* reported on July 30, 1983, "Racial and ethnic jokes have landed in force on the nation's bookshelves under the imprint of such publishers as Ballantine Books, Bantam Books, and Pocket Books. But even as the once-taboo volumes have begun to scale the best-seller lists, social historians are deploring them as a reflection of declining standards." The first, *Truly Tasteless Jokes*, appearing in 1982, so quickly caught on that *Truly Tasteless Jokes Two* quickly followed. They "included," reported the *Times*, "chapters about blacks, Jews, Poles, and white Protestants, as well as jokes about homosexuals, the handicapped and the blind. . . . [They] frequently employ racial epithets. And the punch lines commonly depict minority groups as shiftless and stupid, or as connivers or drunkards." Listed on the best-selling lists for months, this lode of calumny was quickly mined also by other publishers in books entitled *Gross Jokes, Outrageously Offensive Jokes*, and *The Complete Book of Ethnic Humor*. One of the publishers, reported the *Times*, asserted that "ethnic jokes have become a respectable form of ethnic humor." Was this presumed tolerance for vulgarity and insensitivity owing, in part at least, to a softening by the popular television series, "All in the Family," as well as the turn to the right under the Reagan administration?

Sensitivity to allusions to Jews in the mass media in the United States during the Hitler period and for a while thereafter is understandable if one takes into account Freud's observation that "the jokes made about Jews by foreigners are for the most part brutal comic stories in which a joke is made unnecessary by the fact that Jews are regarded by foreigners as comic figures." This seems to have been confirmed even into the 1960s, as shown in a study conducted by Sig Altman of the "entertainment" media of television, film, theater, and the popular novel. In these media the Jew as such has a "comic image."[23] This, Altman says, was one of those "everyday, taken-for-granted social facts that one can hardly see for their very proximity to the observer."[24] After Jews "vanished" from the mass media, according to Henry Popkin's thesis, their "reappearance" began in the 1950s, writes Altman, with the reemergence of "Jewish comedians" in the television talk shows who, Altman holds, formed the "spearhead of Jewish return to the media."[25] By the 1960s, Jews could be found in all the media, Altman writes, and he studied that return in the movies, theater, and television for stated periods from 1964 to 1970. During this period "the treatment of Jews, unlike that of other groups, is almost totally comic," except for "minor segments" of a few plays.[26] He determined numerically the incidence of what he called the "arbitrary" comic image, that is, an image "comic by its Jewish identification alone—the Jew is comic as such." Compared with other ethnic groups Jews were "comic" far more often; in fact, almost always. On television he found the Jewish image "mostly arbitrary."[27] In film he found Jews with one exception, and only one, not arbitrarily so. The evidence led to the overwhelming conclusion that the Jewish image in the popular media was almost always introduced for comic effect and in most cases the humor was "arbitrary," that is, the character was funny just *because* he was a Jew. The Jew had only to make an appearance to produce laughter. No wonder, then, that Hitlerism, which made Jews such a sensitive subject, induced a recession of Jews in the mass media. Altman further found that the Jew was almost alone of all ethnic groups (Blacks were not included in his study) to be automatically comic, and Jews were alluded to in connection with comedy far more often than any other ethnic group.[28]

When one turns to the fiction of the period, the situation becomes more complex. Altman shows that the comic association continues strong in printed material in the 1960s with numerous gratuitous attempts at "humorous" books that discuss Jewish behavior and that, he says, are not essentially Jewish but rather middle-class, but in which arbitrary use is made of Jews to evoke laughter. He suggests that attenuation of Jewishness has reached such a point that the residual Jewish identity is the only element that creates the humor. He adduces instances of advertising for books on serious Jewish subjects that try to exploit the arbitrary image with execrable taste, callous insensitivity, and vulgarity. He instances a shocking lapse in the advertising of a book on the Holocaust, and in connection with the advertising for *Portnoy's Complaint* the conflicts of the book are "souped up" as is "borne out by the laugh-shock-laugh-shock treatment of sexuality. Here are two subjects, Jewishness and sex, ideally suited to popular titillation."[29]

Yet in the same period the Jewish serious writer entered firmly into the mainstream of the country's literary life, so much so that, as we suggested earlier, we may regard the 1950s as the "Jewish Decade" in American literature. This writing, while much of it was punctuated with wit, was part of the most serious of the decade and far indeed from dependence on the arbitrary comic image. The Jew projected as the symbol of alienation pervaded society because he was the historically alienated figure in Christian society. While writers like Bellow and Malamud rejected surrender to alienation, they were certainly not immune from the awesome influence of the horrifying vision of atomic annihilation and the debilitating effects of consumerism and depersonalization. In common with their fellow writers, who reflected a hopeless alienation, they transmitted their thought through the medium of the *shlemiel* character.

The concept of *shlemiel* in classic Yiddish writing is found in Mendele Mocher Sforim's "little man" (*dos Kline mentshele*), I. L. Peretz's Bontshe Shweig, and Sholem Aleichem's Tevye. The *shlemiel* is the concept of the fallible human character who seems to court misfortune but never loses hope. Often he is the wise fool like Don Quixote who suffers blows from without, yet maintains his inner faith in humanity and the possibilities of a good life. The *shlemiel* concept therefore depends on irony for its severe form of humor by its contrast between the actual and the hoped-for good life. In much Yiddish literature it stood for the long-suffering Jewish people, whose faith in God and people did not flag through all its travails. In the post–World War II period the protagonists of Bellow and Malamud were oppressed by the deracination of humanity but embraced life nevertheless. In Malamud's Fidelman, his *shlemiel* protagonist, for example in "The Last Mohican," is subjected to a series of demands and calamities by the Holocaust survivor Susskind until at last he realizes that Susskind is teaching him to surmount and transcend them. Bellow's Herzog flounders in a sea of personal misfortune and intellectual stasis until he acquiesces at the end to the value of acceptance of his lot. The humor of such *shlemiel* stories lies in the irony of the negativity of external conditions borne with inner tranquility.

But much of the postwar *shlemiel* literature is not so benign or hopeful. It is rather bitter satire in which the hope in Bellow and Malamud is absent. It has become known as "black humor," a latter-day version of "gallows humor." Freud cited a typical instance of gallows humor: "A rogue who was being led out to execution on a Monday morning remarked: 'Well, this week's beginning nicely.'" Or, "The rogue on his way to execution asked for a scarf for his bare throat so as not to catch cold."[30] The difference between gallows humor and the black humor of today is that gallows humor pertained to the fatal situation of individuals. Black humor in our day mocks all humanity. Just as gallows humor is an ironical foreclosure of all hope for an isolated individual, so black humor is the specter of hopelessness for all humanity. Its satirical quality lies in its magnification of individual behavior which exacerbates a human situation leading only to total frustration. Nathanael West's *Miss Lonelyhearts* (1933) and *The Day of the Locust* (1939) were anticipations of the full-blown black humor of the postwar period. *Portnoy's Complaint* is one of the most notorious examples of the postwar manifestations. Unlike the classical *shlemiel*, the *shlemiel* of black humor is without hope, a mode practiced by many Jewish and non-Jewish postwar writers. They are far removed from the benevolent *shlemiel* of the earlier Yiddish writers or even of a Kober or Rosten. Of non-Jewish writers of black humor one may cite as an example Thomas Pynchon's *V* (1963).

The half-Jewish Benny Profane's Jewish girl, Rachel Owlglass, tells Benny, "Can't you stop feeling sorry for yourself? You've taken your own flabby, clumsy soul and amplified it into a Universal Principle.... You're not a shlemiel. You're nobody special. Everyone is some kind of shlemiel."[31] According to the postwar black humorists, all humanity is in a condition of *shlemiel.*

The difference in mood between a *Potash and Perlmutter* in the pre–World War I atmosphere and the dark, foreboding black humor of post–World War II times is a measure of the depth of sociocultural crisis into which the world has descended in the interval. This distance is analogous to that between the elementary, naive dialect humor and the sophisticated, merciless satire of the Jewish stand-up comics of the 1950s and 1960s—Mort Sahl, Shelley Berman, and finally Lenny Bruce. The condition of a people can be gauged quite accurately by what is currently regarded as funny, for consensus must underlie what a people finds humorous. That is why some humor is ephemeral and topical, since its currency and consensus pass, while other forms of humor, like the comedy of an Aristophanes, a Shakespeare, a Congreve, or a Molière are permanently funny, since they lampoon enduring human behavior. And that is why the dominant group in American society found dialect humor funny in the days of mass immigration and for decades afterward when sensitivity toward ethnic groups was low and anti-Semitism was close to the surface, and why dialect is no longer considered funny by many people because of the higher level of sensitivity to ethnic sensibilities in our time. That is why minstrel shows flourished nearly until World War II, while Jim Crow was almost universally accepted, and why one would not dare to resuscitate this anti-Black form in our own time. And that is why we must look to the state of society to account for the prevalence of black humor in our day.

The prominence of the Jew in relation to black humor is tied to the symbol of the Jew as the alienated exemplar of humanity. For black humor was an auxiliary expression of the same basic mood and was emphatically practiced by the bitterly satirical stand-up comics, who were virtually all Jewish. In literature it was written by a number of non-Jews as well, such authors as Pynchon, Terry Southern, J. P. Donleavy, and others. One of the earliest black humorists was the Jewish Joseph Heller, whose *Catch-22* may well outlast all other fiction of this genre. While this brilliant and devastating satire of modern warfare is ostensibly set during World War II, it is actually a mordant postwar commentary on war, an anti-war book written after victory in World War II, written after the Korean War in the 1950s and published in 1961. The book contains no Jewish characters but statements in otherwise authoritative sources assert that Yossarian was depicted as a Jew in early drafts of the novel. Heller denies this and has written that "there were no earlier drafts. There were notes containing ideas, one of which was to put a Jewish soldier in a hospital ward. At no time was

Yossarian going to be Jewish." However, just as Dean Corde (in Bellow's *The Dean's December*), a non-Jew, clearly speaks for Bellow himself, so Yossarian must be interpreted as Heller's spokesman. Heller has written to me, Yossarian's "temperament and outlook are consistent with my own; I would not be the one to maintain they are exclusively Jewish."[32]

By the 1960s black humor was a flourishing genre. It is appropriate, in light of the association of both alienation and black humor itself, that a Jewish writer, Bruce Jay Friedman, a practitioner of the genre, was reported to have named the genre. In 1965 he edited an anthology of pieces of black humor and in the preface attempted an analysis of it. The thirteen writers represented, he wrote, had quite "separate" and "unique visions"; but what they all had in common was "the fading line between fantasy and reality in the modern world"; their writing has "a nervousness, a tempo, a near-hysterical new beat in the air, a punishing isolation and loneliness of a strange, frenzied new kind." The source of this mood, says Friedman, "is the calamitous news that daily beset them—the Vietnam War and the wild violence that pervade our society, political assassinations—a new mutative style of behavior afoot; one that can only be dealt with by a new one-foot-in-the-grave asylum style of fiction." To the black humorist, he says, the daily news has itself preempted satire; by now history has become a form of self-satire, so egregiously irrational is it. The black humorist challenges his time—"What in hell is going on here?" Friedman exclaims. Criticism is badly needed, but how can you deal with the absurdity of present events? To do this is "to sail into darker waters" of humor. The writer must ask ultimate questions: he must "take a preposterous world by the throat and say okay, be preposterous, but also be damned sure you explain yourself."[33] The 1960s were the heyday of this fiction, a counterpart of the revolt of youth against the middle-class values of their parents' generation. Among the Jewish writers who shocked their readership with this black humor were Burt Blechman, Friedman, Stanley Elkin, and Jeremy Larner.

Burt Blechman's *How Much?* (1961) subjected the frenzied, insensate consumerism (How much?) to searing satire as epitomized in a young Jewish "mom"; the faddism of her son, second-generation Barney, self-indulgent and self-absorbed; the father, interested only in making money from his business; the nursing home director who mercilessly exploits aged clients; the Black aide at the nursing home interested only in sleeping with men but yet the most human character of all. Blechman has made them patently characteristic products of the period, all fragmented human beings lacking in relationship to one another. Most of the characters are Jewish, who are of course subject to the malaise of the era like anyone else, selected only because the author knew them best. The second-generation Barney conveys the meaning of it all in his "theory of numbers." "From sea to shining sea, everyone was worshipping numbers: swank street numbers, bulging bank account numbers, glittering age numbers. What is their collective name but a number?—that grandiloquent abbreviation, U.S.A., leader in numbers, in popcorn popped, cars vomited, bombs conceived, calculators calculating, 1st, 1st, 1st."[34]

In his *Camp Omango* (1963) Blechman depicts the great outer world in microcosm in a boys' camp with its crude values, ugly individual relations, its few sensitive people, some of whom are finally infected with the aggrandizing spirit. All this reaches its ultimate ugliness in the camp director, promoter of false, chauvinistic national feeling, instilling thinly disguised Cold War hatred and the frenzy to be Number One. Competition to win at any cost is exalted to heights in a war game played with crude, ugly, dishonest tricks and the complete suppression of any idea of cooperation as a social method. Among the camp's Ten Commandments promulgated by the new-style Moses, the camp director, "Thou shalt kill for God and country upon demand.... Thou shalt adulterate the water, pollute the land, and poison the air for the sake of our father's pride," and so on. The boy Randy has a hard time suppressing his decency to fall in with the passion for winning at any cost: "He had to fight something inside him that wanted to lose.... He had to crush it, kill it to win."[35]

Unlike Blechman's brutal exposure of inhumane aggrandizement so close to the surface of contemporary social values, Bruce Jay Friedman depicts fragmentation and depersonalization in the pervading alienation through a pathetic Jewish *shlemiel* in *Stern* (1962). Stern's obsession with anti-Semitism and his fear of it bring out his impotence and inability to connect with others. He is a quite ordinary Jew whose vapid occupation is writing labels for commodities. The pivotal event of the novel is the encounter of his wife and child with an anti-Semitic neighbor who forbids his own child to play with Stern's son, pushing Stern's wife to the ground in the process, and seeing the exposure between the legs of the prostrate woman. When Stern hears about it, he is intimidated by the larger, aggressive anti-Semite whom he calls, "the kike man" and imagines him ridiculing Stern before his friends. The social ineligibilities of Stern, real and imagined, fill him with a timid, troubled awareness. After recovery from a breakdown caused by his unceasing morbid review of events and obsession with anti-Semitism, Stern is sufficiently recovered to challenge his antagonist to a fight; this is aborted and Stern cannot overcome his failure to communicate with other human beings, a *shlemiel* without hope in a time of general alienation. In a later novel, *A Mother's Kisses* (1964), Friedman sets forth a *shlemiel* who is a high school graduate with no awareness of the world at large. He seems shut off from the world by his mother's smothering love and solicitude. When he goes off to college in Kansas, she insists on coming with him. When he asks her to leave him at his destination, he finds he cannot do without her and retracts his demand that she depart. Friedman's wry humor through his fiction accentuates the pattern of the *shlemiel's* predicament, the inability to connect.

A dark view of the ordinary man emerges from Stanley Elkins' volume *Criers and Kibbitzers, Kibbitzers and Criers* (1965), short stories first published between 1959 and 1965. Most of his characters are Jewish, and an air of fantasy hovers over his narratives. The predominant note is a relentlessly negative view of people. The strong, pervasive satiric negativity is cushioned by the grim humor. In the title story the Jewish supermarket owner's dim view of human beings is confirmed when he discovers that his lately dead son pilfered from the cash register. The picture of ordinary humanity at a Catskill resort in "Among the Witnesses" is also most unflattering. After a lifeguard negligently allows a child to drown, it is revealed that the owner had hired the sixteen-year-old lifeguard to save money. In "The Guest" a visiting trombone player is allowed to occupy the apartment of friends. He proceeds to ruin it under the influence of drugs and is then compelled to stand by while thieves remove and take away all the contents of the apartment, including his trombone. In his first novel, *Boswell, A Modern Comedy* (1964), Elkin develops with a clever, fantastically satirical story to symbolize human resistance to mortality, the desire to get the most from life while it is lived. Its black humor, which is pervasive, is the secondhand character of the human quest in terms of the "Boswell" of the story, who is a seeker after vicarious greatness in human history. Throughout the fantasy Boswell meets important people and this culminates in the contrast between his own grandiose aspirations and his small realizations. The novel is in the existential current of the decade with an overlay of absurdist satirical fantasy. The same vein of intense individuals seeking liberation of the self from demands made on human life in his second novel, *A Bad Man* (1967), is again wild, satiric fantasy about Feldman, a department store owner. This novel has considerable Jewish content, which in this instance is a vehicle for the author's exploration into the nature of man, depicted as basically aggrandizing. It recalls Sade's theory, the opposite of Rousseau's, that man is by nature evil. After following Feldman's rise from the role of traveling peddler with his father to ownership of a store, in the familiar manner of the immigrant story, Feldman is in maturity jailed for doing illegal "favors" for others. The vagueness of these illegalities at first suggests the vagueness of the "charges" against Kafka's characters. Jail turns out to be a microcosm of living a "bad life" in relation to his fellow prisoners, for which they beat him up just before he is discharged. While somewhat more explicit than Kafka and replete with black humor, Elkin projects the Jew as the symbol of human alienation of modern man.

Varied as is the approach of each black humorist, the assumption of a dark view of humanity is common to all of them. Jeremy Larner's *Drive, He Said* (1964) pursues this mode of satire on contemporary life and United States foreign policy. He applies to them an untiring fantastic imagination; it is extravagant, free-wheeling, but always directed toward one or another aspect of the life of the times. As in so much black humor, the Jews serve as the agent for this satire concomitant with the Jew as symbol of alienated modern man. Jews are involved in the features of life satirized—athletic puffery, psychiatry, love relations, celebrity, foreign policy. The poles of social behavior are represented on one side by Moses Mandel, immigrant at ten, clothes peddler, City College "idealist," now a manufacturer of missiles, and on the other, his radical, pacifist student opponents. A party at Mandel's turns into a merciless depiction of celebrity and its corruption. Mandel tells the radical leader at the party, "O.K., so I'm evil. How do I live with myself? Wretchedly. But why stop with me? . . . I know these men. I know the President, the Senate, the successful and the fabulously successful of our time. . . . I have seen the most deliberate perverseness and debasement and deflection of morality the world has known, ever, and on such a scale you'd never imagine in your wildest dreams."[36] On the Cold War competition to reach the moon, a ticker-tape parade idolizing "our man on the moon," Larner writes, "New Yorkers had flooded Fifth Avenue from one end to the other to see the man who had beaten the Enemy and done our Country proud."[37] At the end the anti-war students demonstrate against missile manufacture at Mandel's plant, the anti-war leader is killed during the police break-up of the demonstration. Mandel, looking down at the carnage, makes the ultimate dark judgment of humankind: "Life is a horrid farce. . . . A horrid farce! . . . Death, Hector, Death. Death. Death. Death. It's ghastly. . . . Ha Ha: Everything in life is Death."[38] All is illusion. The author is cynical, though tinged with futile acquiescence with any attempted resistance to the "farce" our leaders have made of social life. Only laughter can make life tolerable.

Not a black humorist but worldly wise was the enduring, unique talent of S. J. Perelman, whose basic technique of humor never flagged over a half-century of practice, mainly in brief essay form. He had early joined his talents with those of the Marx Brothers in a few of their movies in the 1930s and wrote for other movies for a period, but he was most at home in brilliantly funny, literate little essays, many of which were first published in that fruitful reservoir of comic material, the *New Yorker*. He then collected them in books with such titles as *Acres and Pains* about country living, *Westward Ha* and *Swiss Family Perelman* about his travels, and *The Ill-Tempered Clavichord*. The titles give a clue to his technique—witty turns to the familiar and to clichés in meticulous, cultivated, elegant terms. He himself defined the salient characteristics of his "work for the printed page" in an essay of reminiscences about the Marx Brothers. Groucho, he knew, liked "my preoccupation with clichés, baroque language, and the elegant variation."[39] His masterful play with words to arrest the reader through startling turns of meaning founded on his wide and deep knowledge of the English language, combining elegance and ease with the popular image, punctuated with swerves of meaning in the use of clichés as well as ordinary discourse aroused explosive laughter. For instance: "I was strolling aimlessly down Fifth Avenue when several dollars which had been burning a hole in my pocket suddenly burst into flame and I found myself in Brentano's."[40] The attitude toward people in this humor is not cruel for the most part, but not kind either, rather sophisticated, tart and worldly-wise. Indeed, he once asserted that he didn't think there was any such thing as "kindly" humor.

Was Perelman's humor "Jewish"? It is true that he left a trail of Jewish allusions and Yiddish in his work, from beginning to end. His injection of Jewish or Yiddish phrases was always appropriate and meaningful. For instance: "at Tunafish College for Women, Ivy Nudnick, sauciest co-ed in the class, she of the unruly locks and the candied eyes, leaned over to impart the latest gossip."[41] Or, much later, in the essay, "Did You Ever See Irving Plain?" concerned with his encounter with Irving Thalberg: "Herewith, and invisibly impeded with a lump in my throat the size of a *matzo-ball*, are my memories of that signal experience."[42] Such Yiddishisms occurred frequently in his writing. But except for such obvious and external signs of Jewishness, it would be hard to define the essence of his humor as Jewish. It is intensely individual and unique. However, because it is so unmistakably and pervasively identified with a Jewish author, an inextricable association with Jewishness clings to it. There is an ineradicable fusion of Perelmanian humor with Jewishness so that the Jew and the humor cannot be separated.

3

Jews as Poets

American Jews produced only one Jew of notable poetic talent before the twentieth century, Emma Lazarus, who died at the age of thirty-eight in 1887. It may be worth noting, however, that the first book publication of verse by an American Jew was that of Penina Moise, *Fancy's Sketch Book* (1833). Verses of the same uninspired kind, usually religious, by some women poets did appear in such English-Jewish religious journals from the 1840s onward as *The Occident*, which began in 1843, the *Asmonean*, from 1849, and Rabbi Isaac M. Wise's *The Israelite*, published from 1854 onwards, as well as a number of English-Jewish newspapers published thereafter. This meager poetry, pious in tone and totally conventional, just about exhausted Jewish poetical activity during the century.[1] Literary production by Jews in the drama and fiction, though still for the most part hardly distinguished, was somewhat more successful and interesting.

But it would obviously be hasty to suppose therefore that Jews were inherently averse to cultural life or to creation of poetry. One need only recall the supreme poetry of the Hebrew Bible, most obvious in the Songs of Solomon or the Psalms, as well as the great Hebrew poets of the eleventh and twelfth centuries, such as Judah Halevi and Ibn Gabirol. Indeed, Robert Alter has asserted that the best of the secular Hebrew poetry of that period in Spain "is, I believe, on a par with the finest lyrical poetry of the Western tradition." He also calls attention to "the astonishing degree of continuity exhibited in Hebrew poetry through its long history and wide geographical dispersal," much of it, though not all, liturgical.[2] In the nineteenth century one need only recall Heinrich Heine as a major modern poet. In recent years the literary community and increasingly the general reading public is being made aware of such Yiddish poets as H. Leivick, Moshe Leib Halpern, and others, most of them working men, toward the end of the nineteenth century and in this century, in Eastern Europe as well as the United States.

How then can we explain the paucity of poetic work by American Jews until well into the twentieth century? The religious leaders of the Jewish community during the last century deplored the lack of an American-Jewish literature and called upon Jews for some transfer of attention from the prevailing American absorption with business toward literary creation. In the old established Jewish community during the first third of the century some plays by Jews were produced but virtually no fiction and only negligible poetry. Among the German immigrants of the 1840s onward some fiction was produced; versifying was mainly the work of women who echoed the current conventions with almost no inspiration, except for Emma Lazarus. However, several male poets were better known, although often for other achievements than for their poetry: Bret Harte for his fiction and Horace Traubel for his Boswell-like relation to Walt Whitman, as recorded in *With Walt Whitman in Camden*. Bret Harte's Jewish connection was as tenuous as his Jewish awareness: one grandfather was Jewish. Traubel's poetic work was Whitmanesque, with long, free lines and poems of wearing length, which are unreadable today. Unlike these two, Emma Lazarus was a passionate defender of the Jewish people at a time of rising anti-Semitism on the world scale and especially in Tsarist Russia; her poetry echoed her deep feeling. The critic George Whicher wrote that during a period of undistinguished poetry in the country at large, Emma Lazarus was "contributing poetry easily distinguishable by reason of its firmness, poise, from that of contemporaries whose only motive was literary."[3]

The genteel tradition, which by the end of the century had done much to sterilize the American literary scene, was exhausted, and new currents were beginning to stir with the spurt of realistic fiction and the spread of Whitman's influence in poetry. By the end of World War II perhaps a dozen Jewish poets had published verse and attracted some general attention, although many more were writing. All had been born before 1900, were native-born and of German-Jewish origin, except for Alter Brody, who was born in Russia and a Lower East Side resident. Jewish writers were now participating in the awakening of American literature, a literature associated with left-leaning politics and Greenwich Village bohemianism, which had enlivened the pre–World War I literary and cultural atmosphere. This was most vividly indicated by their contributions to the socialist-tending *The Masses*, founded in 1911.

One may locate the watershed of modern poetry as 1912, one year after the founding of *The Masses*, through two events. First was publication by publisher Mitchell Kennerley of *The Lyric Year*, in which appeared one hundred poems chosen from submissions from almost two thousand writers. Second was the founding of *Poetry Magazine* under the editorship of Harriet Monroe. The magazine was given a "modern" tone by the cooperation from abroad of Ezra Pound, who also led Yeats and the new "imagistic" poets to contribute. From the beginning it "discovered" and published leading poets and was the standard bearer of experiment in poetry. A new era in modern poetry, as one aspect of the rising literary renewal, had really begun. The fertilization of poetry was such that, as F. O. Matthiessen observed, "there were more expert practitioners of the craft of verse during the twenty-five years before 1940 than during any generation in American history."[4]

Where did the Jews stand in relation to this outpouring of poetry? A small number of Jewish poets were active in the early years of the century. Of the hundred poets who appeared in *The Lyric Year*, five were Jewish, a few forgotten today but including Ludwig Lewisohn and Louis Untermeyer. Yet no Jews appeared in *Poetry Magazine* until Maxwell Bodenheim in Number 4 (1914), with several thereafter. After Number 8, two or more usually appeared in each issue. The sheer number of Jewish poets grew rapidly. The extent of this participation in the life of poetry in America can be roughly gauged from their quantitative appearance in anthologies edited with a variety of editorial tastes. In observing the succeeding volumes, it is interesting to see how tastes changed; some poets in earlier volumes continue to appear; some drop out to be replaced by newer talents.

While numbers are a crude measure, they do serve as symptomatic of trends. The most prolific anthologist of American poetry was undoubtedly Louis Untermeyer. His *Modern American Poetry: A Critical Anthology* went through many editions after its first appearance in 1919. In the 1925 edition Untemeyer noted, "since 1912, more than thirty magazines were devoted exclusively to the publishing of verse. Though the death rate among these gallant *ephemera* has been rather high, there are as I write [1925] no less than fourteen poetry magazines still appearing."[5] If we begin with the first Jewish poet of the past century included in this anthology (we do not here count Bret Harte as Jewish), Horace Traubel, born in 1860, there are about 15 Jews of the total of 118; if we begin with Franklin P. Adams ("F.P.A."), born a generation after Traubel in 1881, 14 were Jews out of the total of 73, or 15 percent. In Untermeyer's Fourth Revised Edition in 1930, again beginning with Franklin P. Adams, the total was increased to 92 and the Jewish figure, reflecting a sharpening of taste and appearance of new poets, dropped to 12, or 8 percent. By the "New and Englarged Edition" in 1962 Untermeyer had drastically reduced the number of inclusions and added new poets. Now the oldest Jewish poet to appear is Louis Untermeyer himself, born in 1885. Of the total of 55 poets, 8, or about 13 percent, were Jewish. Most are not unworthy of their appearance there: Stanley Kunitz, Kenneth Patchen, Kenneth Fearing, Delmore Schwartz, Muriel Rukeyser, and Karl Shapiro.

It is well known that Jewish writers were well represented in the literary left of the 1930s. In the collection of fiction, poetry, reportage, drama, and criticism, *Proletarian Literature in the United States: An Anthology* (1935), the poetry section includes thirty-one poets; of these, nineteen, or two-thirds, are Jewish.

After World War II, an editor with the most severe standards, F. O. Matthiessen, published *The Oxford Book of American Verse* (1950); he allows only two Jewish poets to enter his Pantheon, Delmore Schwartz and Karl Shapiro, and no Black poets, though Paul Lawrence Dunbar, Langston Hughes, and Countee Cullen were well known. When, a quarter-century later, Richard Ellman compiled *The New Oxford Book of American Verse* (1976), he enlarged the list of Jewish poets to six, dropping Karl Shapiro, retaining Delmore Schwartz, and adding the younger poets Anthony Hecht, Louis Simpson, Denise Levertov, Philip Levine, and Adrienne Rich. Finally, *The Oxford Book of American Light Verse* (1979), edited by William Harmon, broadens the scope of such verse to include the musical theater. The editor's "principles of inclusion...comprehend...parodies, burlesques, travesties, satires, nonsense, *vers de société*, occasional poems, and verse that can be called 'familiar.' "[6] The first Jewish writer to appear is Arthur Guiterman, born in 1871, who was quite widely known as a humorous writer in his day. Beginning with Guiterman, there are 119 verse writers, about 24, or about 20 percent, Jewish. In addition to the lighter moments of some serious poets such writers of musical lyrics as Oscar Hammerstein II, Lorenz Hart, Ira Gershwin, and Stephen Sondheim have a place in this anthology. Others like Guiterman, Samuel Hoffenstein, and Franklin P. Adams were famous in the 1920s and 1930s.

Considering the large number of poets among Jewish writers and their stature, it is not unexpected that they were recipients of the several forms of recognition available in the United States. In addition to inclusion in many anthologies, Karl Shapiro received the highest official recognition for poets in America: in 1945 he received the Pulitzer Prize for Poetry, the first Jew ever to receive this award; in 1946 he was appointed Consultant in Poetry at the Library of Congress; from 1950 to 1955 he was editor of *Poetry Magazine*, oldest and most prestigious journal of poetry in the country; and in 1969 he was awarded the Bollingen Prize for Poetry. Not until fourteen years after Karl Shapiro's Pulitzer did another Jew receive the award, and after that many followed: in 1959, Stanley Kunitz; in 1964, Louis Simpson; in 1968, Anthony Hecht; in 1969, George Oppen; in 1970, Richard Howard; in 1973, Maxine Winokur Kumin; and in 1978, Howard Nemerov. These and others received recognition in several forms.

But what of the status of these poets as *Jewish* writers? Has their Jewish origin introduced in their work any difference from that of their non-Jewish colleagues? What is a *Jewish* poet in any case? Or is the designation "American Jewish," applied strictly to poetry, an oxymoron, that is, a contradiction in terms as some may maintain? The answer depends on two interpretations of "ethnic Jewish content" used to justify the dual designation of American *and* Jewish. The American side is apparent—use of American English with all the connections and overtones of the language rooted in this country and its accumulated experience and imagery. The Jewish side would be fulfilled by the introduction of themes relating to Jewish history, culture, milieu, and affairs of special concern to Jews. Some critics, however, would demand a more severe and demanding criterion: in some sense the poetry should be Jewish in spirit and in mode of expression. The difference between these two modes is that one writes *about* Jewish life past and present, in America and elsewhere, in American English; the other is a distinctively Jewish manner of thought and feeling. This second kind of Jewish poet must write out of some sort of immersion in Jewish tradition.

The extent to which such a deeply rooted form of *Jewish* poetry is possible for an acculturated American is problematic. The sophisticated, educated modern personalities who become Jewish poets are so deeply embedded in general American cultural life with its non-Jewish literary tradition, and usually so little concerned with an ethnically cultured Jewish life that, except for a few who lead a devoted religious or ethnic life, the Jewishness of their verse is necessarily of the first kind specifically characterized by *themes* relating to some aspect, whether secular or religious, of Jewish life.

How have anthologists of Jewish verse met this issue? Perhaps the earliest collection of American-Jewish poetry was *Anthology of Modern Jewish Poetry* (1927), compiled by a Jewish versifier, Philip M. Raskin, who included a generous sampling of his own pious work. Aside from uninspired religious poets included, there were some competent ones like Babette Deutsch, Alter Brody, Arthur Guiterman, Emma Lazarus, Jesse Sampter, Louis Untermeyer, and Jean Starr Untermeyer. In his Introduction Raskin wrote, "there is far greater soul-relation between [Louis] Untermeyer, [H.N.] Bialik [the Hebrew poet] and [the Yiddish poet] Yehoash writing in three different languages than between Untermeyer, Lindsay and Frost in the same language." If one takes "soul-spirit" to mean spiritual depth of intuition and feeling irrespective of nationality, Untermeyer is unduly exalted by the comparison with the other poets named. Raskin obviously means something specifically Jewish. But what can be Jewish, or poetic, for that matter, in Raskin's line: "God, though this life is but a wraith."? Raskin goes on to characterize modern Jewish poetry with a string of presumed general, universal traits such as "intense love of children," "tradition jewelled with a halo of adoration," "God-seeking," "clamor for social justice," "Messianic ideal of humanity," and so on. These, he adds, "may not be a monopoly of the Jewish race, but they are the main components of Jewish psychology and the leit-motif of Jewish poetry."[7]

Raskin's book was reviewed in *Menorah Journal* by a genuine poet, Kenneth Fearing, who characterized Raskin's conception of Jewish poetry as "a superstition about the Jewish soul" which "gives it sacerdotal glamour, ...expects of its poetry something mysterious and different." But, adds Fearing, the anthology yields only the "uniformly mediocre" and "extremely dull" because of the "pompous, lifeless, unimportant theories of what Jewish poetry should be." Raskin's view is shared, Fearing sadly observes, by "hosts of superstitious, intellectual intelligentsia."[8] Louis Untermeyer falls into this category in his essay, "The Jewish Spirit in Modern American Poetry." Like Raskin, he similarly ascribes universal qualities to Jewish poetry. Jewish poets possess, says Untermeyer, "certain outstanding racial characteristics"—"troubled energy,... probing dissatisfaction,... almost too intense introspection which is so eternally Semitic." He describes the various types of Jewish poetry—"not necessarily found together": "Poetry of exaltation, of mystical fervor,... poetry of disillusion, of bitter irony and driving restlessness,... of exultation, of sheer physical joy and thanksgiving."[9]

To such theories as those of Raskin, Untermeyer, and others, Kenneth Fearing in his review presented an alternative shared by many who have dealt with the question: "Whatever honest work was written by a Jew was undeniably Jewish poetry," Fearing wrote.[10] Like him, Florence Kiper Frank, a poet and playwright in the first few decades of the century, similarly challenged theories like those of Raskin and Untermeyer. "The Jew in modern American poetry," she categorically asserted, "has nothing to say as a Jew." For his part, Maxwell Bodenheim, she writes, had written about "the intellectual detachment, the destructiveness, the fastidious aristocracy of the Jew in modern writing." In Bodenheim's view, she adds, the Jew who writes as a Jew is a "critic of society" and if he does not write in this vein, he has abjured his heritage and is not writing as a Jew. To such views Florence Kiper Frank replies that such attributes of writing belong rather to the "de-nationalized, de-religionized expatriate of spiritual solidity" as a modern, not as a Jew. While Frank's rejection of belief in "the Jew as Jewish artist" as a "romantic conception" is only partly true, I cannot agree with her total rejection of any Jewish component of any kind in the work of consciously Jewish poets.[11] She was writing at a time when many Jewish intellectuals were assimilationists and believed in the early demise of Jewish ethnic identity.

But critical developments during the interwar period and World War II and its aftermath altered the course of Jewish history and slowed the strong, by then almost unobstructed trend toward full assimilation of acculturated Jews. Nazism, the spectacle of pronounced anti-Semitism in the cultured, developed German nation, the horror of the Holocaust and the establishment of Israel all reawakened and strengthened the sense of Jewish identification of United States Jews. At the same time the rapidly expanding postwar market in both the business and professional sectors drew larger numbers of Jews than ever into the middle class while the necessity of supplying personnel for this expansion helped to break down many previous barriers of discrimination that had excluded Jews from some industries, professions, and, most specifically, from academic life. Limited immigration had also reduced the number of poor working-class Jews with Old World customs and accents. The second and third generations had by this time a high degree of acculturation. At the same time, Judaism had gained general acceptance as one of the religions of bona fide Americans.

While all this was going on, American literature as a whole had indeed developed to such an extent that the literary center of the world had shifted to the United States. The writing of second- and third-generation American Jews, too, had grown in maturity with the literature of the nation as a whole. In this movement Jewish poets participated with increasing recognition. The Jewish writer Delmore Schwartz was recognized as one of the earliest modernist American poets even before World War II, but it was not until Karl Shapiro gained the Pulitzer Prize for poetry in 1945, writing as a soldier during the war itself, that the general public awoke to the distinction of some Jewish American poets.

The entire complex of events, from the murder of 6 million Jews to the establishment of Israel and the general acceptance of Jews as full-fledged Americans, is the concomitant of this participation by Jews in the high technical level of American writing, which gave them confidence in their integral place on the total American scene. This led to the reassertion, sometimes even militant, of their Jewish identity and in some cases even to a return to the Jewish religion. An early material sign of this new status was an anthology of fiction, poetry, and non-fiction published in 1964, *Breakthrough: A Treasury of Contemporary American-Jewish Literature*, edited by Irving Malin and Irwin Stark. The poetry section contained work by Karl Shapiro, Muriel Rukeyser, Howard Nemerov, Delmore Schwartz, Allen Guttmann, Allen Ginsberg, Hyam Plutzik, David Ignatov, Irving Feldman, and Harvey Shapiro. For Malin and Stark there is a "community of feeling which transcends individual styles and genres." There exists, they say, "an American-Jewish context" in writing, which consists in the "quest for values and meanings within a living Jewish ethos and under the auspices of ideas derived largely from the Hebraic tradition." This is a more specific statement of what earlier writers called the Jewish "spirit" in writing.[12] Thus one assumes that the only writer of Jewish origin who could *not* be designated a Jewish writer is the one described in Hyam Plutzik's "portrait," since he lacks the Jewish "spirit": he has minimal Jewish identification and ignores its millennial history.[13]

Ten years after the Malin and Stark volume a bulkier book appeared, *Jewish-American Literature: An Anthology of Fiction, Poetry, Autobiography, and Criticism* edited by the late Abraham Chapman. The editor's introduction is an extended and valuable analysis of the Jewish writer. In salutary manner Chapman emphasized the enormous importance of that "personal imagination" that determines the writer's "unique and distinctive literary qualities." This, however, he cautioned "in no way negates the fact that the culture into which such a writer is born, however much that culture may be a battleground of conflicting values and visions, is a significant element of interacting forces out of which a writer creates literature." Chapman noted that hatred or drastic criticism of that culture may still be an expression of it, just as, he added, Joyce's criticism of Catholicism is still "profoundly Catholic" or Philip Roth's conflict with middle-class Jewish values is still Jewish. We may observe that only the writer who totally ignores his native culture, or tries so to obliterate it from his consciousness that it receives no expression in his writing, is excluded from the category of Jewish writer. Even though Chapman finally stated, "In this anthology I have not applied any restrictive criterion on subject matter or theme" but simply included work by writers "of Jewish descent," his actual practice largely conforms with the conception of dependence on the culture of origin.[14]

The advance of literary sophistication in the general Jewish community by this time is signaled by the fact that in 1975 the Union of American Hebrew Congregations (Reform) published *A Time to Seek: An Anthology of Contemporary Jewish American Poetry*, edited by Samuel Hart Joseloff. Their motive, according to the Foreword by Abraham Segal, the educational director of the rabbinical organization, was to correct the general neglect of Jewish poetry "in all levels of congregational planning."[15] Poetry, he added, "offers a new way to explore Jewish values and concepts, content and subject matter, experiences and concerns."[16] This anthology does not have the parochial character of so much of the 1927 Raskin collection and is generally far superior in poetic quality, numbering among its contributors some of the finest American Jewish poets such as Hyam Plutzik, Karl Shapiro, Stanley Kunitz, Charles Reznikoff, Howard Nemerov, Denise Levertov, Irving Feldman, David Ignatov, Robert Mezey, Muriel Rukeyser—three of them Pulitzer Prize winners. Despite the diversity of these poems, says the editor in his Introduction, "one senses a unity here. It is the reading of one chapter of one book still being written, the varying moods and thoughts of one man still in the process of maturing. These are the poems of a people, of a civilization, of a heritage."[17]

The anthologies are the materializations of an increased interest by Jewish poets in Jewishness. A climax of sorts was reached in 1980 with the publication of a 1,200-page collection, *Voices Within the Ark: The Modern Jewish Poets, An International Anthology*, edited by Howard Schwartz and Anthony Rudolf. The book contains the work of four hundred modern Jewish poets from forty nations, both in the original English and in translation into English from the original Hebrew, Yiddish, and other languages. The United States is represented by ninety-two poets writing in English (I do not include here the numerous American poets whose Yiddish work is here translated into English). "Modern" in the title is construed as work appearing "since the turn of the century."[18] About a dozen of the American poets were born before 1920; about twenty-eight between 1920 and 1945;

and fifteen in 1945 or later (including the senior editor, Howard Schwartz). Of the remaining poets, whose dates are not given, it is apparent that a number stem from the postwar generation.

The editors have on the whole selected the work of poets of whom it could be said that, while their "work resembles, in many respects, that of other poets writing in the same country or language, it should quickly become apparent that the Jewish heritage of these poets has left its distinctive and profound mark on virtually all of them." How much such derivation extends beyond use of biblical or otherwise Jewish themes, as opposed to deeper, more subtle reflections of Jewishness, the editors do not make clear. In addition, the editors introduce a religious and traditional note which would have been unthinkable in an anthology in English before the 1970s. "We did not relish," they write, "the position of having to operate like a *Beit Din*, a rabbinic court of justice," since "almost all of the poets included here were Jewish according to the *Halakah*, the traditional Law." In the "few difficult cases," such as a father as a sole Jewish parent "rather than their mother as called for by Jewish law," the poets "deserve inclusion." This explicit allusion to Orthodox Jewish law is a relatively new phenomenon among Jewish literary people, who were predominantly secular in this century until the post–World War II socioeconomic, cultural, and spiritual crisis. Despite the religious predisposition of the editors, they decided the issue of those who converted to Christianity "on a case-by-case basis," and concluded, therefore, that they would include a converted (*from* Judaism) Soviet expellee like Joseph Brodsky, who still manifested a feeling for the Jewish people, and to exclude Boris Pasternak, who totally ignored Jewish themes. For poets writing in languages other than Hebrew, Yiddish, or Judezmo, "theme became the central determinant." The editors interpret such themes as not only those "based on the laws and legends of the Bible and the subsequent sacred books," but also those "based on superstitions and customs of various Jewish communities," in addition to the Holocaust and Israel.[19] So absorbed are the editors in themes relating to Jewishness as such that recent and current anti-Semitism (other than the Holocaust) do not occur to them for inclusion as subjects.

Who is considered a Jewish poet, we may conclude, depends on the use of a Jewish theme and biblical imagery. We now have reason to discard two extremes—the one that would regard as a "Jewish poet" any poet who is born a Jew irrespective of his attitude toward his identity, or the other, who is imbued with some vaguely defined "Jewish spirit," as Raskin or Untermeyer would understand this, a spirit so vague and general that it is useless for definition. It is understood that a "Jewish poet" is, initially at least, one who is in some significant manner differentiable in some of his work from his non-Jewish contemporaries. By writing in a non-Jewish language, that is, a language other than one unique to Jews, such as Yiddish or Hebrew, a poet is deprived of any *intrinsic* Jewish ethnic quality and is in the end dependent on theme or traditional imagery through which to reveal Jewishness. It can be argued that only in one of the Jewish languages can poetry be Jewish in the full sense, for only in such a language can all the connotations and overtones and cultural accumulations of the group's sensitivities and common experience be embedded. This quality, for instance, makes the difference between English English and American English. And since the English of both nations has developed in a Christian society, the language of *any* poet in that language must to some extent partake of that Christian outlook, even if the poet is an acculturated Jew, and more especially if that poet does not live in a deeply Jewish cultural ambience.

How mastery of language or absence thereof can function separately from the operation of sheer talent is indicated in a live experiment in the shape of the extraordinary and unhappily aborted poetic career of the young Samuel Greenberg (1893–1917). He emigrated with his parents from Vienna in 1900 and was Bar Mitzvah in 1907. The family lived in poverty on the East Side, on Suffolk Street (I was born and lived on that street in my first few years at the very same time!). He left school in 1908 to help support the family and thereafter worked at various jobs until he was stricken with the common ghetto scourge, tuberculosis. He was in and out of hospitals from 1913 until his death four years later, and only during those hospital sojourns was he able to write poetry. Two older brothers were musicians and moved in artistic circles. One of their friends, the art critic William Furrell Fisher, became interested in Samuel, loaned him books, encouraged him to write, and served as his mentor. Greenberg's earliest poems are dated 1913; by the time he died four years later he had completed six hundred poems.[20]

It is interesting to note that his English contemporary, Isaac Rosenberg, poet from the London ghetto, had emerged, and both died within the same year. Rosenberg was killed in the trenches of World War I. But here the parallel ends, for the young Rosenberg was already a recognized Georgian poet while Greenberg was totally obscure and unpublished. Greenberg was extremely talented but fragmentarily self-educated, awkward in his application of poetic techniques little known to him, unsure in syntax and spelling, and simply insufficiently acquainted with the English language. But anyone reading his often inspired phrases could discern an extraordinary native talent without the technical means to bring it to fruition. One senses, for instance—to cite one of many possible examples—the tension of poetic projection striving to free itself from the restraints of ignorance of the English language in the sonnet, "Earth."

After Samuel died his brother Morris turned over all the manuscripts to Fisher, who in turn introduced them to Hart Crane, often considered the quintessential American poet of the 1920s. Crane's response to this poetry is described in a letter to Gorham Munson dated December 23, 1923.

Greenberg, wrote Crane, is "a Rimbaud in embryo." Crane continued: "No grammar, nor spelling, and scarcely any form, but a quality that is unspeakably eerie and the most convincing gusto. One little poem is as good as any of the consciously conceived 'Pierrots' of Laforgue."[21] Indeed, Crane rendered Greenberg the ultimate tribute—he used some Greenberg material as a source for his own poetry. Scholars have since traced some of Greenberg's poems and phrases, which Crane adapted for his own use, in "Voyages" and "White Buildings."[22] Unfortunately Crane never publicly acknowledged his debt to Greenberg, whose suggestive hints he transformed into mature poetry. Crane's poem "Emblems of Conduct" is an extensively revised version of Greenberg's "Conduct," although Crane's version is unmistakably his own. Crane's biographer Philip Horton first discovered this relationship. In Allen Tate's Preface to the first published collection of Greenberg's work he concluded, "Poetry of the twentieth century could not be complete without the publication of the poems of Samuel Greenberg." Tate noted "with astonishment" Greenberg's poem "The Glass Bubbles."[23]

Greenberg's last dated poem (March 14, 1917) is addressed to his brother, Daniel. As he lay on his death bed, he heard death, but life was far away.[24] He died later in the year at the age of twenty-three.

Greenberg's intention was to be an American, not a Jewish poet in the full cultural sense. But it is likely that he was an Orthodox Jew and he inevitably introduces biblical and Jewish thematic material in some verses, as in the first verse of "Thus Be It in Heaven Heavenly." Or the striking line, "Religion's chariot halted for my thought," in the group, "Sonnets for the Hebrew Temple," which would indicate an implicit belief in his ancestral religion. Also in these poems he celebrates his father's vocation of embroidering mantles for the Torah.[25]

Who knows what mark he would have made if he had chosen to write as a poet in his native Yiddish? But like the legions of second-generation Americans, he chose to aspire to poetry in English. Nevertheless, his gift was so irresistible that his poetic invention shone through his awkward, inadequate English. Although he invoked the God of Judaism in many poems, the language was an insurmountable barrier to Jewish expression in the fullest sense and willy-nilly contained Christian overtones. Harold Bloom has suggested that Jewish poets of our century cannot be altogether at home in Jewish themes, since they composed in current styles ranging from those of Pound and Eliot to those of Wallace Stevens and William Carlos Williams, styles that are essentially alien to the Jewish tradition.[26] If American-Jewish poets were to create without reservation in the Jewish tradition, Bloom held, they would have to sever their relation to Christian traditions and styles.

A small number of American poets of this century who were born Jews— or half-Jews, for that matter—did not allude to any aspect of Jewishness whatever in their work. Dorothy Parker was one example. Most of them did allude in one or more of their poems to something of their ethnic origin. A few were, for some periods at least, preoccupied in most of their work with Jewishness and the tradition from which their forebears sprang. In our effort to shed some light on the concept of the "Jewish poet," we have singled out three poets, Charles Reznikoff, born before the new century opened; Karl Shapiro, born before World War I; and Irving Feldman, born a decade after that war, as poets extensively occupied with one aspect of Jewishness or another.

Among these perhaps the least appreciated was Charles Reznikoff, born in 1894 in Brooklyn of immigrant parents. He worked at a variety of jobs and was a resident of Greenwich Village bohemia in the 1920s. He was a leading member of the group of "Objectivist" poets led by Louis Zukofsky, with Ezra Pound as his mentor. Reznikoff was not a Communist in the 1930s like some of his fellow objectivists, but a Labor Zionist, and later was for many years an editor of the monthly Labor Zionist journal, *Jewish Frontier*. Since his death in 1976 his reputation has grown and a two-volume collection of his complete poetry was published in 1976 and 1977. He wrote as a New Yorker and as an American as well as a Jew. It was the Holocaust which later drove him to extensive devotion to the Jewish theme.

His objectivism gives his verse a quiet, restrained, dignified concreteness, with hard objects serving for his images. Many of his themes, even in his earlier poetry, were biblical but the allusions are also to social problems of the Jews. In his tender eulogy to his mother, "Kaddish," his verse has the cadence of a liturgical chant.[27] Another poem, "Hanukkah," reveals not so much his poetic gift as the trend of his thought about the Jewish tradition.[28]

In much of his poetry, word pictures through simple images of everyday experience with material objects, one gets a pervasive, often explicit feeling that the poet is a Jew. Reznikoff's large output of poetry included poetization of quotidian urban experience with a Jewish aspect, biblical allusions, Jewish people's festivals year-round, and other traditional themes. In 1975, the year of his death, he published *Holocaust*, a series of free-verse poems narrating various aspects of the Nazi treatment of the Jews from their rise to power to their defeat, concentrating on specific acts of inhumanity and unparalleled cruelty and brutality and callousness.[29] These accounts are obviously drawn from documented events. Reznikoff makes no effort to make poetry of this human depravity, which in the bare telling is almost too much to tolerate. But in his recall of traditional figures and events in Jewish lore and history his poetry expresses a delicate, even tender feeling and concern for his people. Without being religious or theological his poetic observations reveal depth of immersion in the tradition. His "Meditations on the Fall and Winter Holidays," a series of poems on "New Year's," "Day of Atonement," "Feast of Booths," "Hanukkah," are perhaps one peak of his writing on the Jews and exemplify his attitude.[30]

He accepted his fate as a poet in English in the full realization of its essential incompleteness in expressing his intent. In "The Hebrew of Your Poets, Zion," he wrote that poetry in Hebrew was like "oil upon a burn," while none of the non-Jewish languages of "strangers" can compare to it.[31] More nearly than any American poet writing in English, Reznikoff can be said to have been a "Jewish poet."

In the next generation of poets, Karl Shapiro, born in 1913, was preoccupied for a period with Jewishness in his poetry. Unlike Reznikoff, who was un-self-consciously drawn to a Jewish perspective and manifested an unforced relation to it, Shapiro was driven by outside influences to assert his Jewish identity. "We accept our Jewishness," he wrote in 1949, "because to reject it would be betrayal not of our election [the Judeo-Christian community] but of ourselves."[32] In an essay on "The Jewish Writer in America" (1960), Shapiro related how Jewish professors and others he encountered in workshops tried to remain quiet about anti-Semitism in the work of T. S. Eliot and Ezra Pound. He was at first taken in by these apologetics but was driven to examine the matter further when he was a member of the committee that deliberated awarding Ezra Pound the Bollingen Prize in 1969. He voted to reject Pound for the prize on the basis of his anti-Semitism, "anti-Americanism," and an awareness of what had happened to the Jews of Europe. "Whatever Jewish consciousness I possess," he wrote, "I can trace to the writings of the American classicists [Pound? Eliot?] who made it their business to equate 'American' and 'Jew' as twin evils." This forced attention to the problem then led him to the conclusion that if a writer is to create as a conscious Jew, his work must be "God-centered." This does not, however, require adherence to organized religion, to which he declares he himself was opposed. He rejects as literary material what he calls "sociological Judaism," which I take him to mean what we have called "ethnic" Jewishness, or consciousness of belonging to a social group by virtue of some common cultural awareness deriving from a differentiated social existence. Instead he offers the concept that Martin Buber assigned to Hasidism, "the true hallowing of man is the hallowing of the human in him. ... There is no essential distinction between the sacred and the profane," Shapiro quotes Buber. Consonant with his approach to Jewishness and religion and the novelty of the favorable Jewish situation in the United States, Shapiro created a new psalm to follow the last in the Bible, Number 150.[33] In the "151st Psalm" he invokes the "immigrant God" as his own.[34]

The note of defiance found in Shapiro's work since World War II is again sounded in the title, *Poems of a Jew*, in 1958. In his Introduction he writes that the poems "are documents of an obsession," with "the Jew at its center, but everyone else partakes of it." The reciprocal relationship of Jew and non-Jew through history has been one of "obsession." The poet then tells us that "the undercurrent of most of my poems is the theme of the Jew."[35] In addition to the explicitly Jewish poems, one section of the book is devoted to the confrontation of Judaism with the Christian world. But so pervasively is he aware of it that it intrudes even on the Jewish poems, as in "The Synagogue," where he contrasts Jewish affirmation of everyday life with the Christian sacrament: "Our wine is wine, our bread is honest bread" it is not the body, even though it is food." In "Jew," the word stands for an unending history of persecution. And the sense of eternal confrontation is achieved in the lines of the same poem. In "The Alphabet," too, the elements of the language similarly symbolize the Jewish tradition.[36] The confrontation occurs even in "The First Time," a delicately sensed initiation of a seventeen-year-old boy by a prostitute.[37] She regards him naked and asks if he is a Jew. And finally, in "Israel," a poem to be read in Baltimore at the birth of the State of Israel in 1948, he now can feel on a deeper level about his name and look anyone clearly in the eye.[38]

If Shapiro's preoccupation with the Jew is an obsession, one should not then be surprised that the idea of the Jew he tries to convey is not altogether clear. At one point in his Introduction he asserts that his poems are "not religious poems but the poems of the Jew."[39] But in his essay on the Jewish writer he says, "the consciously Jewish writer...must recognize his obligation to establish this consciousness centrally in his work, the right, so to speak, of the existence of God....If this encourages religious progress that may be good, but I am not talking about religion." But what is this talk about "God" if not religious? Since he rejects "sociological Judaism" as "pointless," one wonders just how clear his conception of the Jew is.[40] In any case, Shapiro's Jewish affirmation in the 1950s stimulated awareness of the growing general acceptance of Jewish writers and content in American literature.

In the next generation of poets perhaps Irving Feldman, as much as any, was concerned with the Jews. He was born in Brooklyn in 1928, and his first book of poems, *Works and Days*, appeared in 1961. His language has an arresting freshness, and his satirical verses show clever satirical command of clichés. A religious undertone pervades his work, though not the resistances of the modern man. In "Scratch," the last poem of "The Wandering Jew" sequence, God sardonically throws the poet back on his own resources as he struggles with a variety of doubts, ending that the response of God is as meaningful as a "scratch" on a record.[41] The poet is finally caught on the horns of a dilemma, as he expressed it in the epigraph to the sequence: If one does not remember Jerusalem, one deserves to die; but if one does remember Jerusalem, "how will I live?" "The Gates of Gaza" poses his perplexity about where and how to settle a Jerusalem in a world beset by human folly and violence.[42] In "The Face of God" a mourning "tumbler-candle" signifies to him the aspiration to be worthy of the sweetness of his selfless mother.[43] In the next two poems of the sequence the mood sharply changes to mordant satire. "The Wailing Wall" bemoans the succession of troubles in his life and he appeals to God to teach him fortitude.[44] The next poem, "Assimilation," is a dream sequence of events in the life of a Jew from boyhood to ignorant wallowing in the vulgar aspects of commercial popular culture, which betokens assimilation to the emptiest phases of American life.[45]

Feldman's next volume, *The Pripet Marshes and Other Poems* (1965), is concerned with Jews under genocidal Nazi actions from the viewpoint of a survivor. "Scenes of a Summer Spring" echoes the guilty feeling for having survived.[46] In his "Psalm," in *Magic Papers* (1970), the poet laments the sterility left by the Holocaust of the murdered millions and looks to his "words" to be their fertility.[47]

There is nothing of facile religiosity in Feldman's poetry, but a deeply felt striving for spiritual tranquillity. He has no illusions about how hard it is to achieve this and never seems to have succeeded. Something of Herman Melville's struggle with belief is suggested by Feldman's less than assertive faith.

If one surveys the roster of Jewish poets in this century, one is struck by the fact that relatively few of them failed to venture into the Jewish theme at some time in their poetic work. Our examination of this phenomenon must necessarily be selective, since there are so many. In the anthologies of American poetry, as expected, there is a core of major poets about whom there is wide consensus, but beyond this the variety is considerable. The poets whose work I shall briefly examine are a selection of those who are for one reason or another relevant to one purpose of this study: to shed light on the Jewish participation in American literature. These poets may be divided into two chronological groups, paralleling two major divisions of our literature. So far as Jews are concerned, there is some work, though not much, prior to World War I. The two major divisions are the interwar period, about 1919 to the 1940s, and the post–World War II period.

It is not as a poet but as an anthologist that Louis Untermeyer holds a significant place in American poetry. It is paradoxical that at a time when the belief that literature in English was somehow beyond the comprehension of Jews was widespread, Louis Untermeyer should have compiled what was perhaps for over half a century the most widely used anthology of modern American poetry. The first edition of his *Modern American Poetry* appeared in 1919; successive revised editions were published in 1925, 1930, 1936, 1942, 1950, and 1962. Untermeyer also edited numerous other anthologies. The first volume of his own poetry appeared in 1911, but not until *Roast Leviathan* (1923) did he devote much attention to the Jewish theme. The title poem is a celebration of God's power over the immense creature which cannot be subdued by man, but God calls on Behemoth to vanquish Leviathan, whereupon the angels prepare a meal for the Hebrews. It is not inspired poetry, and while Untermeyer included excerpts from it in the 1925 edition of his anthology, he dropped them from later editions. Other poems are on biblical themes but are no more impressive. His wife, Jean Starr Untermeyer, seems to me to have been the better poet.

Of those Jewish poets born before the turn of the century, two stand out: James Oppenheim, born in St. Paul in 1882, and Alter Brody, born in 1895 in Russia and an immigrant at eight. Both were socialists of a kind. We have already met Oppenheim in our examination of the fiction of the pre–World War I period. But he was a versatile literary man perhaps better known as an editor of the short-lived *Seven Arts* in 1916 and as a poet than for his fiction. He published a half-dozen volumes of poetry between 1919 and 1923, and was a significant figure during the movement of American literature into the twentieth century. His poetry is in form Whitmanesque with a suggestion of the biblical line but on the whole his verse was bland. That he was aware of his origin is seen in "Hebrews" in *Golden Bird* (1923), which seems to have been a year when Jewish literary men harked back to their Jewishness, perhaps because of the surge of anti-Semitism. "I come of a mighty race," wrote Oppenheim in "Hebrews." After celebrating Adam, Noah, Moses, David, and Isaiah, the poet salutes the heroes who followed in centuries in which they have suffered tragedy and triumph.[48]

Of especial interest is Alter Brody as a poet of the East Side ghetto, where he lived. His one volume of poems is *A Family Album, and Other Poems* (1911); in 1928 he published a volume of plays, *Lamentations: Four Folk-Plays of the American Jew*. His poetic "Album" is a sort of Spoon River anthology of the tenements on the East Side, celebrating streets and people. His poems are informed with a gentle sadness about the physical surroundings and poverty as well as the spiritual life of the ghetto; they convey the feelings of a sensitive young man immersed in their reality. The quality of his verse is conveyed by "Ghetto Twilight" in which he personifies the tenements with the exhaustion of the "tired faces coming home from work" greeting their children.[49] The poet describes relatives as he turns the pages of his family "Album" with quiet realism and affection. As a left-wing Socialist Brody laments the pro–World War I position of the socialist leadership in "The Lost Leader (for C. E. R.)," probably for Charles E. Ruthenberg, the leader of the left anti-war faction of the party, who was to help found the Communist party shortly thereafter. Brody calls the right-wing Socialist leader a betrayer for supporting World War I.[50] Brody greeted the Russian Revolution with ecstasy in "To Russia—1917."[51] Indeed, nearly all the poets of any consequence in the first few decades of the century were socialists of one kind or another. Untermeyer was a founding editor of *The Masses*.

Among the Jewish poets in a later 1930s anthology, *Proletarian Literature in the United States*, none wrote on Jewish themes or even alluded to Jewishness, except for a poem about a Jewish garment worker by A. B. Magil. Of the Jewish poets in this anthology a few have sustained their reputation until our own day—Kenneth Fearing, born in 1902, and Muriel Rukeyser, born in 1913. Fearing scarcely mentioned the Jew in his poetry, except as obscurely implied in his variation on the theme of pawnbrokers in "Afternoon of a Pawnbroker," in which the aspirations and accumulated hopes and fears of humanity no longer seem redeemable.[52] They are no longer affordable by a disillusioned humanity. This is symbolized by the deposit with the pawnbroker of such mythical objects as Gabriel's horn, the apple bitten into by Adam, Aladdin's lamp, Pandora's box, the magic carpet, and others. These have been surrendered by people who have nothing left.

However, Muriel Rukeyser dealt explicitly with Jews in significant ways in some poems. Through her career she incorporated her social concern in her poetry, as sounded in the first poem in her first volume of poems, *Theory of Flight* (1935), as, compactly, Sacco and not Soppho.[53] Her writing career began after the rise of Hitler, and awareness of the Jewish situation became part of her social concern. In comments on patrician cultural critic John Jay Chapman, who became a virulent anti-Semite in the 1930s, she wrote that he had espoused many and various causes and was so changeable in his loyalties that he now calls for revenge on the Jews.[54] World War II intensified her social awareness to include even more Jewishness. In 1944, in "Bubble of Air," she declared that she called on a three-part heritage as a woman, as an American, and as a Jew.[55] She was sensitive to the challenge to her people from Hitlerism and anti-Semitism down the centuries in the poem which is the epigraph in *Creative Awakening*: "To be a Jew in the Twentieth Century."[56] She further comments on the time by excoriating the witch-hunting investigators who violate everything dear and whose targets include women, Jews, and Blacks.[57] In her last decade she returned to the tradition of her mother's family that they were descended from the great rabbi and scholar, Akiba, spiritual leader of the Bar Kochba rebellion against Rome in the second century. In her long poem, "Akiba" (1968), she commemorates the martyred death of this great Jewish scholar who "is identified with Song of Songs."[58]

Among the most important American-Jewish poets is Delmore Schwartz, whose place in the development of American literature we have already discussed as the harbinger of the alienation theme. His relationship to Jewish participation in poetry is more pronounced than is sometimes believed. Allen Guttmann was far too categorical when in 1971 he wrote that "Muriel Rukeyser, Howard Nemerov, and Delmore Schwartz are gifted poets, but their verse is almost without a trace of their Jewish origins, except, perhaps," he adds, "in such poems as Nemerov's irreverent 'Dialogue with a Rabbi.' "[59] We have already seen what a distortion this is with respect to Muriel Rukeyser and shall see the same with Nemerov, but it is equally so with regard to Schwartz. Guttmann seems to have discounted totally what is in effect an immigrant novel in verse in Schwartz's *Shenendoah*, in which the poet describes the Jewish milieu of his early life, nor does Guttmann notice the degree to which Schwartz regarded his Jewish origin as crucial to the alienation exemplified in his poetry and in all his work, nor does Guttmann notice the several biblical subjects among Schwartz's poems, including the poems, "Jacob," "Abraham," and others.

Although Louis Zukofsky, born in 1904 and a protégé of Ezra Pound, was a radical, he did not participate in the "proletarian" literary movement. He was an eccentric and leader of the Objectivist movement, of which Charles Reznikoff was a leading member. His poetry contains only some half-dozen passing allusions to Jews and a few poems on religious themes. His most sustained comment is a two-page passage in his poetic "Autobiography." His poor home he describes with objectivist concreteness and adds, in Yiddish, "Un in hoyse is kalt" (And in the house it's cold). Why, he asks his mother ironically, are Jews supposed always to be hungry for food when we at home eat little? He comments on assimilation. He and his mother, he writes, should be like the Anglo-Saxons and have more color in their cheeks, adding Shylock's statement that if we are like them otherwise, we should be like them in that, too. This section can be viewed as a poetic rendering of the plight of the poor, marginal Jew—a sense of strain in relation to the society into which he assimilates and indifference to his own Jewish community.[60]

Awareness of his marginality was met early by Stanley Kunitz, born in Worcester, Massachusetts, in 1905, who had to wait for full recognition until he received the Pulitzer Prize for Poetry in 1959. When he was graduated with highest honors from Harvard in the 1920s and had received the Garrison medal for poetry, he was "ultimately denied a post as teaching assistant" on the ground that, as we have by now so often seen, "Anglo-Saxons would resent being instructed in English by Jews."[61] He left Harvard "in a rage." The taboo was at last surmounted; he became a teacher of English literature, and in 1969 he became editor of the Yale Series of Younger Poets.

Kunitz rarely introduced any semblance of Jewishness into his verse. Only during the anti-Nazi era and in his later years did he return nostalgically to his origin. In "Father and Son" (1944) he implores his father to "Return!" from the dead and instruct his son "In the Gemara of your gentleness."[62] Again, in 1971, he returns to the theme in "Journal for My Daughter," when he tells her how her grandfather used to have visits from Maxim Gorky, Emma Goldman, and "the atheist Ingersoll," which conveys the excitement of youthful radicalism. Obviously the poet's father was a Jewish radical, although nowhere does Kunitz use the word "Jew."[63] But there is no need of this. Again, during World War II he returned with "Reflections by a Mailbox" about his forebears.[64]

Among the other gifted poets before World War II who were more than casually interested in their Jewishness were Hyam Plutzik and David Ignatov. Plutzik was born in 1911 and died in 1962. A modern who respected T. S. Eliot as a poet, he chides him for his anti-Semitism in "For T. S. E. Only" (1959), suggesting Eliot's technique of quotation within poetry, echoing phrases from Skylock and Eliot's own anti-Semitic lines about Bleistein. Plutzik then reminds Eliot that they are all victims of alienation and, in a refrain running through the poem, that Eliot and all of us should be weeping in exile. With gentle love and understanding Plutzik holds out his hand to Eliot.[65]

A number of Plutzik's poems are based on biblical themes but not in celebration. They are instead a call for compassion and mercy. In "The King of Ai" the poet recalls the slaughter, rape, and sack by Joshua's army at the city of Ai and gently scolds the Jews for these inhumanities. He contrasts the fragrance of flowers with the "swaying shape in the air."[66] The poet concludes with a plea to God for the evil committed. So also in the latter-day "On the Photograph of a Man I Never Saw," his grandfather, a stern, pious man, the poet quietly asks of the *minyan* that they be merciful in judgment.[67] But in "Portrait" Plutzik is unsparing in his judgment on the assimilated Jew who "personally resembles nothing." He imitates his middle-class non-Jewish neighbor scrupulously in dress and mode of life. But his father, according to rumor, was an old-clothes dealer. The assimilationist himself wears a shirt he has borrowed, his borrowed mode of life, the shirt of Nessus, which, according to the myth, poisoned the wearer.[68]

Like Plutzik and nearly all poets preoccupied with the Jewish theme, David Ignatov, born in 1914, wrote poetry that built on biblical stories, universal observations about humanity, brief and pithy. In his "Noah" on the return to dry land humanity will not have learned anything but at least will have the assurance of God's Covenant that it will never be utterly destroyed.[69] In "Job's Anger" (1958), the poet celebrates the mutual relationship of God and man. For "God hath vexed my soul" (Genesis 27:3), Job had complained, but by his works Job had "challenged God" and put God on the defensive until "God came down," wrote Ignatov, after Job established his integrity.[70]

Like so many of the poets, Ignatov comments on the contrasts between his paternal immigrant generation and his own in "Europe and America" (1948), contrasting the poverty-stricken life of the former with the affluent, secure life of the latter.[71] He delves into his father's plight in Russia in "1905." His father had been a passive sufferer who in 1905 simply left the condition where he was a bookbinder. He lived in material poverty but was rich in culture.[72] In "Kaddish" he attends his mother's last illness when he was young and gains consolation from the thought of all that he derives from Mother Earth.[73] In addition to such weighty writing, some of his verse has a quietly humorous aspect. In 1977 Ignatov received the Bollingen Prize for Poetry.

As the number of poets generally increased, so also did the number of Jews writing among the thousands of versifiers. During the 1950s and later a large crop of poetry magazines appeared and rather quickly expired. Richard Howard, born in 1929, a poet and translator of *Les fleurs du mal*, published a study, *Alone with America: Essays in the Art of Poetry in the U.S. Since 1950* (1969), in which he discussed forty-one poets. Of these about fifteen, or over one-third, were Jewish, all born after World War I. After the 1950s, Jews who were poets increasingly asserted their Jewish identity in their work under the combined impact of the Holocaust and the creation of Israel. One way of doing so was to provide English translations from the Yiddish for the *A Treasury of Yiddish Poets* (1969), edited by Irving Howe and Eliezer Greenberg, and the translators included some of the leading younger poets: John Hollander, Adrienne Rich, Irving Feldman, Harvey Shapiro, as well as Stanley Kunitz from the older generation. This is a sign of poetic as well as ethnic maturity on their part.

The temptation must be resisted to explore the work of a large number of this generation of poets, for there are so many. We can comment only on a small number. We have already noted the work of Irving Feldman as well as, in an earlier chapter, that of Allen Ginsberg, born in 1924. Ginsberg remains probably the outstanding and most durable of the "Beat" poets of the 1950s, precursors of the 1960s revolt of the young. Although he has been writing poetry since the late 1940s, he entered into public attention with explosive force through "Howl" in 1956, with its now famous first line, "I saw the best minds of my generation destroyed by madness, starving hysterical naked." In a powerfully effective revival of the Whitmanian line and a modern-day version of the Whitman spirit, the poem sheds a lurid light on some of the desperate expedients used by sensitive spirits of the younger generation against the complacency and crass materialism and intolerance of dissent in the first years of the postwar era. Although Ginsberg was more strongly drawn to oriental religion than to Judaism, he was for a period absorbed in the Kabbalah. His religion was eclectic, including an awareness of Judaism but he seldom made allusion in his poetry to Jewishness. In his eulogy to his mother, "Kaddish" (1958), which he says he wrote under the influence of drugs, he relates the trying reality of life with a psychotic mother in her last days. He alternates between the prose poem and the Whitman line through the excruciating strains of coping with a paranoid mother. The poet's love and compassion inform his restless narrative and tribute. Ginsberg did not fade with the passing of the Beat movement but continued as a poet and activist, as well as a practitioner of Buddhism, for decades thereafter, and commanded respect as an artist from most of the literary community.

Perusal of Howard Nemerov's poetry shows numerous allusions, from the serious to the humorous, based on stories from the Hebrew Bible. "Lot's Wife" projects her at a city gate and a warning, "a hard lesson to learn."[74] In a later poem, "Lot Later," Nemerov retells the story of Genesis 19 of two angels leading Lot and his wife and daughter out of the condemned city of Sodom to safety in a cave, where his two daughters think themselves the only ones left in the world.[75] To perpetuate the family they ply their father with wine on successive nights and beget his children. The poet casts the story in a contemporary setting and language. In a fifteen-line poem, "The

View from Pisgah," there are a half-dozen verbal allusions to the imagery of the original story in Exodus, again with modern terminology and references.

In "Moses, the Finding of the Ark" the basket with the child found by Pharaoh's daughter is magically preserved, and the poem concludes with a condensed intimation of the future persecution of the Jews in Egypt.[76] A subtle use of a biblical idea is "The Icehouse in Summer (See Amos 3:15)."[77] It recounts an experience in a boy's life whose meaning is illuminated by the lines from Amos: "And I will smite the winter-house with the summer-house; / And the houses of ivory shall perish, / And the great houses shall have an end, / Saith the Lord," events in punishment for transgressions. Told of the drowning of a horse and wagon by breaking into thin ice while collecting ice for the icehouse, the boy in a dream is reminded of the Pharaoh's men and horses in the Red Sea.

Nemerov was nothing if not contemporary. A clergyman in 1957 hailed ours as the greatest spiritual age ever because of our material progress. This moved the poet to write "Boom!" which gives this idea the satirized treatment it deserves.[78] Delicate satire marks his "Money," which purports to be an introduction to the study of symbolism "basic / To the nature of money." Then ensues a mock-serious lecture on the iconography of the nickel coin: on one side an Indian who was conquered a century ago and his descendants kept on reservations, which he likens to concentration camps. The bison, on the other side, was killed off. The poet says he hopes the symbolism conveys the real meaning of money.[79]

We have mentioned only a few of Nemerov's poems that use biblical themes to point a modern moral. In his "Debate with a Rabbi" Nemerov cleverly debates his loss of religion, and at the same time the poem implies that absence of religion does not necessarily mean abandonment of Jewish ethnicity. At the end the exasperated rabbi charges the poet with being stubborn, and the poet replies that Jews are like that.[80] Nemerov was also a writer of fiction, but it was his poetry that received recognition in 1963–1964 with appointment as consultant in poetry to the Library of Congress, and he received the Pulitzer Prize for poetry in 1979.

The Jewishness of three noted postwar poets is problematic, though all three consider themselves Jews in some sense. Louis Simpson, born on the island of Jamaica in 1923 and Pulitzer Prize winner for poetry in 1964, immigrated to the United States as a young man. Not until he visited his maternal grandmother in Brooklyn did he discover that he was a Jew. He had known only that his mother was "Russian." His father was not Jewish. After he met the Jewish side of his family, he still "didn't feel Jewish."[81] But he didn't feel like a Christian, either, so he decided that he was a Jew because others thought he was. Nevertheless, he wrote several poems purporting to recount his maternal grandparents' life in Russia. "A Night in Odessa" deals with the hazards of Jewish life in Russia;[82] "Meyer" was a

Communist in Russia who was killed;[83] "Isadore" is a revolutionary in constant danger of arrest.[84] In "Adam Yankov" the poet contrasts the life of his immigrant grandparents and their families with his own broader American life.[85]

Also born of a mixed marriage is Adrienne Rich, whose mother was Protestant and her father Jewish. "I would be considered a Jew by anti-Semites," she has said, "and a non-Jew by Jews.... Although my Jewish father had great influence on my reading and writing while I was growing up, he was himself an assimilationist and sent his daughters to the Episcopal Church." She herself married "an agnostic Jew" and felt herself a feminist alienated from all "patriarchal religion.... I would identify myself whenever Jews were under attack or threatened, [but] I have never felt myself to be a Jewish writer."[86] Accordingly, she makes no allusions to Jews in her poetry, although she does in "Prospective Immigrants Please Note" caution those entering the country that immigration gives no guarantees, since it is "only a door."[87]

Denise Levertov poses quite another view. Unlike Adrienne Rich, who does not consider herself to be a Jewish writer, Levertov like Rich "also half-Protestant, is able to identify with her Chassidic forebears, and can use that identification in her poetry."[88] Levertov was born in England in 1923 and came to this country with an American husband, Mitchell Goodman, in 1948. Besides being a highly regarded poet, she is a leading peace activist. Her father came of a distinguished Russian Hasidic family and prepared for the rabbinate. Instead, he converted to Christianity in the belief that Jesus was indeed the Messiah, and he became an Anglican priest as a sort of Jewish Christian. In "Illustrious Ancestors" the poet writes sympathetically of her Hasidic ancestors.[89] Levertov has here captured the spirit of the Hasid who tries to live the holiness of the everyday, as Martin Buber taught. In three sensitive half-Jews, thus, we have three modes of relation or non-relation to Jewishness: Levertov identifies with the Hasidic past of her father, Simpson feels himself an outsider with relation to Jewishness, while Rich makes no pretense of feeling any Jewishness.

There were many more respected Jewish poets who began to write in the post–World War II decades. We shall cite only a few to convey some idea of their range and variety in relation to Jewishness. It is particularly strong in Harvey Shapiro, born in 1925 and influenced by Objectivism. He is said to have accepted Hayden Carruthers' characterization of his work. Carruthers said it reflects "the tensions between his orthodox religious background and his experiences in war and modern living." His *Battle Report* (1966), for instance, includes many poems on Jewish themes from Auschwitz to the Hasidic Rabbi Nachman. In "The Prophet Announces," a picture shows to the poet the Prophet Elijah "with the shofar to his mouth." But everything looks so quiet to him that he can hardly hear—there was still hope for religion then, a hope we now know not realized.[90] In "Death of a Grandmother" the poet summons his thoughts of her in the later years with thoughts of the coming generations, her heirs.[91] (It is striking how second- and third-generation Jewish poets hark back to their grandparents for their Jewish feelings, rather than to their acculturated parents!) Jewish themes recur throughout Harvey Shapiro's poems, though not as numerous in the later as in the earlier volumes. As the poet sadly remarks in "The Synagogue on Kane Street" (1971), he laments the departure of the young from the synagogue in Brooklyn and the few who remain in large temple.[92]

Less committed religiously and less devotional, if not basically secular, is the poetry of John Hollander, born in 1929. Robert Alter has called him a "technical virtuoso" whose problem has been to escape "the avidness of mere virtuosity." As a result, Alter continues, "poem after poem reads like a distanced, abstractly conceived 'treatment' of some idea or situation."[93] One of Hollander's technical stunts is a poem, "Graven Image," ironically in the shape of the Star of David.[94] However, his poetry attracts by its extraordinary finish and the sheer interest engaged by his images. For instance, in "Ninth of Ab" the poet is in the country at summer's end.[95] In this, as in other poems, there are occasional biblical allusions in a basically secular poem. His "At the New Year" is the occasion for the development of the thought that "Every single instant begins another new year" no less than, among other things, the year initiated by the shrill sound of the horn and the start of harvest.[96] Typical also of the poet's secular use of the Jewish theme is his "Letter to Jorge Luis Borges: Apropos of the Golem." In translating a Borges poem on Prague, visions return to the poet of his grandfather's tales (always the grandfather!) about that city and especially of the Golem.[97]

Not so elegant and polished as John Hollander's poetry is the work of the youngest of the Jewish poets here considered, Robert Mezey, born in 1935. His style is rather rugged and conveys a sense of some perpetual inner conflict between what he writes and what his mouth can utter.[98] In the long poem "The Wandering Jew" we can follow the peregrinations of Mezey's own history. The conforming Bar Mitzvah boy uncritically loves God "fiercely" because he loves the Jews and hates the Philistines. Then, he cannot recall when he stopped going to the synagogue with "its habitual old men praying and swaying on the Bima." He was, he writes, "adrift." Entered on mature life, the poet experiences conflicted sex, marriage, divorce, return to unresolved thoughts about God, and an everyday life of pain and frustrating experience contemplating the history of persecutions which caused him to doubt his faith. These sufferings give rise to questions in "anguish of the spirit." The poet studies the Pentateuch for clues to his spiritual predicament and concludes that the best he can do is survive in obedience to the Law.[99] There seems to be resolution of a kind in "The Great Sad One": the poet's faith returns when he realizes that he can grieve for the cruelty of life, but that God does not have even this consolation.[100]

Like so many Jewish poets Mezey pays his respects to the Holocaust victims in a piece like "Theresienstadt Poem." In watercolors drawn by the thirteen-year-old inmate the poet can discern the various facets of the suffering with a "heart on fire."[101]

Many other poets of the century could be discussed as well as those taken up here. Our purpose, however, is not to anticipate the judgment of the future, but rather to afford some hints as to how the minds of Jewish poets of various persuasions worked as the century wore on. It is interesting to note that the tendency toward use of Jewish themes at the least, and the tendency to look for solace to Judaism, became stronger and more explicit than among prose writers, since poetry lends itself more readily to intimate personal expression than fictional narrative. But what of the quality of the poetry? In a review of the immense Schwartz and Rudolf anthology of world Jewish poetry of this century, Harold Bloom ventured the opinion that "the more than ninety American poets represented here include no single figure who so far matters urgently or overwhelmingly in the poetry of our century," that "only about a dozen of them have written authentic poems," and that "none of these alas has earned a place in the canon, though one or two yet may."[102]

Bloom may be right. We shall see, or rather our progeny will see. But in another place Bloom raises an interesting question when he judges with considerable plausibility that "several Yiddish poets writing in the United States—Moshe Leib Halpern, Mani Leib, H. Leivick, and Jacob Glatstein—are more impressive poets in my experience as a reader, than any American-Jewish poet who has written in English."[103] Considering the eminence of some Jewish fiction and drama writers in English in this century, who stand with the best of their non-Jewish contemporaries, the reason for this is interesting to explore. Is it simply that poetic talent comparable, say, to a Bellow in fiction or an Arthur Miller in drama has just not emerged by the chances of such emergences? Perhaps there is a reason directly stemming from the nature of poetry itself, as it differs from the qualities called forth by fiction or drama. Can it be that the exquisite sense of the English language, reaching deep within the consciousness of the Jewish poet is not sufficiently and absolutely native and unobstructed and bred in the bone as it is in the non-Jewish poet to whom the language is as natural as breathing?

4

The Jew in Drama

BEFORE WORLD WAR I: 1900–1918

Culturally speaking, the twentieth century did not arrive in the United States until its first few decades were over. Enormous changes in economic and political life occurred in the opening years. Industrial expansion was rapid. With the power of Big Money came also the countervailing forces of populism and a widely influential "progressivism." But cultural changes were slow to follow. In the opening years of the new century the theater continued as usual. The long-lived invidious stereotype of the Jew was unimpaired. As M. J. Landa wrote of the British stage, equally applicable to the American, "the twentieth century was reached with the stage Jew helplessly debased. If anything, his status had declined; he was simply an enslaved buffoon, condemned to outlandish gesticulation, to a specific make-up which must at least border on the foreign."[1] Jewish writers for the stage were few until the second decade. Jews did not, in fact, enter American literature in a major way until later in the century.

Interestingly enough, however, there had been four Jewish dramatists in the first third of the nineteenth century, Mordecai M. Noah, Isaac Harby, Jonas M. Phillips, and Samuel B. H. Jonah. Noah and Harby commanded considerable respect in literary circles, and drama historian Arthur Hobson Quinn has written that Noah was "probably the most important American playwright of the period next to James Nelson Barker" as a proponent and practitioner of a theater of American nationality.[2] But none of these included the contemporary Jew in their plays (with one minor exception), probably because they refused to portray their fellow Jews in the invidious conventional stereotype on the stage. An occasional Jewish playwright appeared, like Samuel Yates Levy, of Savannah, in mid-century.

The situation of the Jew in the theater can be gathered from an article of 1901 in *The American Israelite,* reprinted from the *Indianapolis News*:

It is a curious thought that, with the growing influence of Jews in theatrical matters, so little respect on the stage is paid to the Jewish character or the Jewish traditions. It seems curious to people of this age who are of Hebrew stock among successful leaders in all branches of endeavor, that racial prejudice ever militated against those people, as a people. Everywhere, except on the stage, the Hebrew today is rated at his true worth, and it is well recognized by thinking people that the old gibes and smears have lost their point and force. It might be imagined that with the great preponderance of the theatrical business of this century in the hands of the Jews, that the frightful caricature of the Hebrew that has long served as a buffoon for the amusement of the unthinking would disappear, but there are no signs of any such change.[3]

No doubt the article exaggerates the extent to which Jews were "everywhere" treated according to their "true worth." But it did confront the reality and persistence of the "Hebrew" stage comic throughout the nineteenth century. It is not surprising that most of the Jews in the "theatrical business" at the close of the century did practically nothing to curtail use of the stereotype. They were entrepreneurs and, like the usual businessman, aimed to please the public in the interest of maximum returns. In the theater this meant easy laughter from traditional Jew-baiting clichés and continuing along conventional channels. Hebrew comics, who specifically exploited these mannerisms, further reinforced the invidious notion of the Jew, and they extended dialect humor to its outer limits to serve as a constituent of the stereotype. That the Jew had "growing influence... in theatrical matters" at the time is indeed true. One writer on the American theater wrote that in 1900 the "leading producers" were "Charles Frohman, David Belasco, Klaw and Erlanger, David Frohman, Liebler and Company, Weber and Fields," and a few others, nearly all Jewish.[4]

A stimulus for the currency of the Hebrew comic was the flood of East European Jews of the mass emigration from the 1880s onward from the *shtetlach* and ghettos with their strange language and customs, making them an easy butt for "humor." During this period the Hebrew comic was added to the German and the Irish as well as the Black comic figure in the wholesale exploitation of ethnic humor. Jewish comedians sometimes resorted to blackface in their vaudeville skits and theater appearances, and they most often lapsed into demeaning Jewish dialect humor which, whatever their intention, infringed on the dignity of the Jewish people. These comedians were nevertheless immensely popular. One-act plays and "monologues," with some aspect of Jewish life as their butt, proliferated in the first few decades of the new century. How popular they were can be gauged from the fact that Edward D. Coleman's bibliography of the Jew on the English stage (both British and American) listed 116 "Hebrew monologues" by

William McNally from 1915 to the 1930s[5] and 61 such monologues and one-acters in the 1920s and 1930s by Arthur Leroy Kaser.[6] These must obviously have elaborated on the stereotype and used pseudo-dialect speech. In addition to dialect, these comics assumed a "grotesque Jew make-up"[7] which consisted sometimes of "tall, rusty plug hats, long black coats, shabby pants, long beard which ran to a point," and at others to "crepe hair, misfit clothes, hat over ears."[8]

There was occasional protest in the general as well as in the Jewish press in English against this denigrating treatment of the Jew. In 1912, a certain Montefiore Bienstock published a passionate protest against "The Hebrew Comedian" in *The American Citizen*; in this he fantasized a scene in which a Jew interrupts a Hebrew comic in action on the stage with cries of "This is an outrage" and "If the Jews have to break up every show in the country, it'll break up such slander as this." The audience encourages him to speak and he exclaims, "We have gone through bitter sorrow; we have been massacred; we have been tortured; and in America, ... where all people are free and equal, it is vicious to mock us; to sneer at us; to make us ridiculous; to infer that we are criminals." He urges Jews to the civil disobedience of breaking up all such performances. The theater manager, represented as a decent man who has now come to realize the offense to the Jews, comes to the stage and promises never again to engage such comics.[9] But it was not until after World War II that the extraordinary rise in ethnic sensitivity and general awareness of the dubious humor of the ethnic comedians—Black as well as Jewish and other ethnics—lost public approval, and they gradually almost disappeared from entertainment and the theater. (Unhappily the early 1980s witnessed a relapse into "ethnic jokes" in the cheap paperback books.)

Such militancy on the issue as Bienstock's fantasy was rare in those earlier years. No doubt much resentment was privately expressed and sometimes broke out into print. But there is a division of opinion as to the negative quality and effect of ethnic and dialect humor even down to our own time. An acute critic like the late Henry Popkin deplored the passing from favor of this type of humor while others welcomed its falling out of use. For instance, in Elmer Rice's autobiography, *Minority Report* (1963), he looks back with regret at its passing. Writing about the days of "vaudeville fare," he observes that "One feature of vaudeville was the dialect comedians, German, Irish, Swedish, Jewish, Negro (the last often in blackface). They imitated accents and speech patterns and poked fun at characteristic traits and usages. There was nothing malicious or inimical about the caricatures; they were often enjoyed most by those who recognized their own idiosyncrasies."[10] While Rice was accurately reporting the fact of enjoyment, he seems not to have realized that, however intended, such "caricatures" made fun of denigrated groups already the target of prejudice that was thereby reinforced.

The sense of Anglo-Saxon superiority was so pervasive that even ethnic groups took it for granted like good assimilated Americans. The severity of the damage it inflicted on an ethnic group varied with the status of that group within the general society. Imitation of such accents as the German or Swedish was not damaging to the group concerned. While they were the objects of anti-foreign prejudice when this prejudice flourished, they were not marked out for prejudice when acculturated. The case with other groups, like Blacks or Jews, was quite different. Caricatures of Blacks have always, down to our own day, been denigrating because equality is far from realized. The case of the Jews is similar though not nearly so extreme. The Irish caricature was damaging at a time when the Irish were harassed and a target of prejudice, but in more recent times this prejudice has been almost completely erased. As we have noted, however, in the wake of World War II with its searing demonstration of the evil of ethnic prejudices, dialect humor largely lost for a time its effect as "comic." Elmer Rice notes, "Today such good-humored raillery is taboo. Every racial, national and religious group has its zealous spokesmen who object to any allusion that might conceivably offend the most hypersensitive of their constituents. Where animosity does exist, censorship intensifies it. Ridicule, even invective, is often a safety valve." Rice himself was a political dissenter and even at times a radical, but he was, he said, "a thoroughgoing assimilationist."[11] It is not, therefore, difficult to understand his insensitivity concerning the validity of ethnic humor. Dialect humor is stereotypical because its use immediately identifies the mocking thought of "the Jew" with the prejudiced connotations it inevitably bears. But such portrayal can be deliberately hostile as well, without humorous intent. Both types survived well into the twentieth century.

Invidious Jewish stereotypes appeared conventionally in the plays of many non-Jewish dramatists in the first decade of the new century. One of the most popular playwrights of the pre–World War I period, Clyde Fitch, included a Jew in a few of his plays, once as a money lender in his eighteenth-century comedy of manners, *Beau Brummel* (1890), and again as a gambler, vulgarian, and generally shady character in *The Lady in the Case* (1905). In C. W. Hancock's *Down on the Farm* (1906) comic relief is provided by an "old clothesman," described in the play's stage directions as wearing "Black suit, shabby, black beard, Jew make-up."[12] An extremely bad play, Franklin P. Norton's *Financier of New York* (1915), portrays a pawnbroker who combines the worst features of Shylock and Kit Marlowe's Barabas. A pawnbroker also appears as an appendage to Sing Sing prison in Winchell Smith's and John E. Hazard's *Turn to the Right* (1916); he alternates between straight English and dialect speech and caters to the clothing needs of released prisoners.

The fact that these plays were written by non-Jews does not by any means suggest that Jewish writers did not also resort to the stereotype and dialect humor on the stage. Indeed, the plays that most extensively exploited this type of humor at that time were those of the Potash and Perlmutter series. Originally published in 1909 as an extremely popular series of short stories by Montagu Glass, the adventures of the Jewish garment business partners Potash and Perlmutter were collected into a book in 1910, and additional books appeared in succeeding years with the two "funny" men as partners in various other industries. In 1913 they first appeared on the stage in *Potash and Perlmutter* with great success, and these characters continued to appear on the stage into the 1930s. The two men do not speak in dialect so much as in rather outrageously ungrammatical English and Yiddishized word order. The mood of the play is relaxed and bland and purports to be amusing. Their business dealings are pervaded by an atmosphere of petty dishonesty, which is meant to invite indulgence. Sometimes the situations are funny, but throughout the onlooker (and the author) necessarily feel superior and condescending toward the patently harmless, well-intentioned joking pair. But sharp practice seems second nature to them and somehow pertains to their Jewishness.

Despite this persistence of the invidious treatment of the Jew on the stage, an awareness of its nature began to penetrate to the playwrights themselves early in the century. It would indeed have been remarkable if the "Progressive Era" in United States history in the early 1900s had not somewhat influenced the theater and, specifically, the treatment of Jews there. These were the years of the settlement houses, the social gospel, the muckrakers, and of social legislation introduced after Teddy Roosevelt, who became president in 1901, carried forward his "trust-busting" campaign. At the same time the wave of pogroms in Tsarist Russia created widespread sympathy for the Jews. One of the effects of the progressive and reform movements was to give playwrights pause concerning their treatment of the Jewish character in their plays. It dawned on them that Jews, too, were complete human beings with individualities and sensitivities that might be bruised by ridicule and by judgment via the stereotype. What ensued was a parade of plays that playwrights thought would at last do justice to the Jews. One might assign symbolic significance to the fact that the very first play presented in the first year of the Harvard Dramatic Society in 1908 was Allen Davis' *The Promised Land*, the play that won a competition judged by George Pierce Baker, Winthrop Ames, and *Boston Transcript* critic H. T. Parker ("H.T.P."), and was dedicated to George Pierce Baker. The central character of the play was a transparent representation of Theodor Herzl from his shocked awakening to the anti-Semitism in the Dreyfus case to his organization of, and work for, world Zionism.

The issue of the Jewish character in the theater was thrust into public discussion by one of the leading dramatists of that day, Augustus Thomas, in a speech in May 1908. He created a sensation by declaring, "The next great play will deal with the American Jew, the far-seeing, philanthropic, sweetly domestic Jew." He was even more specific. "Not the Jew of Shakespeare, not the Russian Jew"—meaning the revolutionary or poverty-stricken immigrant type—"or the persecuted Jew but the American Jew, who is philanthropic, far-seeing and, above all, sweetly domestic"[14]—meaning the rich, socially acceptable, civic-minded, family-loving, kindly Jew—in short, the ideal, middle-class Victorian Jew. Thomas continued to urge his conception in Chicago early in the next year, although this time he added a sanitized "socialism" to his demands. "Great plays," he said, remain to be written about the American Jew and about socialism. "I mean," he added, so there would be no mistake, "the American Jew of fine qualities as we know them, and I don't mean the dull kind of socialism one hears from platforms and in speeches but a sort of celestial socialism that we sometimes read about."[15]

Thomas' call for plays about Jews was widely discussed in the press, and an article in Chicago suggested that Thomas himself was the playwright who could best answer his own call—as indeed he did a few years later. But the writer acutely warned that such a play should, besides being good theater, "avoid flattery."[16] Another writer in *Theater Magazine* noted that Thomas' appeal "aroused much comment." "There had been plenty of plays," he continued, "with Jews presented in both favorable and unflattering lights, but Mr. Thomas' conception of the Jew as the hero of an impressive drama of our national life came home to the people of the theater with the force of a moral idea."[17]

A spate of plays with "favorable" Jewish characters followed Thomas' call, whether in response to it or whether the authors were responding to the same atmosphere that prompted Thomas himself to issue the challenge. A writer in *Current Literature* (August 1909) remarked that "the continuous influx of Jewish blood has aroused playwrights to the dramatic possibilities of interest in the question of intermarriage between gentiles and Jews." And many indeed were involved in this issue, which proved so common in fiction as well, because of its actuality in the life of the two peoples. Israel Zangwill's *The Melting Pot*, in which intermarriage was one aspect of Zangwill's thesis about intermarriage as one phase of the desired amalgamation of all ethnic groups into one American nation in which the original ethnic character of each would be "melted down" into a single national character, had opened in 1908 in Washington to great acclaim. The play as such was poor melodramatic "clap-trap," as some critics called it, but had sociological importance in popularizing the notion of the melting pot and the assimilation of all immigrant groups. Two other plays, more likely to have been inspired by Thomas' challenge, focused their dramatic centers on intermarriage. Thomas Addison's *Meyer & Son* (1909) makes all its characters very, very good, and the *American Hebrew* noted that the author "means well" and that "if there is offense in flattery, Mr. Addison is an offender, but probably an unconscious one."[18]

Another play, *The House Next Door* (1909), by Hartley Manners, is set in England. The son and daughter of an impoverished English baronet fall in love with the daughter and son, respectively, of their wealthy Jewish neighbor, a financial genius who has just been knighted and has bought the house next door to the baronet. The baronet is a Jew-hater and the parents of both families reject intermarriage. But by some incredible reversal, the parents of both couples agree to the marriages and all ends harmoniously. The original Austrian play from which the Manners play was derived was, appropriately enough, a farce. Philip Hale in Boston on February 20, 1909, said of the play that it contained a Jew who was "a saint-on-earth, who preaches mercy, drips forgiveness, and speaks copy-book platitudes of peace, goodwill and generosity, while his Gentile [is] in his old age, proud, irascible, tyrannical toward his family, utterly unbearable, after having squandered his money and reduced his wife and children to poverty." Most of the reviews, however, were favorable. In 1911, Louis N. Parker provided the famous *Disraeli* as a vehicle for which George Arliss became famous for many years on the stage and in film. This favorable portrait of Disraeli virtually identified Arliss for decades with the glorified likeness of the famous man.

All these attempts to portray a human Jewish figure foundered on lack of real knowledge of the Jews and the problems they faced, or on the depth of prejudice endemic in the Christian world, as well as limitations of play-writing talent. Would Augustus Thomas do any better when he turned his own hand to the "great play" of his conception? The highly selective nature of both the character and class on which he projected his challenge would lead one to doubt the adequacy of his vision. His *As a Man Thinks* (1911) confirms these doubts. Like so many others, the action of his play centers on intermarriage. The Jew who is intended to meet Thomas' criteria, Dr. Seelig, was a wealthy, highly respected doctor. His daughter, Vedah, is at first nearly deceived into a marriage with a Jewish scoundrel, De Lota, but then falls in love with a non-Jewish sculptor Burrill, whose father admires Dr. Seelig as a physician but blackballs his application for admission to an exclusive social club. Vedah tells her father that she wishes to marry Burrill, but he objects, chiding her, "Whenever the daughter quits us the religious welfare of the whole world is the loser."[19] The couple marries nevertheless. Then Burrill's father is brought around to agree quite magically; Dr. Seelig's approval, if indeed he ever gives it, which is left unclear, is tacit only. The play is well intended but genteel, weak in its motivations and dramatically unconvincing, since the arguments for and against intermarriage are scarcely confronted. All these limitations were really implicit in the content of the author's original challenge.

In his review of the play in the *American Hebrew*, the American Zionist leader Louis Lipsky remarked, "Thomas has certainly missed writing the great American Jewish drama."[20] Another reviewer noted that Thomas had "begged the question" and the play was hardly "a great drama."[21] Clayton

Hamilton wrote that Thomas failed to "say anything significant" about the "status of the cultured Jew in present day New York society," and that he had indulged in "rhetorical eulogy of the Semitic race."[22] On the other hand, "H.T.P." in the *Boston Transcript* was enthusiastic over the portrait of Dr. Seelig.[23] Perhaps Thomas' defense of the wealthy cultured Jew was animated more strongly by loyal fellow class feeling than by goodwill toward the Jew as such. An anecdote by Edna Ferber arouses our suspicions. She relates that while Thomas was directing her McChesney play in 1915, Thomas stumbled on her name after having seen her every night for weeks. She told him her name, and he replied, "Yes, yes, of course, Ferber, Ferber. I never can remember those Jewish names." Ferber adds that she stalked out, slamming the door.[24]

A more realistic effort to abandon the tradition as regards the idealized, favorable female Jewish character is John Corbin's *Husband* (1910). Rebecca Levine is a "Jewish lady from the East Side." She is a social activist, participant in politics, a "free-love" advocate, writer of a book on "Socialism and the Family." The author's own notion of marriage is also the final view of Beatrice Levine, who awaits her lover, a political prisoner, on his release from jail. "Free love," she exclaims. "Since Noah and the Ark, men and women have talked and tried it and still go in couples."[25] The play is superficial and largely rhetorical but is interesting as an early effort to create a contemporary "advanced" Jewish woman on the stage. A notable effort to create a Jewish character with an occupation like that of an ordinary human being is Max Rosenbaum in James Forbes' play about show business, *The Show Shop* (1914). The play has no other special distinction for us. Max is good-natured, shrewd, careful to show a maximum profit like any other theater manager, Jewish or not. He received no invidious treatment or any special positive or negative qualities. Human treatment of the Jewish character was also achieved by Rachel Crothers in her *A Little Journey* (1918), in which a Jewish traveling salesman, an ordinary, decent man, is treated no differently from other passengers on a transcontinental train. When the train has an accident, he rises to the occasion and is helpful in rescuing and comforting the injured. But even in this friendly vignette of a Jew, Crothers has him say that the first thought to occur to him after the accident is that he has no life insurance and must get it at once after his return home.

It is not surprising that, when Theodore Dreiser turned to the theater, he should make the same break with the past as he did in his fiction. In his *The Hand of the Potter* (1918) he applied the new realism to his interest at the time in Jewish life on the East Side. Mike Gold had earlier led Dreiser on a guided tour of the ghetto and even invited Dreiser to a Friday evening meal at his Orthodox home. The plot of the play centers on a mentally unbalanced twenty-one-year-old Isidore, son of an immigrant Jewish family. Already guilty of child molesting, Isidore again assaults an eleven-year-old girl and kills her; he is pursued by police and hides out; and he finally follows the paternal advice to commit suicide by gas.

While critics granted that Dreiser drew the East Side background with authenticity and greeted his courage in tackling this bit of psychopathology, they faulted the clumsiness of his plot structure. There is no special reason why the family should have been Jewish except that, as Dreiser once told Gold, he wished to write about the East Side Jews. The term "tragic" was often applied to the play. However, this seems dubious, since Dreiser makes amply clear that there is no freedom of will in this young man's behavior— an essential element in tragedy. His behavior is uncontrollably determined by his nature. Dreiser puts his theory in the mouth of the policeman, Quinn, who finds the young suicide. Isidore and those like him are "no more than any other person with a disease. He can't help it. There's something that pushes him in spite of himself." Indeed, Quinn goes so far as to enunciate Dreiser's theory about "chemisms" of human behavior. "Sometimes," says Quinn, "I think we're naht unlike the formula they give you in the chemical laboratory."[26] While the play left the impression, wrote Ludwig Lewisohn, of the purposeless display of mere pain, "it failed to rise from an immediate vision of the protagonist's depravity to the height of the tragic idea he was representing."[27] There is no suggestion in the play of the anti-Semitism that Dreiser was later to exhibit.

There were practicing Jewish dramatists in these early two decades, though far fewer than were to emerge in the post–World War I years. Elmer Rice produced his first play, *On Trial,* with great success in 1914, but his most important work dates from the 1920s. No other Jewish dramatist before the war produced plays of more than ephemeral interest. We should recall, however, that a burgeoning Yiddish theater flourished during this period. But Jewish dramatists in English received greatest popular recognition earlier than in other major literary genres, fiction and poetry, if we except Edna Ferber's Pulitzer Prize for *So Big* in 1923. No Jewish writer again gained the prize for fiction until 1951, and the first for poetry was given to Karl Shapiro for *V-Letter and Other Poems* in 1945. But Elmer Rice won it in 1929 for *Street Scene,* and Jewish playwrights received the award for drama again in 1932, 1934, 1937, 1945, and 1950.

How does one account for the more rapid entry of Jews into the theater, first as producers and then playwrights as acculturation advanced? Perhaps a glance at the occupational trends among the more adventurous immigrants from both the German-Jewish immigration from the mid-nineteenth century and the later Eastern European immigration might give a clue. The more able and adaptable ones engaged in small businesses, which they quickly expanded into large scale, from peddler to department stores, or from immigrant garment worker to garment manufacturer of this new mass production industry, or the exploitation of mineral resources of the West like copper, or from small businessman to movie tycoon. All these were marginal, innovative projects by virtue of their novelty and the consequent risk. Like these ventures theatrical production was marginal and risky, and perhaps in that sense attracted acculturating Jews seeking upward mobility. But playwriting is radically different, though intimately related to producing, but it did share the element of risk and marginality, with promise of large reward if successful. Not all professions or business areas were yet open to Jews at that time, but the theater was wide open to producing and playwriting, and younger Jews availed themselves of the opportunities provided, once they achieved acculturation.

Among the Jewish dramatists, a few departed from the stereotype. A very popular play, *Cheating Cheaters* (1916) by Max Marcin includes a crooked Jewish lawyer in collusion with a gang of thieves, who finances their robberies and recruits thieves for the gang but lives in perpetual fear of exposure and arrest, which finally happens. Some Jewish playwrights depicted Jews as ordinary, fallible beings. Joe Weinstein in Edgar Selwyn's *The Country Boy* (1917) is one, a theater ticket speculator, but not essential to the plot. He is on his way to achieving financial interest in the movies and is an active participant in the play's banter. However, a line spoken to him by a Black domestic is significant in light of the relation of Blacks and Jews. She complains to Weinstein, "White folks don't appreciate what I do," and adds hastily, " 'Course I don't mean you, Mr. Weinstein. If all the folk were like you—!"[28]

The best-known and most successful Jewish playwright in the pre–World War I period was Charles Klein. He was born in 1867 of a wealthy Russian-Jewish family associated with the arts in England. He immigrated to the United States in 1883 and successfully produced his first play in 1891. Of the thirty plays he wrote, twenty-two were produced, and eight or ten were successful. His "melodramas," wrote Arthur Hobson Quinn, "were among the most successful of the first decade of the new century."[29] So active was he in theatrical affairs that he became president of the Authors' Producing Society, whose aim was to protect the author from producers' tampering with their original texts. Klein was a master of commercial theater technique and was a play doctor, as well as a play reader for the producer Frohman. As one New York paper said of him on October 2, 1901, he had a "monopoly of technique... and... is... so to speak, a theatrical trust of stage trickery." In 1906 the press reported him as an "ardent follower of the Christian Science crowd." Among his successful dramas were *The Music Master* (1914) and *The Lion and the Mouse* (1905). Some of his plays, like *Maggie Pepper* (1911), include Jewish characters. In this play a Jew is a stock figure, a dress jobber whose function is to provide comic relief in a particularly objectionable way. In 1915 Klein sued to be named as co-author of the highly lucrative *Potash and Perlmutter* play, for which one may assume that he was the play doctor. He then embarked for Europe on the ill-fated *Lusitania*, and the case became moot.

From our examination of the plays with Jewish characters in the first two decades of the new century, we see the beginnings of the breakup of the conventional, invidious figure of the Jew that had rigidly prevailed in the theater for centuries. This trend was fused with the germination of a mature American drama in these decades which was to emerge in the period between the world wars. The way was being prepared in the 1910s by the spirit of revolt in the several literary genres. Heretofore playwrights for the United States stage could hardly be said to be producing work that could properly be called literature. The post–World War I period began to change that with the emergence of Eugene O'Neill.

AMERICAN DRAMA COMES OF AGE: EUGENE O'NEILL

World War I was a watershed in both American life and the American theater. The nation emerged from the war as a full-fledged world power, and the maturity it gained in its economic and political position on a world scale exerted profound influence on its intellectual, social, and artistic life. By the 1920s the nation found itself a literary as well as an economic giant. The brilliant efflorescence of the novel with Hemingway, Fitzgerald, Faulkner; of poetry with Ezra Pound, T. S. Eliot, Robert Frost, and others, also had their counterpart in the drama of Eugene O'Neill. All these figures were trailed by men of considerable talent. Just as the new work marked a sharp break with the immediate past, so the new currents flowing through the stage changed the theater. Until now, the country had never produced a single major playwright—in this respect contrasting with fiction, poetry, and criticism.

Joseph Wood Krutch has succinctly characterized the period opening at the end of World War I with respect to the theater.

During the last fifteen years [1915 to 1930] the American drama has become, for the first time, a part of American literature. Whatever success previous generations of native playwrights may have achieved in the popular theater, their work had little interest outside of it, and they neither earned nor found any place in literary history. About nineteen hundred and fifteen, however, a new dramatic movement began. A well-defined group of playwrights consciously revolted against the timid artificialities of our stage and began to compose work intended for the theatre but written with the sincerity and passion which had hitherto been found only in other literary forms. . . . By common consent, Eugene O'Neill is acknowledged to be the most distinguished of the group which created the current American drama. He was one of the first to emerge, . . . and the best of [his] work is also the best of our contemporary dramatic literature.[30]

Not only would this estimate be unchallenged half a century later; O'Neill's stature has increased in the interim, and his like has not yet been seen in the American drama.

The renaissance of fiction was incubated in the cultural, social, and political revolt against corporate power in the Progressive Era and against the emasculated culture generated by the "genteel tradition." The cultural revolt had its dramatic development in the foundation of such non-commercial theaters as the Neighborhood Playhouse on the East Side in 1915, the Provincetown Players in Greenwich Village in 1916 which nurtured O'Neill's plays, and the Theater Guild in 1919.

For whatever reason, the contemporary Jew never appeared in O'Neill's plays. From the evidence available to us it would appear that O'Neill was less subject to ethnic prejudice than many of his novelistic and poetical contemporaries. His biographers, Arthur Gelb and Barbara Gelb, offer no evidence of anti-Semitism, but on the contrary supply evidence of freedom from prejudice. So deeply did he hate Hitler and his works, for instance, that he told the actor Eddie Dowling, "If the Holy Father could just tell Hitler off, I'd go back to Church."[31] They write of the deep feeling O'Neill felt for Mrs. Lena Cominsky, sister of Emma Goldman, who served as a warm, motherly comforter to him during a sojourn in Rochester. The dramatist once told Mrs. Cominsky's daughter, "If I had a wife like your mother, everything would be fine."[32] A touching incident in 1916 is recorded by the Gelbs: "Sometimes Mike Gold would walk with them [O'Neill and Dorothy Day] and when they moved out on a pier, [Mike] Gold would sing melancholy Jewish songs."[33] One cannot, however, overlook a lapse of his sensitivity about the Jews when one reads of his light-hearted "editorial conference" about the Jewish Question with his colleagues on *The Spectator* in 1935 in which Dreiser expounded his anti-Semitic ideas. O'Neill did not demur from Dreiser's anti-Semitic views.

Very important was O'Neill's attitude toward Blacks in several plays. When *The Emperor Jones* was produced in 1920, it concerned a Pullman porter who becomes dictator of a small Caribbean island and is finally murdered by the fellow Blacks he oppressed. In this play O'Neill broke ground in several ways: it was the first American play with a Black as central character, and it was the first play in which a Black actor, Charles S. Gilpin, played the central character. The usual practice would have been for the part to have been done by a white actor in blackface. Gilpin gave a great performance. But when the Drama League invited the company to an honoring dinner, Gilpin's invitation was withdrawn because some Drama League members objected to dining with a Black. In a fury O'Neill persuaded the cast to refuse the invitation unless Gilpin was included, and the league had to agree to include him.[34]

When O'Neill presented *All God's Chillun Got Wings* in 1924, a play in which there is intermarriage of a white woman with a Black man and a white woman actually kisses the hand of a Black man on stage, the sky fell in. Paul Robeson played the Black husband. Such intermarriage treated on the stage was unprecedented enough, but to have a Black and white play their own parts shocked the public, whose indignation was unrestrained. The play was considered "immoral." The city could have had the play shut down if it had been playing at a public theater, but since it was played to subscription performances at the Provincetown, it was outside the city's jurisdiction. The mayor then charged that the play could incite riots and could then have acted against it, but he refrained. Hearst's *New York American* suggested that maybe the situation could be eased if an "octaroon" played the part of the white wife.

O'Neill replied to the bigots with a statement: "Prejudice born of an entire ignorance of the subject is the last word in injustice and absurdity." Robeson played the part, said O'Neill, because he "can portray the part better than any other actor could." The play is not a " 'race problem' play, but portrays the special lives of individual human beings. . . . Nothing could be farther from my wish than to stir up race feelings." On the contrary, the play "will help toward a more sympathetic understanding between the races." The Ku Klux Klan, then at the height of its influence, intruded its ugly face into the situation in its press and threatened the author and participants in open letters. O'Neill received letters from "infuriated Nordic Kluxers who knew I had Negro blood, or else was a Jew pervert masquerading under a Christian name in order to do subversive propaganda for the Pope!"[35]

Four days before the opening O'Neill told a press interview, "I admit that there is prejudice against the intermarriage of white and blacks, but what has that to do with the play? I am never the advocate of anything in my play—except humanity toward humanity."[36] In 1925 Augustus Thomas made a different comment on the play, shedding further light on his own real outlook on minorities. "In the first place," he said, "I should never have written a play" like *All God's Chillun*, "and in the second place, I should have been willing to do what is usually done in such cases, to permit a white man to play the part of a Negro. The present arrangement, I think, has a tendency to break down social barriers which are better left untouched."[37]

O'Neill did one play with Jews in it—*Lazarus Laughed* in 1925—several times revised but never presented on Broadway because it was too elaborate and fantastically expensive to produce there. The play is a paean to the conquest of life over death, based on the author's reconstructed sequel to the miracle of Lazarus' return to life in the New Testament story. In a way the play could be interpreted as the affirmation of life at the center of the Jewish tradition. The title, "Lazarus Laughed," O'Neill once told someone, was inspired as a counterpoise to Jesus' statement, "Jesus wept," in the gospel story. For the play celebrates not the non-material "eternal life" which Jesus taught, but a conquest of material life over death of the body. Laughter is the symbol of such life in the sense that it signifies the defiant liberation from death in *joie de vivre*. The materiality of O'Neill's conception can be gathered from such a verse as the paeon to cosmic laughter by the play's Chorus.[38] But the ancient Orthodox Jews in the play condemn Lazarus' liberated spirit. The father of Lazarus curses "the great mocking devil that dwells in Lazarus.... I curse the day he [Jesus] called my good son, Lazarus, from the grave."[39] That the liberation gives no license to corruption of any kind is made clear in the second half of the play, which opposes Caligula, the self-proposed "Lord of Fear! I am Caesar of Death,"[40] to Lazarus as Lord of Life and Laughter. Caligula does succeed in the end in killing Lazarus but is stricken with grief after the deed. He "proved there was death" but begs Lazarus to forgive him, so his victory is Pyrrhic.[41] While the inevitability of death is confirmed, the longing in humanity for long life and laughter remains supreme even if unattainable. While he affirms life in the Jewish mode, Lazarus' doctrine diverges from Jewish Orthodoxy in its abandonment of Law, but is also distinct from paganism and its multiplicity of anthropomorphic gods.

O'Neill emphasizes the Jewishness of most of the characters. His stage directions say that all characters are masked according to type of character and age, of which O'Neill indicates forty-nine categories. All other characters are masked, each category with a different type of mask, but Lazarus, "freed now from the fear of death," is not masked.[42] O'Neill directed that the "masks of the Jews in the first two scenes are pronouncedly Semitic."[43] The followers of Lazarus "wear a mask that, while recognizably Jewish, resembles him in fearless expression of life and laughter."[44] In further scenes of Athens and Rome the masks of the crowd are Greek and Roman "types of faces."[45] Moreover, in Greece and Rome Jews are explicitly referred to as such and on occasion in Rome are Jew-baited, while Caligula calls Lazarus "a dog of a Jew."[46] The reason for the explicit Jewishness is primarily historical, since Lazarus and Jesus actually were Jews, but partly that Jews represent a third world view different from both Christian and pagan. Yet Lazarus' viewpoint can be said to derive from Judaism and Christianity simultaneously, through Jesus, though different from both.

While there is general agreement that O'Neill was the greatest dramatist produced by the United States, the socioliterary atmosphere out of which he grew also produced other important playwrights, just as the Elizabethan period produced not only Shakespeare but also a cluster of important dramatists. The 1920s marked the entry of American playwrights into the world drama and into world literature for the first time. Jewish writers were among the dramatists who emerged in the 1920s. The late distinguished theater director and critic Harold Clurman wrote in 1970 that since O'Neill, four dramatists stand out—Clifford Odets, Lillian Hellman, Tennessee Williams, and Arthur Miller. Of these four, only one, Williams, was not Jewish. And beyond these four a number of other Jews made substantial contributions to a mature American dramatic literature.

We return to our rough quantitative method of estimating the extent of such a contribution by Jews, this time through the medium of the annual volume *Ten Best Plays*, initiated by Burns Mantle for the 1919–1920 Broadway season. In the fifty years up to the 1968–1969 season, as recorded in the *Ten Best Plays* for that season, five hundred plays had been selected. Of the thirty-two dramatists authoring "best plays" over this period who were cited four or more times, eleven, or one-third, were Jewish. George S. Kaufman was cited eighteen times; Moss Hart, eleven; S. N. Behrman, nine; Lillian Hellman, nine; Arthur Miller, seven; Sidney Kingsley, six; Joseph Fields, five; Clifford Odets, five; Elmer Rice, five; Jerome Chodorov, four; Rose Franken, four. Of the 217 plays by all authors cited four or more times, 83, or more than one-third—about 37 percent—were by Jewish authors. When musicals were first named among the ten best plays in 1930–1931 with *Of Thee I Sing*, of ten dramatists cited at least twice as authors of musicals, all but one were Jewish. Inevitably many, if not most, of the plays cited as among the ten best proved ephemeral.

What had emerged in the 1920s was nothing short of a flowering of American drama for the first time in American history, together with the contemporary renaissance in fiction. The theater nurtured a realistic trend which broke with the genteel, moralistic tradition in drama. Realism had already achieved much in fiction beginning with William Dean Howells and his followers Stephen Crane and Frank Norris, who went far beyond him, and through Theodore Dreiser, coming to climax in the galaxy of 1920s writers. This trend became manifest in the theater with the early plays of O'Neill and others in the 1910s and became full-blown and dominant in the 1920s. Wrote John Gassner, "One of the achievements of the nineteen twenties was the liberation of the stage from the proffered ministrations of the blue-noses and bigots."[47] The playwrights tended to be bohemians, political as well as artistic radicals, satirists, and critics of current society. This sociopolitical strain can be traced onwards from the 1920s. It intensified as the 1920s wore on and continued into the Depression 1930s. Some were socialists and even Communists while others were unaffiliated radicals like O'Neill himself. Among these writers were a number of Jews, but whether Jewish or not, most included Jewish characters in their plays. For the most part their realism extended to their Jewish characters' departure from the stereotype.

It should be noted that Jewish dramatic talent at this time was not limited to expression in English. A Yiddish theater, enormously popular among the Yiddish-speaking, had flourished for decades after the mass immigration. At first it was excessively sentimental and pandered to the worst tastes; this type of theater, known as *shund*, conquered the early Yiddish stage. When the dramatist Jacob Gordin immigrated in the 1890s, he succeeded in lending dignity and quality to the Yiddish theater. That theater then presented an impressive number of serious plays. Yiddish actors, some among the best in the country, emerged from them. About the same time as the non-commercial theater in English began, such excellent Yiddish art theater companies were founded as Maurice Schwartz's Yiddish Art Theater in 1918, and, finest of all, the Artef in 1928, a left-wing theater modeled on the Moscow Habimah company. These theaters and others in cities with large concentrations of Jews presented not only classical and contemporary plays in translation but also original Yiddish dramatic works by such dramatists as Jacob Gordin, Leon Kobrin, David Pinksi, Perez Hirshbein, Sholem Asch, H. Leivick, and S. Ansky.

Shut off as Yiddish culture was from the general American cultural scene, the English press from time to time noticed impressive artistic achievements in the Yiddish theater. Some actors from the Yiddish stage were co-opted by the English theater or the movies (Paul Muni was one of the most widely known). But the closest connection with the English theater was created when some Yiddish plays were presented in English translation there with great success. Leivick's *The Treasure*, about the degrading effect of love of money in a stilted translation by Ludwig Lewisohn, was presented by the Theater Guild in 1920. Peretz Hirshbein's *The Haunted Inn*, an idyllic play about the *shtetl*, was produced on Broadway in 1922. Other Yiddish plays also appeared on Broadway in English, but undoubtedly the most notable was S. Ansky's *The Dybbuk*, produced by the Neighborhood Playhouse in 1925, which became the sensation of that theater season. The play was a beautifully presented study of the exorcism of a "Dybbuk," an evil spirit possessing a young woman. The production was saturated with an authentic folk spirit and was profoundly human in its impact. The general audience, both Jewish and non-Jewish, found the play a deeply moving experience. Burns Mantle commented that "Only the pre-determined policy of the Neighborhood Players not to permit any one play, however great its success, to dominate a season, interfered with the run of the Ansky drama. Otherwise it could easily have continued indefinitely."[48] What moved the audience so deeply was the austerely sincere manifestation of profound human belief and feeling which uncovered the deepest layers of human insecurity in a human environment that presented manifest temptations to violate the compact with their God. The play was a compelling revelation of an intimately human Jewish past.

In time the best work of these American-Yiddish playwrights will be seen in clearer perspective as a product of the new burst of creativity which gathered strength in the 1910s and came to full fruition in the 1920s. The realism of the theater was to some extent a continuation of the social tradition in the novel.

LEADING PLAYWRIGHTS, 1920s TO WORLD WAR II

All the outstanding playwrights who emerged between the 1920s and World War II, except Tennessee Williams and Edward Albee, dealt with

Jewish characters in at least one of their plays. A few sometimes distanced themselves from such characters, and some Jewish dramatists did not abandon the stage stereotype. But for the most part there is little difference between the Jewish and non-Jewish playwrights in the treatment of their Jewish characters. It is a salient fact that, despite the prevailing anti-Semitism, the leading non-Jewish dramatists, unlike their novelistic colleagues in the 1920s, seemed immune from anti-Semitism, perhaps because they tended to be radicals who identified anti-Semites as among the enemy.

We shall first deal with the Jewish dramatists—Elmer Rice, George S. Kaufman, John Howard Lawson, S. N. Behrman, Lillian Hellman, Sidney Kingsley, and Clifford Odets—to be followed by the non-Jewish—Maxwell Anderson, Sidney Howard, Robert E. Sherwood, and Philip Barry. We cannot examine the entire *oeuvre* of these authors but shall look only at those plays with Jewish characters as we try not to lose perspective on their total work.

Elmer Rice

When Elmer Rice enjoyed his first success on Broadway with *The Trial* in 1914—one of the outstanding hits of that year—he was the first of the modern Jewish dramatists to emerge. He drew attention to his experimental talent in this play by introducing the flashback, which he said he did not consciously derive from the movies.[49] He was born in New York City and practiced as a lawyer for a short time; then his success with *The Trial* freed him for the theater. He was, as we observed, an assimilationist, and legally changed his name from Reizenstein to Rice, although he never had any thought of concealing his Jewish origin. In his personal life, he has written, he was "never...influenced by race, nationality, or religion," and never, he said, met any discrimination in organizational life except for a Jewish "quota" imposed by Jewish parents at a private school to which he wished to send his children.[50]

Rice was well aware of the break with the theater's past in the 1920s. At that time, he wrote,

a whole group of playwrights made its appearance, rapidly superseding the older group and bringing freshness and vitality to the American theatre. After half a century of industrial development unparalleled in history, America was beginning to pause for breath, to stop and look at what it had wrought. Self-satisfaction still prevailed; but self-criticism was beginning to intrude. Sensitive observers were revealing the cruelties, fatuousness, corruption and maladjustments that lay behind the grandiose facade. I do not mean that all these new writers were satirists or social critics—though many of them were; but they all surveyed the American scene with a sharp and sceptical eye.[51]

Like most of the new wave of dramatists and literary people, Rice was a political and social radical, and this viewpoint was reflected in his plays without his losing sight of his characters' humanity. In an experimental, expressionistic play in 1923, *The Adding Machine*, he exposes popular prejudices while dramatizing the mechanization of humanity in modern life. A chorus of his dehumanized characters respond to one of their number's cry, "America for the Americans!" with "That's it! Damn foreigners! Damn dagoes! Damn Catholics! Damn sheenies! Damn niggers! Jail and shoot 'em! hang 'em! lynch 'em! burn 'em!"[52] This was an *omnium gatherum* of the prejudices that bedeviled the 1920s.

A number of Jewish characters were included in Rice's plays, and he did not confuse authenticity with the stereotype. His most successful and probably most durable play, *Street Scene* (1929), is a microcosm of multi-ethnic East Side tenement life peopled with Italian, Swedish, Irish, and Anglo-Saxon as well as Jewish characters. Rice received the Pulitzer Prize for this play, the first ever awarded to a Jew for drama. The action centers on the Kaplan family. Samuel is a law student in love with the non-Jewish Rose Maurrants; Shirley, Samuel's sister, is a school teacher who has sacrificed her personal life and her chances for marriage to enable Samuel to graduate from law school; Samuel's father Abraham is a writer for the radical Yiddish press. The mood of the play is somber and frustrating but the dialogue has enduring vitality. The marriage of Samuel and Rose is prevented by objections to intermarriage from both families.

Some anti-Jewish prejudice is manifested by the Kaplans' fellow tenants, as well as anti-gentile prejudice by Jews. Jewish and Italian dialect speech is not offensive because the context is serious and dignified. Shirley suggests to Rose that "It's much better to marry your own kind. When you marry outside your own people, nothing good ever comes of it. You can't mix oil and water." This belief is obviously contrary to Rice's own, for he later stated that "intermarriage . . . [is] one of the best means of breaking down sectarian barriers and religious prejudices."[53] While the mood of the play is depressed, it is informed with compassion.

Perhaps Rice's most "Jewish" play is *Counsellor-at-Law* (1931), which was a hit and launched the former Yiddish actor Paul Muni on his English stage career. A variety of Jewish characters are treated naturally and without strain. The titular character is George Simon, born and raised on the East Side, a prominent lawyer with an Italian partner, married to a blue-blooded wife who elopes with one of her own social set. George has been politically corrupt in the distant past and is not above sharp practice on occasion but he is basically decent, certainly more so than his non-Jewish enemies. What the play conveys is that Jews are much like other people, no better and no worse. It is very clever and has often been revived.

Both the Depression and Nazism received Rice's dramatic attention. His keen social sense and conscience led him to help organize the Federal Theater of the Works Progress Administration (WPA) in 1935. In *We the People* (1933) he innovatively attempted a panoramic view, with fifty actors, of the effect of the Depression on several groups—the unemployed, the academic community—and the harsh police treatment of demonstrators. As he often did, Rice had dual protagonists, a Jewish and a non-Jewish professor, the latter of old New England stock, who participate in a faculty committee to join in promoting a protest demonstration. As a result, the Jew, Morris Hirschbein, is fired, while his colleague, Sloane, is only reprimanded; however, he resigns in protest against the anti-Semitism involved.

Rice also wrote several anti-Nazi plays. *Flight to the West* (1940) takes place on a plane from Lisbon. On it are a Jew from an old New York family with his non-Jewish wife, a German-Jewish woman refugee, a Nazi spy, several non-Jewish American businessmen sympathetic to Hitlerism, a Nazi diplomat and a reactionary United States army officer. The spy is exposed and arrested; a Belgian woman whose family was slaughtered by the Nazis tries to shoot the Nazi diplomat, but the Jew interposes himself between them and is wounded. The Nazi is unhurt but the incident has not changed his theories about Jews. While the play must have been moving in the atmosphere of the 1940s, it is so melodramatic as to be dated today. The play reiterates Rice's belief in the desirability of intermarriage through the harmonious intermarriage depicted. Whether or not one agrees with Rice's assimilationist views, his treatment of the Jewish characters—or any other, for that matter—cannot be faulted for any kind of prejudice. He displayed admirable respect for the dignity of the individual.

George S. Kaufman

The most commercially successful playwright of the period was George S. Kaufman. He was, wrote his biographer Scott Meredith in 1974, "second only to Shakespeare in the number of appearances and revivals of his plays throughout the United States and much of the rest of the world."[54] Like so many of the Jewish writers who emerged before the 1930s, he was born of German-Jewish parents established in this country. His mother was religious, but his father was an assimilationist because he thought differences among people separated them instead of uniting them. His father was also liberal and strongly pro-labor in that period of intense labor struggles. The divisions between his parents caused George to be ambivalent about religion. When he was twenty-four in 1913, he got an indelible lesson in anti-Semitism. He was then writing a daily humorous column for the *Washington Times*, patterned after Franklin P. Adams' "Conning Tower" in the *New York Tribune*. The publisher, Frank A. Munsey, was an intense anti-Semite but hired Kaufman on Franklin P. Adams' recommendation. One day, after a year of successful publication of the column, Kaufman's biographer relates, the columnist accidentally ran into Munsey in the composing room, throwing him to the floor. "Who is that Jew in my composing room?" asked the irate Munsey. When told the man was in his employ, Munsey ordered him fired. Kaufman "heard Munsey's words in stunned silence, suffused with all the feelings of Jewishness his ancestors felt as they, too, had faced savage and unwarranted anti-Semitic cruelty."[55]

No evidence appears to show that Kaufman thought deeply about Jewishness except that he unquestionably accepted his Jewish identity and on occasion would not allow anti-Semitic allusions to pass without comment. After Nazism was installed in Germany, he never in his life allowed his plays to be performed there. He quietly helped literally thousands of German Jews to escape and then supported many of these refugees from Nazism. After his wife Beatrice died in 1960, he burned a *Yahrzeit* candle in his bedroom each anniversary, but his funeral was held in the non-sectarian Campbell Funeral Home. Kaufman, writes his biographer Meredith, "always despised racial, religious, and national prejudice, ... and he realized that he might himself have been one of the Jewish intellectuals hauled off to prison or dragged into an alley and beaten to death."[56]

Kaufman was the collaborative dramatist par excellence, having been paired with twenty-two collaborators in the course of his writing career. This is not to say that he was incapable of writing a successful play alone, as he proved definitively by his solo performance in *The Butter and Egg Man* (1925). He was from first to last a highly talented writer of comedy. Since he wrote a number of plays about the entertainment industry, it is no wonder that Jews were included in them, as they were actually densely represented there. There are Jewish characters in about a half-dozen of his plays about Broadway and Hollywood pictured as directors, managers, producers, actors' agents, song writers, and movie tycoons. Curiously enough, none is a writer, except for the brief appearance of Hollywood writer Mr. Getzel in *Stage Door* (1936), written with Edna Ferber as first-named author. In this play there is also the dramatist Keith Burgess, who seems to be a satire of Clifford Odets, who had in reality just been proclaimed the great hope of the American theater. The play traces the transformation of a poor, informally dressed, bohemian, aspiring young writer to the author of a successful first play who, after his success, is "wearing tails, white tie, white muffler, platinum and gold cigarette case."[57] He now has a Hollywood contract, but his girl protests, "You said you would never go no matter how broke you were, and now your play's a big hit you're going." He replies that he will "use Hollywood" to get money for his real writing. "I'll write garbage in the daytime, but at night I'll write my own plays." His girl rejects him saying, "He's one of those fellows who started out on a soap box and ended up in a swimming pool."[58] The satire is too broad to do justice to the reality of Odets' personal history. Kaufman's wife Beatrice later wanted him to collaborate on a study of a new-name playwright "rather like Saroyan or Clifford Odets who is surrounded by sycophants but turns out to have few real friends," but there is little sign that anyone then remembered the *Stage Door* version, if it was indeed intended as an Odets satire.[59]

If Kaufman's pictures in these plays were not flattering, neither were they simply good or bad. They were like most people, a bit of both. The features of their personalities are based on accurate observation and are in many cases part of the truth about the Jews in the entertainment industry of this century. In the first of these plays, *Merton of the Movies* (1922), the movie director, Sigmund Rosenblatt, and a Mr. Walburg of the Straussenheimer company, each wants to steal the services of the unexpectedly successful neophyte comic actor Merton. In *The Butter and Egg Man* (1925), the erstwhile vaudeville agent and present play producer Joe Lehmann, whose "clothes are not of the kind known as loud, and yet has the knack of making them seem a bit exaggerated," does indeed have a "butter and egg man" (a financial sponsor for a play), a Mr. Ackerman, a bootlegger whose money is unavailable at the moment.[60] Lehmann's wife, Fanny, a vaudeville juggler who has money of her own, refuses to invest in a musical play her husband wishes to produce. Lehmann inveigles a gullible young Westerner, just arrived in town with a $25,000 legacy, to invest in his musical. The musical is a flop, but the young man, Jones, buys the play from Lehmann with the balance of his money, revives it, and it becomes a hit in New York. By now Jones has become Broadway-wise and sells the play back to Lehmann for $100,000. Lehmann is depicted as a rather pathetic if shrewd figure scrambling to survive.

Quite different is the picture of the actor's manager Oscar Wolfe in *The Royal Family* (1927), again by Kaufman and Ferber. The play was a broad, extremely clever takeoff on the noted Barrymore theater family. Wolfe is described as "a figure of authority: dark, stocky, slightly gray, dressed with picturesque richness. A rakish velour hat. Altogether the entrepreneur."[61] Wolfe keeps the family lives and finances on as even a keel as their mercurial temperaments permit. He extricates them from their tantrums or follies and scrapes and manages to keep their reputations as respectable as reasonably possible. He is loved by his capricious and wayward charges, as is evident from the family dowager's, "Oscar, what a grand person you are!" He tells her that he began as a "call boy at Daly's Theater for two dollars a week" and has been in the theater ever since."[62] The play was a great success and has often been revived.

Kaufman turns to the song writing and publishing branch of entertainment in *June Moon* (1929), with Ring Lardner, who supplied the idea for the play, as first-named author. The play is again a spoof—too good-natured to be called satire—of song writing and Tin Pan Alley. Whatever criticism is in the play is embodied in the career of Sammie Schwartz, a talented musician whose efforts to succeed at song writing have failed, but who is highly proficient at revising others' songs to make them salable. He is cynical by now but easy-going, kindly, and a valued employee of a music publishing house. When he is offered a drink by an aspiring song writer, he replies, "I don't drink. After listening to songs all day I don't want liquor. I just go home and take a general anesthesia."[63] Maxie enlightens a naive new song writer on the gold-digging intentions of a girl who wants to extract his money and sends him back to his hometown girl.

Satire of movie-making in Hollywood was Kaufman's next theme in *Once in a Lifetime* (1930), this time with the gifted Moss Hart as first-named author. Targets of their humorous shafts are several rival movie tycoons. The twelve Schlepkin brothers had, with immense success and illimitable future prospects, just brought out the first talking picture, a project which Herman Glogauer, the most important movie producer, had shortsightedly rejected. The Schlepkins offer to amalgamate their interests, but Glogauer turns them down because he recalls their earlier cutthroat competition. "All my life," says Glogauer, "they have been trying to get me! Way back in the fur business already, when I had nickelodeons and they had pennylodeons!" But a vaudevillian named Lewis wants to be on the ground floor of the talkie business and offers Glogauer to "teach your people to talk."[64] Glogauer puts Lewis in charge of his first talking picture, saying, "That's the way we do things out here—no time wasted in thinking!" For as Glogauer remarks of his actors in silent pictures, "They're beautiful people but unspeakable."[65] Although the picture made is a comedy of errors, it is a huge commercial success. Finally, in *Dinner at Eight* (1932), by Kaufman and Edna Ferber, Max Kane appears as the manager of a dissipated, superannuated movie and theater star who is on the point of being turned out of his hotel for non-payment of bills. The actor is enraged at his manager when he is offered a minor role in a play. When he insults Kane with the taunt, "The double-dealing kike!"—one of the few direct anti-Semitic epithets in Kaufman's plays—Kane tells him that he is finished.[66]

In all these portraits of Jews on the business side of the entertainment industry Kaufman is reasonably faithful to the realities of their functioning, except for the romanticized picture of Oscar Wolfe. It cannot be said that Kaufman in any manner succumbed to the comic stereotype of the Jew beyond the vocational traits necessitated in them. He never stooped to caricature of a Jew.

When Kaufman turned his lampooning talents to politics in the 1930s, the satiric edge was so dull that he had to resort to the ridiculous. When the Depression set in and a new presidential election was in the offing, Kaufman, with Morris Ryskind, exposed the vacuous hullabaloo involved in electioneering and the fatuities of the inaugural as well as the deliberations of the party bosses in smoke-filled rooms and the happy acceptance and participation of an electorate in the meaningless diversion from the issues of the political campaign. However, what we got in *Of Thee I Sing* (1931) was a lampoon, not a satire, a reduction to the absurd of superficial aspects of the matters at hand without any probing thrusts into their true nature and meaning in the life of the people. The ensuing play was favorably received by the public and by many critics. Only Robert Benchley dared to convey his disappointment. He found it "not particularly fresh satirically. The whole thing, during great stretches, was reminiscent of an old Hasty Pudding 'spoof' in which *lèse majesté* was considered funny enough in itself without straining for any more mature elements of comedy."[69] The main slogan of the campaign, "He's the man the people choose—/ Loves the Irish and the Jews," was not far from popular lore. Nor was the conception of a Jew, Louis Lippman, as a member of the National Committee in tandem with Francis X. Gilhooley as "representative of the two races which the candidate loves," a departure from the common stock of jokes.[68] Lippman becomes secretary of agriculture—a clever turn.

That Kaufman had no gift for genuine satire was even more evident in the sequel (again with Ryskind), *Let 'Em Eat Cake* (1933). The same characters are engaged in the reelection campaign but are defeated. The play then proceeds to caricature both right and left purely in terms of the color of their shirts, the blue and the black. When the election is lost, Mrs. Lippman persuades her husband to go into the shirt business together with the other defeated candidates, since the 1930s world is one of shirts—brown for the Nazis, black for the Italian fascists, red for the communists. This country should join the parade of shirts by wearing blue shirts, she urges, and Lippman would get rich by selling the shirts to the "revolutionists" he has joined for the purpose of promoting his business. The extreme right takes to black shirts. "By God," says Lippman, "if the American people want a revolution, we can give it to them. We've got the shirts for it."[69] He even suggests that he could make the business more efficient by reducing the number of buttons from six to five. But the revolutionary leader goes over to the counterrevolution and jails Lippman and his shirt business partners for having started the revolution. "Who started the whole thing? The shirt business!" To which Lippman replies, "The shift business—yes! But not the revolution business. That was your idea. A typical goy idea—revolution."[70] The Lippman group finally returns the country to democracy.

The critical reception of the musical was deservedly unfavorable, and it had a short run. Joseph Wood Krutch commented with restraint that "the trifling conclusion [was] almost an evasion of the issue the authors themselves have raised."[71] Kaufman and Ryskind were clearly out of their depth in attempting to satirize fascism or revolution. It should be added that in any case satire was not a flourishing genre in the deadly serious 1930s. For penetrating satire of American politics one would have to turn to a model like Hugh Henry Brackenridge's *Modern Chivalry* (1792–1815) or Mark Twain's *The Gilded Age* (1873).

Kaufman was more at home when in the next year (again with Moss Hart) he produced *Merrily We Roll Along* (1934) about song composer

Sam Frankel, said to be modeled on George Gershwin. Cyrus Winthrop (né Simon Weintraub) has become a millionaire through his invention of cellophane (called "cello paper" in the play). Other characters are vaudeville agent Sam Kraine and the commercial playwright Richard Niles. The play, like all of Kaufman's work, exhibits the tangled, rather heartless personal relations among theatrical people with Niles the least scrupulous with women and with his art.

All his life Kaufman was a liberal. So important was this to him that he found himself unable to collaborate any longer with Morrie Ryskind after that writer had veered to the right. But he could not convert his liberalism into genuine social criticism. His gift was for popular comedy, and he demonstrated that gift more consistently than any American playwright, but he was no Molière. He had a keen sense of the structure of the "well-made" play, and his primary talent was for clever dialogue. As a practical matter he was a commercial playwright in a period of mass commercial art, which relied on the banality and vulgarity of easy appeal to the mass audience. Although Kaufman never stooped to that banality and vulgarity, he never strained his audience beyond the superficial, and his social and political comment never cut deep. While the times cried out for criticism, there was no live American tradition that Kaufman could invoke or follow.

John Howard Lawson

The significance of Lawson for the American theater was more in his practice and his influence in his day than in the lasting character of his work. He was one of the earliest radical dramatists, having already written a play of social criticism, *Roger Bloomer*, in 1922. He was an early exponent of expressionism on the American stage, not only with this play but also with *Processional* in 1925, when Joseph Wood Krutch called him "obviously a man to keep one's eye upon." By 1934 Harold Clurman wrote that Lawson's aim was to "work toward remaking the world" and to further "the struggles to forge the future" and regarded him as "the most promising playwright in America."[72] A year later Lawson was to be replaced by Odets in Clurman's estimation. However, Lawson soon afterward shifted his energies to writing for the movies.

Processional, subtitled "A Jazz Symphony of American Life," produced in 1929, was a bold expressionistic experiment. Lawson explained in his introduction that only vaudeville and musical revues could genuinely mirror American life on the stage at that time, and he proposed to incorporate its techniques into his effort to achieve something of the quality of American consciousness. Without attempting individual characterization, the play takes us to a West Virginia mining town where harsh labor and human relations are depicted through a strike situation. Two Jewish characters are important to the action: Isaac Cohen, owner of the general store, and his daughter Sadie. The workers are a multi-ethnic group, Polish, Black, Irish, Italian. The hero is Jimmy, strike leader and lover of Sadie. He is finally blinded by the Ku Klux Klan and marries Sadie. All the characters are cardboard figures intended to bring out social issues. The targets of Lawson's bitter comment on the coal operators, the Klan, the bourgeoisie, and others are displayed in terms of jazz and vaudeville modes.

Blatant anti-ethnic and anti-foreign sentiments are exposed during the Klan hunt for Jimmy, which are scarcely an exaggeration of the widespread anti-foreignism rife in the 1920s. At a Klan meeting the white-hooded men are addressed as "Native-born American patriotic Protestants, regular citizens," and exhorted to "exterminate foreigners. . . . Clean up dirty foreigners; make 'em kiss the flag." Unfortunately Lawson's adoption of the vaudeville mode leads him to adopt uncritically the ethnic stereotypes of Jews and Blacks as well. The Black character is given the minstrel show name of "Rastus." The Jewish storekeeper is described by the author as having a "lisp that makes his speech a little ridiculous. . . . The vaudeville type of Yiddish figure." The Black "Rastus . . . plays a banjo and sings most of the time for good measure." "Dago Joe" is described as a "greasy Italian."[73] Cohen's language is the ungrammatical vaudeville Yiddish of the stage Jew.

That Lawson's insensitivity here was not an aberration is unhappily confirmed by *Success Story* (1932), a more conventionally well-made play and perhaps Lawson's best. His main character, Sol Ginsberg, is a successful lawyer determined to get rich at any cost, who climbs over others on his way up. He is not a simple character like Sammy Glick, who has no redeeming features, for he is actually in conflict about the climb. He had been a radical in his younger days, but abandoned this when it proved an obstacle to his passion to accumulate riches and to rise high in his profession. Harold Clurman remarked of this character that he was a man of "unusual energy, imagination, and sense of truth" who can find no way of living "in harmony" with his society because it is only by becoming "society's enemy and betrayer of his deepest values that he can succeed in it."[74] It was not the character itself but the timing of presenting such a Jewish character to the public that gave evidence of Lawson's insensitivity, for the horror of Nazism specifically in relation to the Jews was now only too evident, and the audience was repelled. The Group Theater, which produced the play, was therefore not reluctant to cut short the play's run. In the case of *Processional*, so egregious were the stereotypes of both Jew and Black that the Federal Theater felt obliged to modify the invidious Black and Jewish characters when it revived the play in 1937. Even in Lawson's *Marching Song* (1937), a Jew is introduced for comic relief and arouses a laugh when his name is introduced as Woodrow Wilson Rosenbaum. *Gentlewoman* (1934) has a Jewish psychiatrist, an intelligent, dignified man in a thoroughly middle-class environment, who is socially eligible but is a supercilious and quite unpleasant character. Why were all of Lawson's Jewish dramatis personae either stereotypes or unpleasant?

Lawson was one of the few playwrights of the 1920s and 1930s who can be charged with insensitivity regarding ethnic characters in their plays, especially the Jews. About Lawson's personal enmity to any form of anti-Semitism and anti-Black manifestation or any hostility there can be no doubt. One can only conjecture that his insensitivity derived from his upbringing in a middle-class Jewish family in which the father had changed the family name to Lawson. The dramatist seems to have been unaware of the significance of what he was doing and allowed his pen to operate unconsciously in this regard. This and similar paradoxes are not uncommon in all radical movements. It would be utopian to expect perfect consistency.

S. N. Behrman

Behrman was a master of elegant comedy who came from a lower-middle-class Jewish family in Worcester, Massachusetts, where he was born in 1893. He began to produce plays in the late 1920s, but his best work dates from the 1930s onward. Although his plays often dealt with current problems, since those were so pressing as to be unavoidable, his heart was not in the social theater in the sense in which Elmer Rice's or John Howard Lawson's was. Elmer Rice, who knew Behrman well from their association in the dramatists' cooperative, The Playwrights Company, wrote, "Behrman in spite of his wit and social talents, shrank from unpleasant problems and avoided, as far as he was able, contact with the crude realities of life. This awareness, conscious or unconscious, of his inability or unwillingness to be tough-minded is reflected in his plays, which usually portray an encounter between a clever, hypersensitive woman and a blunt, dominating man of the world, even when she eventually triumphs."[75]

We should not therefore be surprised that in the first play in which an important Jewish character appears, Sigmund Traub in *Serena Blandish* (1929), he is a wealthy jeweler in London's Bond Street and an urbane, intelligent man. This character did not reveal a more intimate knowledge of Jews, which Behrman did possess, than would such a character by a non-Jewish playwright. In a Soho restaurant Traub is struck by the beauty of young Serena Blandish and offers to allow her to borrow an expensive diamond ring for one month as an "investment...in the expectation of profits" because the ring "should have an offspring." Serena is invited, at Traub's suggestion, by the hostess of a high society party. The hostess explains to some of her guests, "Old Traub. Fancy! I'll wager he capitalizes on her in some ways. These Jews make money out of everything."[76] Contrary to Serena's expectation, possession of the diamond ring does not elicit any proposals of marriage from anyone in the wealthy set. At the month's end she is conned out of the ring by a fellow bus passenger on her way to return it. Her story to Traub is that she has given the ring to a needy poet. Traub proposes marriage to Serena, but she rejects him and marries her true love. Although Traub as a Jew is no vulgar money-grubber and the portrait is quite civilized, it is conventional without being invidious.

Two other plays besides *Serena* are located in Europe, and both have to do with Nazism and the Jewish issue as a major component. So close was the impact of Nazism on any sensitive person in those years that all serious playwrights, Jewish or non-Jewish, were irresistibly impelled to incorporate consciousness of its inhumanity at some point in their work. In *Rain from Heaven* (1934) Behrman approaches the problem from three directions. Lael, relative of a titled English lady, is engaged to a British Antarctic explorer, Rand Eldridge, whose brother is a Fascist trying to organize a Fascist youth movement; Lael rejects Rand because of their conflicting attitudes toward Fascism, and Rand decides to help his brother with his organizing.

Hobart's daughter Joan is in love with a talented Russian pianist, Sascha Barshaev, who is Jewish but tries to conceal this. Joan discovers that he cares more for his career than for anything else. She also chides him for being ashamed of his Jewishness, and he evades the issue. Joan tells him, "Instead of being proud and thrilled about it, you are ashamed. That's contemptible, Sascha," and she rejects his proposal. The third approach is that of Lael to the German Hugo Willens, a one-eighth Jew who has been in a concentration camp for writing a satirical playlet on the last Jew, whom the Nazis save from death because he is too valuable as a scapegoat. Willens, a noted musical critic, tells Lael that he is proud of his "speck" of Jewishness. "This odd and mysterious strain—did it give me sympathy and flavor, intellectual audacity and intensity? I was Nordic with an interesting racial filip."[77] Much as he and Lael wish to marry, he feels he must return to Germany to continue his anti-Nazi work. In his perceptive book, *The Political Stage: American Drama and Theater of the Great Depression* (1970), Malcolm Goldstein has written of this play, "No matter how much Behrman might have wished to maintain a neutralist position, he could not as a Jew ignore the Nazis. In sending Willens back to Germany, he joined the outcry against them."[78] Arthur Hobson Quinn suggested that the relation between the critic Willens and the Fascist brothers in the play was based on the "repudiation by Gerhardt Hauptmann of Alfred Kerr, the [Jewish] critic who had been a devoted disciple, but whom Hauptmann cast off because he did not subscribe to the nationalistic and Fascist wave in Germany."[79]

During the anti-Nazi war itself, in 1944, Behrman adapted for ironic comedy an actual anecdote he had heard about the early days of the war in 1940. In the play, *Jacobowsky and the Colonel* (1940), as the Nazis are approaching Paris, an anti-Semitic, aristocratic, traditional Polish colonel, not too bright, enters into a pact with the shrewd Jewish businessman, Jacobowsky, who will obtain a car and guide them through France to safety from the Nazis. By Jacobowsky's quick-wittedness and uncanny ingenuity they elude capture and reach London. The two widely contrasted characters grow quite fond of one another in the course of their adventure. The Pole's anti-Semitism gives way before knowledge of his Jewish fellow traveler, a resilient, five-time refugee from anti-Semitism who has escaped from Poland to Germany, from Vienna to Prague to Paris and finally to London. This grim situation is depicted entertainingly without diminishing its seriousness, and the play was a success.

Behrman based his late play, *The Cold Wind and the Warm* (1958) patently on his own adolescence and young manhood. The play presents the Jewish neighborhood in Worcester where Behrman grew up. The Yiddishized English of the older generation; weddings planned by the *shadchen* (matchmaker); the grocery store of the family; Toby, the young bohemian, who probably stands for the playwright as a young man; the sad frustrations of young lives, with suicide for one and unrequited love for another—all these ensue. The play is drenched in nostalgia and the double aspect of the cold and the warm in human relations. Toby becomes a composer in New York (read dramatist), and tells his friend, before his suicide, that the "near things, the admirable things, the warm winds of affection, of friendship, of love, don't touch you any more."[80] The combination of advancing age and the widespread reawakening of a sense of Jewishness in United States literature may have prompted the playwright to revive these early memories in dramatic form.

Lillian Hellman

In my view Lillian Hellman should be reckoned as among the half-dozen leading American dramatists of the century. She came from a middle-class New Orleans Jewish family. Although her participation in Jewish life outside her family has, to my knowledge, been non-existent, she would never dream of denying her Jewish origin and identity. She passionately hated greed and fascism and expressed that passion in her plays. On her return from the Spanish Civil War in 1937 she exclaimed, "I am a writer. I am also a Jew. I want to be quite sure that I can continue to be a writer and that if I want to say that greed is bad or persecution is worse, I can do so without being branded by the malice of people making a living by that malice."[81]

Her early play, *The Children's Hour* (1934), dealt with the malice of small-minded gossip-mongers. It was an immense hit, running for nearly seven hundred performances, and established her as a formidable dramatist. However, her next play, *Days to Come* (1936), about employer-union conflict, was a failure. She hit her stride again with the powerful *The Little Foxes* (1939). The play was concerned with greed for money in a Southern woman presented in such a way that this greed might also stand as a symbol of the animating force of capitalism. Following her experience in Spain and later in Europe she produced her moving anti-Nazi play, *Watch on the Rhine* (1941), in which the malignancy of Nazism is played out by a group of German refugees and Nazis in the United States and a non-Jewish German anti-Nazi activist who leaves the safety of the United States to return to Germany to resume clandestine anti-Nazi work. She introduces no Jewish character in this or any other play. Perhaps she considered a Jew in this position would be taken as special pleading. It is unlikely that her plots just happened to provide no occasion for Jewish characters. This may have resulted from the view that Jewishness was irrelevant to the predominantly non-Jewish nature of the American experience with which she was concerned.

Sidney Kingsley

The longest running play produced by the Group Theater was *Men in White* (1933), a first play by Sidney Kingsley. This play launched that theater on its brilliant career and won the Pulitzer Prize for 1933. Kingsley was born in 1906 of a middle-class Bronx Jewish family, so that the central Jewish character in the play was familiar to him. While there is much general social comment on the medical profession in this realistic play, interwoven with it is the implacable objection to intermarriage by an Orthodox Jewish mother. Dr. Levine is an extremely promising doctor who is believed to be a strong candidate for a research position as assistant to a distinguished scientist, Dr. Hochberg. At the non-Jewish hospital nearly all the senior doctors are Jewish while nearly all the interns are not, probably by anti-Semitic design. Dr. Levine falls in love with a gentile girl and marries her against the strenuous objections to intermarriage of his mother. She cuts him off from money in her displeasure, and he is forced to give up all hope of further study, thus becoming ineligible for the desired research position. Instead he has to become a general practitioner on the East Side. He tells his wife: "Katherine! The East Side! Tenements! Fifty-cent patients! Poverty! Dirt! Struggle! . . . Jehovah and Aesculapius! They both demand their human sacrifices. . . . Medicine! Why do we kill ourselves for it?"[82]

Kingsley's next play, *Dead End* (1935), was a landmark for naturalism in the theater. Set in the New York slums among a group of impoverished teenaged boys of several nationalities, the play and dramatist boldly have the boys use their vulgar street talk. So vivid and shocking were the events projected on the stage—murder of an adult by a teenaged boy in an altercation and the subhuman conditions under which the boys live—that the public conscience was aroused. Senator Robert Wagner credited that play with the impetus for the passage of slum clearance laws by Congress. One of the boys in the gang is the Jewish Milty. When the police look for Tommy, the young murderer, Milty yields to Tommy's sister's plea to reveal his hiding place, but the police find Tommy otherwise, through betrayal by another one of the gang. Kingsley went on to write other plays, but his most important work was done with *Dead End.*

Clifford Odets

To the mediocre actor and aspiring playwright Clifford Odets, 1935 was the *annus mirabilis.* In that year he was acclaimed the leading American dramatist of the decade, and three of his plays were simultaneously drawing crowds on Broadway. His mentor, Harold Clurman, a founder and director of the Group Theater, had read an earlier play by Odets but had not suspected the lurking talent of his friend. Clurman "hardly thought... its author a potential playwright." When in three days Odets wrote a one-act play for submission to a contest by the left-wing New Theater League, *Waiting for Lefty* won the contest. The prize was a one-night performance, which proved a sensational success and launched Odets as a promising American playwright. In 1935 Clurman wrote, "Odets became the central figure of the so-called Left movement of the theater."[83]

Odets was born in Philadelphia in 1906 of a comfortable middle-class Jewish family, who moved to New York when he was six. His Jewish education was sparse. As his thirteenth birthday neared, his father tried to provide Clifford with a crash course of instruction in preparation for a Bar Mitzvah, but for some reason this was never completed. Instead, his father fatuously dressed himself and his son up in formal clothes and had them photographed as if at a Bar Mitzvah reception. But if Odets had little religious training, he was intimately familiar with the special qualities of the ethnic Jewish life of middle-class Jews and the milieu of his family and friends, as his pre–World War II plays attest.

As a young actor and aspiring dramatist in New York he was associated with the growing left movement and passionately shared their socialist views about overcoming the Depression and about the need for radical social change. He even joined the Communist party in 1934, but found the demands of the party on his writing intolerable and dropped out after a few months, although he continued for some years as a sympathizer. He joined the Group Theater and was devoted to Harold Clurman as a friend and critic, as well as the director of his first half-dozen plays. These plays cannot be regarded, strictly speaking, as "Communist," but rather as generally Left in direction.

Of all the important Jewish dramatists of the 1920s and 1930s, Odets' pre–World War II plays were unquestionably the most ethnically Jewish, most deeply rooted in the Jewish milieu. If life in this milieu was more or less acculturated, it yet retained recognizable differences from the non-Jewish. Language acculturation was often incomplete, and there was occasional resort to Yiddish; the sense that they were less than totally accepted by fellow Americans was ever present and sometimes broke out into the open; there were occasional residues of immigrant modes of thought and in some cases greater or less adherence to the ritual diet and behavior bequeathed by Orthodoxy. No other dramatist of those years exemplified these ethnic features as well as Odets. This approach expressed Odets' own inclinations. According to Harold Clurman, who should know, Odets was also influenced in this direction by Lawson's *Success Story*, which "brought Odets to an awareness of a new kind of theater dialogue. It was a compound of lofty moral feeling, anger, and the Jewish argot of the big city. It bespoke a warm heart, an outraged spirit, and a rough tongue."[84] While in general American-Jewish life the religious aspect and the historical perspective of Jewish culture were superficial at best, American-Jewish life does have a distinctive social character whose special qualities tend to become attenuated with the growth of acculturation and a weakening of cultural ties with the Jewish past. However, so long as awareness of identity is present, some difference from the rest of the community persists. In this sense Odets' plays have ethnic Jewish content.

As has been noted, Odets is primarily a dramatist of the middle class, actually the lower middle class, and this is apparent from his first produced play, *Waiting for Lefty*. It deals with lower-middle-class people declassed to the working class by the harsh Depression conditions. A laboratory assistant and a Jewish doctor, Benjamin, have been forced to drive taxi cabs for a living. They are so badly paid that they and others attend a meeting to decide on taking a strike vote. Inspired by the burgeoning union organizing of the CIO, the play is a moving declaration of labor militancy. Several members of the strike committee recount in flashbacks how they came to the determination to strike. Dr. Benjamin tells his story, which does not deal only with his family's economic situation, but also with the unrestrained anti-Semitism and upper-class privilege that forced him out of his profession and into taxi driving. He was a good surgeon but was displaced to make way for the incompetent son of a senator. His colleague, Dr. Barnes, from an old New England family, makes it clear to Dr. Benjamin that he was chosen for dismissal because he had criticized the treatment of poor patients and because he was a Jew. When Benjamin demurs ("Such discrimination," he says, "with all those wealthy brother Jews on the board?"), Dr. Barnes replies that it "doesn't seem to make much difference between wealthy Jews and rich Gentiles. Cut from the same piece." Benjamin tells Barnes he had thought of going to Russia, but had decided to stay because "Our work's here—America!"[85] In the end, after news of Lefty's murder is announced, all cry out for a strike. The audience often joined in.

Overnight Odets emerged as the most promising playwright on the American horizon. The play was repeated all over the United States and indeed in many other parts of the world as well. Odets had ready a full-length play, *Awake and Sing*, which the Group Theater then quickly produced and which reinforced the impression created by *Lefty*. The new play was an exploration of a decaying Jewish middle class during the Depression. The theme and dialogue were more suggestive of Sean O'Casey.[86] The distinctive technical feature of Odets' plays is the ebullience and vitality of the dialogue with its unexpected turns of speech. It would be difficult to place this dialogue anywhere but in New York City's second-generation Jewish milieu, no matter what the subject matter. This quality is unmistakable, for instance, in Odets' script for the movie, *The General Died at Dawn*. One finds here an occasional incongruity between the Odetsian figures of speech in the mouth of a non-Jewish American, played by Gary Cooper, and Madeleine Carrol (with an English accent, to boot). This dialogue is at its most un-inhibited and characteristic in the early plays. For example, in *Awake and Sing*, Moe asks Hennie, "Where are you going?" to which she replies, "For my beauty nap, Mussolini. Wake me up when it's apple blossom time in Normandy."[87]

The Bronx Jewish family in this play was so vivid in its authenticity that Alfred Kazin at twenty could wonderingly be moved by the sight of the likes of his own father and mother on the stage. The Berger family is struggling to survive the Depression. The strong mother, Bessie, desperately claws her way to keep the family afloat; her old father, Jacob, is a radical, sensitive and principled, but ineffectual; her husband Myron is an inoffensive nullity; her daughter Hennie is independent, hard, and pregnant by an unnamed man, maneuvered into marriage with an unsuspecting, naive young suitor; Ralph, the sensitive son, is unable to marry his sweetheart because he's too poor to support a family; Moe Axelrod, one-legged World War I veteran, a racketeer, is in love with Hennie with whom he runs off at the end. Jacob sees in his grandson Ralph a chance of carrying on his radicalism and makes Ralph his insurance beneficiary, then commits suicide, making it look like an accident so that Ralph can collect. Odets was thoroughly at home in this situation, and he filled the play with a vitality that can still be felt, even though each of the characters is in one way or another frustrated. But hope at the end lies with Ralph, recalling his grandfather's admonition, " 'Awake and sing.' . . . The night he died I saw it like a thunderbolt. I saw he was dead and I was born! I swear to God, I'm one week old. . . . We're glad we're living."[88]

In the next year Odets produced *Paradise Lost*, again the Jewish family in straits because of the Depression. But the Gordon family starts at a higher level of acculturation than the Bergers, represented by the move to 111th Street from the Bronx. Unlike the earlier play, the diction is unaccented, except for Sam Katz, who retains his Yiddishized English. The family's fall into poverty is their "Paradise lost," for the handbag business of the partners, Gordon and Katz, is near bankruptcy and the family is bewildered by the loss of income and together decline in status. As a whole they represent the declassing of the middle class, and each character brings out a different response to it. The mother, Clara Gordon, neither dreams nor speculates but simply makes the best of what they have; her son, Julie, hopelessly ill and devoting all his sparse energies to playing the stock market without money, represents a self-deluding, sick capitalism scrambling to survive; her husband Leo, the liberal; Pearl, the daughter, a pianist trying to escape and lose herself in music; another son, Ben, an Olympic athlete who cannot find his place in a harshly competitive business society. Leo Gordon's partner Sam Katz stands for the cheating, sterile small capitalist who will stop at nothing to survive, while the janitor, Mr. Pike, an elusive figure of New England family, embodying the rebellious American tradition of the common man, functions more nearly as a symbolic commentator than as an individual character. In an interview at the time, Odets told a reporter that "my interest was not in the presentation of an individual's problems, but in those of a whole class."[89]

The milieu is still unmistakably middle-class Jewish even if less obviously so than in *Awake and Sing*. But Jewishness is throughout taken for granted. In a typical Odetsian phrase: Ben's wife Libby says, "I want fun out of life" to which the earthy Clara responds, "Fun is in the dictionary!"[90] At the end, when Leo offers to give a $10 bill to the destitute men who are returning his furniture from the street after an attempted eviction, Leo Gordon explains why he is doing so. "People like me," he says, "are responsible for your condition." His insistence on the promise of equality and democracy prompts the tough-minded leader of the group returning the furniture to say, in Odetsian phrase, "All over millions dreaming of democracy and liberty which don't exist. That's how it comes out of my knitting machine."[91]

As the 1930s wore on, Odets' projection of hope became weaker as his personal problems became more difficult. The social aspect of his work became more implicit rather than the explicit allusions of the first plays. An omnivorous Hollywood offered Odets a financial reward he could not resist. The Group Theater was coming on hard times and Odets saw the prospect of Hollywood money as an important contribution to the maintenance of the theater he loved. He promised to continue to write plays and to return soon. He did fulfill both his promises—he sent back much-needed money and then returned within a year with a play, *Golden Boy*. But he was a troubled man. More and more his plays turned toward conflict within the individual. This struggle was in all likelihood exacerbated by his capitulation to Hollywood. Indeed, *Golden Boy*, produced in 1937, was his greatest commercial success. It can be interpreted as symbolizing his own travail over the rival claims of art and money.

Odets passionately loved music, so that he could easily identify himself with Joe Napoleon, protagonist of the play who has a promising career as a talented violinist. But Joe is also extraordinarily talented as a prize fighter and can be a champion and make big money, just as Hollywood promised big money for Odets the writer. Joe destroys his talent as a violinist by breaking his hand in a championship bout. This marks his final farewell to music and descent into affiliation with sponsoring gangsters and virtual abandonment of his family, who are now ashamed of him because of his destruction of his art. In full realization of this destruction and, after he has killed an opponent in a fight, of his surrender to the corrupt values of society, he catapults to death in an auto crash with the girl he loves.

In actuality Odets traveled both courses simultaneously: he wrote his plays, and he wrote for Hollywood with large monetary reward. The conflict was not solved; it was intensified, and how deep it ran is exhibited in *Golden Boy* and later plays. At the same time, while social implications remained in his plays, they were less explicit and the dramatic focus was on internal conflict. Also, the ethnicity of his plays became less pronounced until it virtually disappeared—at least until the final play, *The Flowering Peach*. The values contrary to those to which Joe succumbs are represented in *Golden Boy* by his old father and his brother, a CIO organizer. The father is a close friend of a Jewish neighbor, Mr. Carp, and the two older men discuss the dilemma confronting Joe and by implication, all men. Mr. Bonaparte says, "Don't expect Joe to be a millionaire. He don't need it. . . . A good life's possible—," Mr. Carp replies, "For men like us, yes. But nowadays is it possible for a young man to give himself to the Muses? Could the Muses put bread and butter on the table?"[92] This is Odets' dilemma, and he was finally impaled on its horns.

Over and above the specific symbolism is the more general conflict of which this is a part, namely, the conflict within the individual who wishes to rise above the spurious values of money and competition and celebrity and to pursue his own bent with integrity, a struggle which Joe had lost. More and more one comes to the realization of one's authentic individuality and the conflict with a world worshiping false values. But in Odets' next play, *Rocket to the Moon* (1939), social conditions, the Depression, and the struggle to extricate oneself from their effects are even farther in the background than in *Golden Boy*. The personal problems of a declining middle class under these conditions advance into the foreground. The central character, Ben Stark, a dentist, is making a fair living but is aching for love, which he does not get from his anemic, barren wife. His assistant, Cleo, is the pivotal figure in the play, much younger than Ben, also looking for love, security, and mutuality in her relations. "I'm a girl and I want to be a woman," she says, "and the man I love must help me be a woman." Three men are in love with her, Ben; his father-in-law, Mr. Prince, who is well-to-do; and the glamorous, unscrupulous Mr. Wax, to whom Cleo says, "You make love very small and dirty." None of the three arouses her love. She easily rejects Wax; Mr. Prince has already lived his life and is too old for her; and the married Ben is not free to love her as she would wish. So she walks out of the lives of all three. But the future is not hopeless for her, for she says as she leaves, in an Odetsian phrase, "None of you can give what I'm looking for, a whole, full world, with all the trimmings," and then adds, "Experience gives more confidence. . . . I have more confidence than when I came here."[93]

From *Rocket to the Moon* and on to the next four plays we see the attenuation of Jewish characters; where they appear at all, as in *Rocket*, they are thinned out and recognizably Jewish only by name. Indeed, there are no major Jewish characters in any of the following plays as they intensify their preoccupation with the inner personal problems of love and marriage and the corrupting influence of a commercialized Hollywood and theater. Why, then, did Odets return to Jewish ethnicity in his last play, *The Flowering Peach* (1954)? Several reasons may be suggested. First, we may believe that Odets was surely affected by the return to Jewishness experienced by many writers and intellectuals during the 1950s as the realization of the Holocaust and the establishment of the State of Israel bore in upon them. We should recall that the Jew as writer and character became central to American literature in the 1950s. At the same time the threat of annihilation from the atomic bomb hung heavy on society.

In the 1950s Odets seemed to have fused these concerns by evoking the biblical story of the end of the world, with hope for the future lodged in Noah and his family. Odets superimposed on the biblical story a modern-day Bronx Jewish family, somewhat in the manner of his plays of the 1930s, except for the bitter overtones of the later Odets. The story of the flood is transposed into the language and feeling of the 1930s. The English is heavily Yiddishized, and the family relations are unsparingly quarrelsome. Noah is a heavy drinker—somewhat untypical for the Bronx milieu—and there is much unseemly squabbling. But in their common adversity the family gets together and survives the flood. Again, as in the 1930s, Odets emphasizes the centrality of the family. And despite the bitter tone, the hope that pervaded the earlier plays is still present. On return to dry land the family sees a flowering peach. Like survival after World War II and the Holocaust, the family sees the flower as a symbol of a new beginning and as hope for the future despite the threat of the bomb. "This," says Noah "is ahead—a fruitful world. . . . The people need happiness."[94]

Odets' internal struggle to keep his integrity as man and artist intact had a number of phases as reflected in his plays. Among them was the tension between his playwriting and the allure of Hollywood which he straddled (our greatest playwright, O'Neill, never even considered Hollywood as an alternative) by engaging in both. Another conflict that must have caused him anguish in his last years was his decision to testify as a "friendly" witness before Congressional committees on "subversion," after public assertions that he would not capitulate to them. How he dealt with such contradictions within himself and what they imply for his plays merit study. What, in my view, is clear, is that Odets' work was among the enduring literary treasures of the century in the United States.

We pass now to the leading *non-Jewish* dramatists, who understandably included fewer Jews in their plays than their Jewish confreres. It should be recalled that in these earlier decades Jews were not so familiar, either personally or through literature, as they were to become after World War II, and more especially after the 1950s. In the drama before 1940, therefore, the Jew was still treated as something of an exotic by non-Jewish playwrights.

Maxwell Anderson

Like most of the leading dramatists of the period, Anderson was something of a radical in his early days. He was a pacifist during World War I and was therefore fired from his teaching post at Whittier College. His antiwar play (with Laurence Stallings), *What Price Glory?* in 1924 was an indictment of the inhumanity of war. This play also developed Anderson's position as one of the pathbreakers in the drama of the 1920s. Its free use of profanity was shocking on the stage of the time, as was the ruthless naturalism of its scenes in war-torn France in 1918. The soldiers in the play, as in so many war plays, novels, and movies since, are multi-ethnic. One of the soldiers is a Jew, Lewisohn, who is a minor character and is killed in action. But this character, like similar ones in every other Anderson play until *Winterset* (1935), was Jewish in name only. However, in *Winterset* no observation of any kind is made by anyone of the Jewish identity of the character. Perhaps the non-Jew Anderson was aware that he knew too little about Jews to venture into these matters. At any rate, the same is true of *Saturday's Children* (1927), which includes the middle-class Halevy family, and a rooming house owner, a Mrs. Gorlick, both of whom must be Jewish judging by the name, but no mention or comment on Jewishness is made.

When Anderson (together with Harold Hickerson) turned to the Sacco-Vanzetti case for his play, *Gods of the Lightning* (1928), several Jewish figures again appear. One of them, a panhandler named "Ike," tells a Salvation Army lassie who is trying to convert him, "I'm a Southern Jew and Jesus himself couldn't touch a Southern Jew, not ever. He might be willing to do something for one of them New York Jews, but I never met anybody who didn't draw the line at an Israelite hill-billy."[95] This sounds like a highly improbable bit of dialogue. In the play, too, a Jewish woman is blackmailed into testifying against the innocent anarchist defendants but retracts her testimony. Most important, however, is Gluckstein, an idealistic Jewish lawyer, who is a typical enough figure not only in the actuality of the Sacco-Vanzetti case, but in many other defenses of imprisoned radicals.

Just as *What Price Glory?* pioneered in breaking down Victorian restraints in language, so *Winterset* in 1935 was a heroic effort to revive poetic drama, and Anderson continued this attempt for several plays thereafter. In this innovation he had few followers, but it is now generally recognized that Anderson's gift was not for poetry. He took a lively current topic for his theme, once again the Sacco-Vanzetti case, since his earlier effort had been a failure, and also chose to center his play on the Jewish Esdras family in New York. The son, Garth, a witness to the murder whose testimony could have absolved the defendants, had never been called to the stand. At the time of the action years after the execution of the innocent anarchists, the confession of a prison inmate had reopened the case in the public mind. Converging on Garth's home in New York are the real murderer; the son of one of the defendants, seeking to clear his father's name; and the judge who had deliberately avoided calling Garth to testify. Each has his reason for preventing or urging Garth to testify: the judge wants justification for not having called him; the murderer wants reassurance that Garth will keep quiet; the son wants to persuade Garth to vindicate his father. As the play develops, Garth's sister, Mariamne, falls in love with the victim's son, Mio. Theirs is a Romeo-Juliet situation, children of implacably feuding families, and like Shakespeare's ill-starred lovers, both die at the end. The Esdras father is the equivalent of a Greek chorus who comments philosophically on the action.

Why should a Jewish family be located at the center of the action? No specific reason is indicated. It may have been that Anderson wished to convey the notion of ancient Talmudic wisdom in the comments by Esdras on the happenings of the play. If so, the Jewish tone of Esdras' language is not apparent. In light of the evidence from this play one can draw a dual conclusion about Anderson's relation to the Jews. First, nowhere does he show any sign of ill-will; and second, he was probably, for all his good intentions, not very familiar with Jewishness.

Sidney Howard

Like most of his theater colleagues, Howard was strongly pro-labor and was even the author of the most widely publicized investigative exposure of espionage against trade unions in his *The Labor Spy*. An auto accident in 1939 cut short his life at forty-eight. Of this non-Jewish dramatist's four plays in which Jewish characters appear, from 1929 to 1934, only the last exhibits positive, friendly feeling, and this perhaps because the character is a radical. In *Half Gods* (1929), the psychoanalyst Dr. Mannering "has a manner . . . a shade too sympathetic. And he has not quite got rid of the last traces of his Jewish accent."[96] A few years later, in *The Late Christopher Bean* (1932), Howard presents a Jewish art dealer, a profession for Jews to which literary men seem to have some partiality almost as if that were the only sort of Jew with whom the author was acquainted. Rosen is "an oily and affable Jewish gentleman."[97] One should perhaps be thankful that Rosen is at least honest, if a hard bargainer. Again, in *Dodsworth* (1934), a dramatization of Sinclair Lewis' novel, the rich middle-western businessman, Dodsworth, and his romance-starved wife travel to Europe, and on the boat they encounter several Jews who do not endear themselves to us. After conversation with "two Jewish gentlemen" in the bar, Fran Dodsworth chides a friend for "talking down Americans in travel," adding that she "only know[s] two peoples who run down their own race, Americans and Jews." More serious is the complaint of seduction of Fran by a financier and fancy man Arnold Israel, "the perfect international Jew."[98] After an affair with Israel, Fran returns to her husband, but he refuses to take her back after she has had another frustrated affair. It would be hard to infer that this consistently mild but hardly friendly depiction of Jews arises out of a consciousness that is equably disposed toward them.

In *Yellow Jack* (1934), which was in fact written in 1928, the Jewish character is heroic—perhaps also because he is a committed radical. The play was written in collaboration with the noted science popularizer Paul de Kruif, from whose *The Microbe Hunters* the play was drawn. The play memorializes the heroic experiment in Cuba in 1900 by Dr. Walter Reed who discovered the mosquito to be the carrier of yellow fever. The actual experiment's subjects were four American soldiers, one of whom, Levi E. Falk, was Jewish. Named Busch in the play, he is "a city chap of Jewish extraction and intensity" and a radical from Chicago who got his "ideas out of Karl Marx." He wishes he were "back in Chicago furthering the interests of the radical movement." The soldiers are offered $300 each if they will allow two of them to be bitten by an infected mosquito and the other two to be unbitten control subjects. They profess to serve for the money, though they refuse to accept compensation after the experiment is finished. While waiting to discover which two have been infected, Busch says, "I ain't ashamed I'm scared of this! I'll take on any man twice my weight! I may be Jewish but I got guts! Would I be a radical if I didn't have? Put me up against anything and I'll show you." As to the payment, he says, "You can't be even a good radical without dough. If I had three hundred dollars, ... I'd go back to my printing shop like my old man before me that the cops smashed when I was a kid. And I'd get out a paper that'd tell the workers the truth."[99]

Thus in the one instance in his plays when the Jew was a heroic figure, Howard gives him appropriate stature. At a time when Howard himself was something of a radical whose commitment was signaled by his book, *The Labor Spy*, the radicalism of the Jewish character places him in a situation from which other Jews in Howard's plays were distant. We may conjecture that the dramatist's indifference to Jews and resort to literary custom in the assignment of Jews in the earlier plays can be ascribed to unfamiliarity.

Robert E. Sherwood and Philip Barry

We pair these two dramatists not because they are similar but rather because they are both non-Jewish and born in 1896; each treated Jews in a single play, both of which were produced in 1930.

Sherwood's *This Is New York* is one of his lesser plays and concerns nativistic Westerners, the Krulls, whose attitude toward New York is hostile, since they believe the city to be full of "foreigners" and "corruption." Their young daughter Emma becomes innocently embroiled in a lurid situation from which she escapes unscathed and with credit as a human being. The Jewish character, Harry Glassman, is the likable bootlegger, "an urban gorilla, attired in a stylish double-breasted dinner jacket with a soft silk shirt." He has "sleek black hair" and sports "a good cigar."[100] He lives with a woman who is a drug addict. He has been erroneously accused of a murder—actually a suicide—to which Emma is a decisive witness, and she courageously volunteers to take the stand to exonerate Glassman. For his part, the author presents Glassman in a favorable light despite his dubious manner of making an affluent living.

Although Philip Barry was primarily a playwright of elegant comedy, *Hotel Universe* is as serious as the title implies. The characters are the middle-class smart people of his comedies; now they are no longer amused, but world-weary and at their wits' end over what to do with their lives. One of these is Norman Rose, a highly successful Jewish Wall Street financier, a reputed "financial genius." Risen out of East Side poverty, Rose is, at one point in the talk, Jew-baited by other occupants of Hotel Universe, a symbolically named house on the French coast where the play's characters are assembled to find themselves. An actress, Lily, in love with Rose, petulantly tells him that "there are times when I can't stand this damned Jewish superiority of yours.... The way you look down from your eminence of three thousand years—honestly, who do you think you are, Disraeli?" After more banter, Rose engages Pat in an exchange between Catholic and Jew. To Pat's "You are a Jew, aren't you?" Rose replies "proudly," "Of course I am. What about it?" Pat then makes the charge that the Jews are a deicide people, followed by, "oh, you think you know everything. All you do is sit around and read books, little Ikey." As the group's stagnating visit approaches its end Rose wants to go to Andorra and leave finance behind for "time to think." In order further to clarify Rose's character an interpolated scene reenacts events from his early life and his first job in a fur shop. He vowed he would never marry a "*schicksa*—me? Whose uncle is a rabbi—? I guess not.... I'll get up in the world."[101] But in the end, as the company scatter, each to his or her own attempt at a new start, Rose goes off to Andorra with one of the women—a "*schicksa*." The Jew in Barry's play is an interesting study of an individual though the characterization is not sharply delineated. Clearly, Barry does not share the prejudices of the play's personae.

Expressionism, Realism, and Dissent

Our observations on the treatment of the Jew in drama among both Jewish and non-Jewish dramatists between the world wars deal with only a fraction of the total work of these dramatists. These writers are in any case only the top layer of their genre. Before radio and television arrived on the scene, theater was a widely flourishing institution. Its extent may be judged from such figures as these: in the 1899–1900 season there were eighty-seven new plays on Broadway. In the 1920s, the theater was especially popular, and by the 1927–1928 season the play openings numbered 264. While the number fell drastically during the Depression year of 1931–1932 there were 207.[102] Consequently one can perceive that the sampling of plays on which it is feasible to comment, in which Jews appeared or which were written by Jews, is a still smaller percentage of the total output. Yet this small number is indicative of the main trends such as realism, expressionism, and various plays of dissent. Thus far our sampling has been limited to the work in these trends by leading figures. Our view would be incomplete for the panorama of theater if we did not also adduce instances of these trends in the work of other dramatists.

The new century witnessed the gathering strength of realism in the theater in such dramatists as Bronson Howard, James A. Herne, occasionally in Clyde Fitch and Edward Sheldon. It is not then surprising that when one of the earliest and greatest realists or even naturalist writers, Theodore Dreiser, turned to drama with *The Hand of the Potter* (1918), he was bringing the same break with the past into the theater with which he approached fiction. The realistic trend was carried forward mainly by playwrights of the left or of dissent through the pre–World War I period. In addition some such plays were written by others during the 1920s and 1930s. However, as might be expected, most of the plays in this period were conventional entertainments.

In the 1920s, when so much of the country basked in the aura of prosperity and paid little attention to the struggles of labor and the superficiality of daily life, some writers did respond sensitively to middle-class complacency, cultural stagnation, and commercialism. In the drama this social and cultural rebellion found a home in the non-commercial stages of the little theater movement and in occasional plays of dissent on Broadway. O'Neill was nurtured by this non-commercial theater. At the Provincetown Playhouse in the 1920s there were a number of one-act plays performed. In 1920 this theater produced Michael Gold's one-act play, *Money*. This little play, set in an East Side cobbler's basement, had five sleeping boarders, all Jews. The play contained no hint of the stereotype but exhibited that same deep sympathy for the Jewish poor which was to pervade his *Jews Without Money*. The shoemaker's money had been stolen from its hiding place under his mattress and one of the boarders confesses to the theft and restores the money. Why did he do it? One says, "Because you are one of those Jews who have a lust for money, ... one whose religion is to steal and die and kill and betray—all for money!" The thief tries to explain his motive: "I was afraid of—afraid of Money! What was it—this Beast that God has put into the world? It was in many men, making them cruel to each other." He had become a "slave" of money. Another boarder tells them of a speech by a Jewish working man who said, "one day there will be no money, no rich and poor, only everyone working together like brothers and sisters."[103] Perhaps nothing reveals Gold's sensitivity for the Jewish poor more than his technical solution of the language problem, which anticipates the method used by Henry Roth in *Call It Sleep*. Gold renders the Yiddish speech of his characters in appropriately emotional English. But when the men speak English to the policeman who has come to inquire about the disturbance in the cellar, their English is broken and primitive without any decline in dignity.

As the 1920s wore on, radicalism increased among writers, given added impetus by bitter strikes and most especially by the agitation around the Sacco-Vanzetti case. Unlike Gold, however, not all radical writers rivaled him in ethnic sensitivity. Paul Sifton's *The Belt* (1927) was an interesting expressionistic experimental play, produced by the New Playwright's Theater. It is an acerbic critique of working conditions on the Ford factory assembly line. The "Belt" effectively symbolized the inhumanity of the assembly line as a backdrop to the workers' rising determination to strike. Unfortunately the two Jewish characters are among the villains of the piece. Aaronson is a sycophantic secretary to the hypocritical auto tycoon (Henry Ford?) and perpetrates fraud in deceiving both public and workers about the character of his boss. The other Jew, the worker Jacobson, is a survival of the vaudeville Jew, speaking an outrageous dialect, mimicked with extreme hostility by other workers.

While Sifton's condemnation of anti-Semitism in the play is clear, he shows the not infrequent ambivalence of the radical or liberal who does not sensitively apply his generalized disapproval of anti-Semitism to his own conception of Jewish characters. Also lacking Gold's sensitivity is Em Jo Basshe's rather pretentious and rhetorical attempt at a panoramic view of Jewish tenement life in *The Centuries: Portrait of a Tenement House* (1927) developed in a naturalistic manner. In *Earth*, an earlier play, Basshe had tried to dramatize the adjustment of Blacks to American life. His method was not on the whole to dramatize events but to describe them in dialogue so that he can run through the gamut of aspects of that life through descriptive dialogue. These descriptions range from the life of immigrants and the growing up of the second generation to become gangsters, lawyers, and corrupt politicians, to a telescoped account of the Triangle Fire, Jewish gangster attacks on unions, and rabbis' support of the bosses. The final scenes depict material success and migration to the Bronx and Brookyln.

Far more sensitive to Jewish issues than his fellow writers on the left, Jews included, was the non-Jew John Dos Passos. Although he was a major novelist in the late 1920s and 1930s, his plays are decidedly minor. Jews appear in two of his plays. *Airways, Inc.* (1929) revolves around a protracted strike. There are several minor Jewish characters, real estate agents who appear briefly and oppose the strike because it is bad for their business. But the central character, Walter Goldberg, is 88 strike leader in love with Martha Turner, sister of several anti-labor workers. She rejects Goldberg's marriage proposal, ostensibly because she refuses to leave her widowed father and brothers. But Goldberg believes—and she finally thinks he may be right—that prejudice is at work. "You'd have to be a jew [sic] like me to understand.... We've been in prison for two thousand years. I have the mind of a jail bird.... That's why I feel the slavery of the workers. I feel it as a worker and lived it as a Jew.... On the East Side ... we were all jailed in poverty and Judaism and in old customs and hatred and worn out Laws."[104] Goldberg is framed for murder and executed, and Martha then realizes how impoverished her life is without him. In *Fortune Heights*, dated 1933 and never produced, Dos Passos has a Jewish character who is a detective for stolen cars, a writer of crime stories, and finally has his own detective agency. He turns out to be a dubious character, apparently betraying a friend to the police for selling bootleg whisky, and helps dispossess a farmer. It is a poor play, inferior to *Airways*. These plays, however, like his fiction, indicate Dos Passos' freedom from prejudice.

A moving and effective play about the Scottsboro case, in which six young Blacks were falsely accused of raping two young white women on a freight train, was the Jewish dramatist John Wexley's *They Shall Not Die* (1934). The trial and surrounding events are accurately portrayed in highly dramatic form. The two main figures in the legal defense, Rokoff and Rubin, were counterparts of the actual International Labor Defense lawyer who brought to public notice the injustice of the case and Samuel Leibowitz, the famous criminal lawyer from Brooklyn who all served in the case without fee or expenses. The dramatist vividly brings out both the red-baiting and Jew-baiting that the prosecution used in the actual trials. Typical was the prosecutor's plea to the jury, "Tell 'em, tell 'em, that Southern justice cannot be bought and sold with Jew money from New York" and the court audience shouts at the defense lawyer, "Let's get the goddam Jew bastard."[105]

The anti-war movement of the 1930s was powerfully represented in Irwin Shaw's one-act *Bury the Dead* (1936). Six soldiers, about to be buried, rise mysteriously from the dead and "refuse to be buried" in protest against their futile sacrifice. One is a Private Levy. Ministers and a rabbi are present to officiate at the burial. For some curious, unexplained reason, the sergeant tells the rabbi, "There ain't no Jewish boys in those." The rabbi replies, "I understand one of them is named Levy." "Yes, but he's no Jew," replies the sergeant, but the rabbi officiates anyway.[106] The soldiers' wives are brought in to try to persuade their husbands to allow burial. Only a worker's wife refuses to cooperate, since she understands their protest. The powerful play has never been performed since the Nazi-Soviet Pact in 1939 because Shaw has refused to allow it, a prohibition that still stands. In Shaw's passionately anti-fascist 1939 play, *The Gentle People*, two old men, a Jew and an Italian, manage to do away with a fascist gangster on Long Island after he harasses them with extortion and threatens them in language and ideas obviously fascist. The old men lure him into a boat and, since he cannot swim, dump him overboard to his doom. The play is an allegory of a united front against fascism. In the context of the play the old men's notions seem quixotic and suggest the mock heroics of the hero of Shaw's war novel, *The Young Lions.* Shaw's theme is anti-fascism and also an uncompromising struggle against anti-Semitism. But the fascist in the play is an unsubtle, formulistic type of fascist character, making for facile statement.

In the anti-war atmosphere of the mid–1930s which produced a play like *Bury the Dead,* the non-Jewish Paul Green's *Johnny Johnson* (1936) preached against war in the character of the saintly Johnny Johnson, whose experience in World War I converted him to a life of self-abnegating brotherhood even toward the enemy. This gets him arrested by the military during the war and then confined after the war to a mental hospital. Yet even in this Jesus-like attitude toward war, a Jewish soldier at the front briefly enters the action for comic relief. Private Goldberger is "a little squabbly Jew." He rescues a spent bullet as a souvenir and Private Kearns remarks, "Abie here likes the war. He was a junk man back home." To complete the stereotype, Goldberger later replies to talk about epitaphs, "teasingly," that he "sold him one."[107]

Varieties of Jewish Characters

The Jew as dramatist emerged in the front ranks by the 1920s. But what had happened to the character as depicted on the stage? We have seen that a residue of the stereotype remained in some plays of dissent. But what was he like in the more conventional plays of the day? The stereotype continued to be the comic or villainous stereotype of the Jew, which was still widely accepted as a valid presence in the theater. Only occasional protest was made in the Jewish or general press. On the other hand, there was an increasing awareness of the problem, and we have seen how attempts, blundering and misbegotten as they turned out, were made in the early years of the century to counteract the practice of the stage Jew.

When in 1920 Samuel Shipman and Victor Victor presented their *The Unwritten Chapter,* an inflated and erroneous, if well-intentioned, representation of the role of Haym Solomon and other Jews in the American Revolution, a reviewer in the *American Hebrew* could write, "These days there is so much loose talk directed against the Jew that it is a pleasure to find a play which deals with Jewish achievement in America." However, the reviewer deplores "a few lapses of dialect which . . . seem obviously the work of a stage manager with a penchant for local color."[108]

Throughout the 1920s, invidious Jewish stereotypes played their way through the American theater. The stereotypic comic Jew was most evident in vaudeville, where a number of talented Jewish comedians conformed to the current modes of ethnic humor to the great acclaim of the American public, not least its Jewish sector. But awareness of the socially injurious nature of the stereotype grew and by 1929 the *B'nai B'rith Magazine* could write that "the proverbial stage Jew who was set up as an exotic exhibit, supposedly representative of the race, whose mere appearance engendered merriment, is becoming more and more rare." The writer attributed this "possibly" to "justified resentment" and a "general raising of the artistic standards." While the Jew on the stage was given a "more dignified presentation," the Jewish vaudeville and musical comedians, this writer asserts, also supplanted the stage Jew with "native Jewish humor and by frequent recourse to Yiddishisms, which in themselves are natural and healthy."[109]

This statement registers an advance of sensitivity on the issue, but it was not until after World War II that growth of understanding had matured to the point of rejecting the "condescension to Yiddish implied in so much use of Yiddish for comic purposes—indeed, whose mere appearance engendered merriment." Sometimes there is some distance between verbal text and mode of acting, as was apparently the case with Bella Cohen and Samuel Spewack's *Poppa* (1928). From the text one would judge this to be a light entertainment about East Side life without ill intention. But one may conclude from the comments on the actual performance that it was played in such exaggerated fashion as to be a "gross burlesque."[110]

Plays by non-Jewish authors in the 1920s tended to include, with a few exceptions, Jewish characters who were either favorable or neutral. Several projected Jews as neo-Jesus characters or in some relation to the Christ story. *The Light of the World* (1920) by Gay Bolton and George Middleton offers a Jew in an obviously symbolical scheme of the Christ story in a Swiss town that traditionally enacted the Passion Play. The actual Jew in the play, Nathan (the only character in the play without a second name), is a salesman for the sculptor who is to play the role of Jesus. Nathan is himself a saintly, forgiving character. His friendship with the sculptor is used by the rival for the part of Jesus, who has been assigned the role of Judas instead, to discredit the sculptor. But the deceptions of the Judas character are exposed, the sculptor retains the role of Jesus, and Nathan's formerly good reputation is restored. The play is really a sermon full of high-flown rhetoric. It was not well received by the critics in spite of obvious good intentions.

A few years later a better-constructed play, *The Fool* (1922) by Channing Pollock, was a great popular success. This time a minister, who tries to live by the precepts of Jesus, is abandoned by his financée: she cannot face the poverty in which he lives and marries a prosperous and corrupt man. When she tries to return to the minister, he sends her back to her husband. The minister is visited by a poor man, very mysteriously, in a brief, hardly natural, appearance, who urges him to remain indifferent to the material in life. Asked who he is, the mysterious visitor replies, "I am a Jew," and does not leave but disappears—suggestive of the supportive role of a supernatural Jesus who never died. Later, in 1939, *Family Portrait* by Lenore Coffee and Joyce Cowen, is an effort to depict Jesus and his family as ordinary people in modern dress and colloquial dialogue occupied with commonplace affairs. Jesus is leaving home for his final crusade, and his brother James asks, "If he wants to preach, why won't he be a rabbi?" His mother Mary replies, "He doesn't agree with all their ideas."[111] She steadfastly supports Jesus against the family and against rabbis.

As the opposite pole from such reverent attitudes toward the Jew, emphasizing Jesus' Jewish identity, is a spate of dialect plays in which the stage Jew and the stage Irishman combine their dubious talents in a succession of vaudeville skits and demeaning situations, which the public found vastly amusing. *Abie's Irish Rose* (1922) by Anne Nichols, became one of the most phenomenally successful plays on Broadway, running literally for years, and spawned some ugly progeny.

Some non-Jewish authors of the 1920s treated their Jewish characters in neutral fashion or even favorably. In Owen Davis' *The Detour* (1921) the play's directions describe a Jewish furniture dealer as "smiling and friendly," and by an unfavorable character as "a rather dreadful person named Weinstein."[112] He speaks with an accent, is called to buy furniture from an old house, and bargains in an old-fashioned way.

A popular non-Jewish playwright of the 1920s, Martin Flavin, depicts the Jew in a vocation frequently used in plays—indeed, he was frequently so in reality—as a play producer in *Lady of the Rose* (1925), a piece of romantic claptrap. Flavin's portrait of this successful entrepreneur of the theater is not unfair. Max Lubin is "a short, stout, middle aged Jew, who has always the appearance of having just stepped out of a bandbox. He is shrewd and unctuous; voluble and bristling. With his employees he is brusque; with his performers, whom he fondly calls 'my artists,' he has an air of fraternal indulgence. His English is a little loose in spots, but all in all, he is by no means a bad fellow."[113] A few years later the same author's *Criminal Code* (1925) includes a Jewish prison doctor who befriends the convict-protagonist and is depicted as a decent person of rare understanding. In George Kelly's *Behold the Bridegroom* (1927), a doctor of mental diseases, Dr. Loebell, is called in as a consultant in an entirely neutral manner.

Thus, with a few departures, some non-Jewish dramatists of the 1920s treated their Jewish characters favorably. This continues through the decade. John Emerson and Anita Loos' *The Whole Town's Talking* (1926) (the junior author is Jewish) has a Jewish dancing teacher whose accidental association briefly draws her into shenanigans of the leading character. Several melodramas in succeeding years yield favorable images of Jews in a criminal environment. Most interesting is the anticipation of the existential notion of freedom in *Four Walls* (1927) by Dana Burnet and George Abbott, set on the East Side, where an ex-gang leader Benny Horowitz, released from prison, has renounced crime. Through melodramatic circumstances, during a fight in self-defense, his antagonist falls to his death from the roof. Although he could have an alibi, Horowitz gives himself up to the police and confesses. "You see," Benny explains to his brother, "ever since I came home I been kiddin' myself I was a free man. . . . I guess because I made up my mind to go through with it. I've been runnin' away. I been hidin' from things. But all at once I ain't afraid of nothin' or anybody. God! It's so simple. . . . since I decided to give myself up in the last few minutes. I'm happy. I feel free. For the first time in my life—free!"[114] In other words, Benny is expressing the existential view that freedom to choose, freedom as such, irrespective of circumstances or consequences is the prime value. Another play, *Night Hostess* (1928) by George Dunning, includes a gambling house and speakeasy owner, Ben Fischer. In this trashy gangster play the Jew Fischer is represented as scrupulously and honestly adhering to a strict code of honor in his dubious business. In another gangster play, *The Rocket* (1927) by Bartlett Cormack, the disbarred Jewish lawyer Sam Meyer makes a brief appearance as a "leg man" for racketeers.

Jewish dramatists of the period do not on the whole differ significantly from their non-Jewish peers in depicting the Jew both favorably and unfavorably. They do differ, however, as might be expected, in their greater intimacy and detail of Jewish life. Significant, too, is the fact that the only plays with Jewish characters which won the Pulitzer Prizes in the 1920s and 1930s are three plays by Jewish dramatists: Elmer Rice; George S. Kaufman, Morris Ryskind, and Ira Gershwin; and Sidney Kingsley.

Among the plays written in the 1930s by Jewish writers, the earliest was by the prolific vaudeville sketch writer, Aaron Hoffman, in an unhappy venture into a full length play with *Welcome Stranger* (1920). Isidor Solomon moves to a small New Hampshire town to escape anti-Semitism in Boston. His attempt to set up a store is frustrated by prejudice, but with cleverness and enterprise he overcomes this and gains the respect of the townspeople. Another town resident is a crypto-Jew who is in fact the instigator of the anti-Semitic campaign against Isidor, much as in a similar situation in Augustin Daly's popular *Leah, the Forsaken* (1862). Hoffman's vaudeville notions, however, dilute the play so that, as the *Jewish Forum* remarked, the laughs generated "awaken into absurdity many of the play's best moments."[115] In the next year Hoffman's *Two Blocks Away* attempts an East Side play. A Jewish shoemaker changes with great facility from a generous man moved by compassion for his poor multi-ethnic clientele to a grasping, greedy man after acquiring wealth from a legacy mistakenly assigned to him. When the mistake becomes known, he is deprived of his riches and returns to his poor, generous self again. The play relies heavily on laughs through Jewish vaudeville antics with Yiddishized English.

One of the most important plays of the decade—for sociological, if not for dramatic reasons—was Samson Ralphaelson's *The Jazz Singer* (1925). Adaptation of the play for movies was the first commercial talking film and opened the talkies era on Yom Kippur night in 1927. George Jessel played the leading role in the theater version and Al Jolson in the talkies production. The story is simple and dripping with sentimentality. A young son of a cantor is groomed by his father to succeed him. But the boy wants to perform in the great world, breaks away from home, and becomes a famous "jazz singer." He is rejected by his father but a reconciliation takes place when he fills in as cantor for his sick father at the Yom Kippur services, thereby missing his own opening night on Broadway. The play may have provided the first protracted and intimate view of Jewish life in the English-speaking theater in a highly overdramatized, sentimentalized version, and in some ways transferred the mood and type of plot of the Yiddish theater to the English stage. In a Preface to the published play Raphaelson enlarged on his intention. It was, he held, to establish the connection between the Jewish cantorial sound and the development of "jazz." In an overblown flight of rhetoric, he declared that "Jazz is prayer. . . . It is distorted, sick, unconscious of its destination."[116]

The author discloses why he introduced a "Jewish youth as my protagonist" for his theory is that "the Jews are determining the nature and scope of jazz more than any other race—more than the negroes, from whom they have stolen jazz and given it a new color and meaning." This assertion is mistaken on two grounds. Jews were not in fact more determinative of the future of jazz than Blacks, who were not only the originators but the developers of the medium down to our own day. And, second, the "jazz" that Raphaelson is really talking about, the "Mammy" songs, for one, which he says his jazz singer is doing in blackface, is not jazz at all but a commercial, sentimentalized, and diluted form derived from the original. The playwright believed that the Jewish blackface singers were transferring their cantorial passion into their jazz. The singer's father, in hearing him sing, realizes this: "Don't you hear how he sang? The same sighs, the same tears I taught him in the synagogue—that I put in his voice that he should sing to God—now he uses them to sing in his jazz music."[117] The non-Jewish girl who "discovered" him in a Chicago movie house says that his voice has "something like the intensity of Billy Sunday," which may indeed be close to the mark.

Another play whose main interest lies in Jewish sociology rather than dramaturgy is Ludwig Lewisohn's *Adam* (1929), and it derives its significance from its author's identity. During the 1920s and thereafter Lewisohn devoted his life to propagation of Jewish affirmation, Judaism, and Zionism among his fellow Jews. He consecrated all his talents in fiction, essays and analysis to this cause. In 1929 he briefly turned his attention to theater. In *Adam* he advanced his thesis that the Jew who has abandoned his Jewish identity is a lost soul and doomed to unhappiness and misery. This is exemplified in the play by a millionaire who marries a non-Jewish wife and finds life with her unendurable after a few years. He commits suicide by a leap from this private plane over the English Channel. The meaning is symbolized in the Prologue in which Rabbi Akiba envisages a future in which Jews try to become Greeks at the risk of dying as Jews. He adds that if they follow the Torah instead, "they will become unalterably themselves— they and the Torah will be so utterly one, that each will live the Torah even though he knows it not and that the apostate in his apostacy will practice the law."[118] Lewisohn demonstrates the truth of this prophecy from the life of Adam in the play. The play and its thesis are simple in the extreme. Although Lewisohn was an eminent dramatic critic in the early 1920s, his talents obviously did not extend to the craft of playwriting.

While conventional drama and comedy of the 1920s were on the whole friendly or neutral in their depiction of Jews, there seemed to be less friend-liness in this type of play in the 1930s. Not all the writers of the decade were radical. Among the non-Jewish playwrights who were not were How-ard Lindsay and Clare Booth (Luce). Howard Lindsay's *She Loves Me Not* (1933) caricatures the left in this desperately deprived period that affected such a large part of the population at the depth of the Depression. The play superficially portrays the son of a Wall Street broker at Princeton and a Jewish radical, Liebowitz, who has an outlandish accent and dialect resem-bling no language. The issue the students and radicals are protesting is disciplinary action against the harboring in the Princeton dormitory of a night club dancer who witnessed a murder but does not know the identity of the murderer, and is afraid of police interrogation. Liebowitz is impris-oned during a protest against expulsion of a student for harboring the girl and, unintentionally, in order to provide comic relief for the prisoners and authorities while he is in jail. He is regarded as so funny that he is offered a job in Hollywood as a comic, which he refuses, saying, "Noo, I cuddn' be heppy avay from t' Red comrades of t' Revolution." When the jailer orders him to "pipe down," he replies, "Even in jail we ain't got free spiech." If the play is intended as a spoof of the radical play, it succeeds only in being silly and a little malicious.[119]

A far better play is Clare Booth's *The Women* (1936), a devastating satire on wealthy middle-class women. There are two Jews among them who are no more and no less the author's targets than the others. Miss Shapiro is the head saleswoman of a fancy women's clothing shop and is formal and imperious with models. The other, more important, is Marian Aarons, one of the group of gossiping women who is a "breezy, flashy red-head," loud, vulgar, a "gold-digger" like the others but perhaps more vulgar in her language. Unlike the others, she is a "cynic," as she is called by them, and regards Cupid as "the double-crossing little squirt! Give me Donald Duck!"[120] No comment is made on anyone's Jewishness.

If Lindsay caricatured the Jew of the left, John L. Balderston and J. E. Hoare do the same for the Jew of the right, "A Belgian Jewish financier," who gets advance information that Christ is returning to earth for the Second Coming. The financier alerts his world financial empire to make a killing in the stock market from the ensuing panic. He orders his agents to sell all his armaments stock, since Christ's coming will bring disarmament, and with the proceeds to buy up thirty-day options for all places of assembly, all material commodities relating to the Christian religion like prayer books, church supplies, and publications. "The Jew cashes in on the Christians' Messiah!" he exults.[121]

Jewish playwrights showed themselves hardly more sensitive to depiction of Jews. One case is that of Rose Franken. Her *Another Language* (1932) is a transparent picture of a middle-class Jewish West Side family named Hallam, whose externals are non-Jewish. They have weekly family gatherings each Tuesday (not Friday, as is customary for Jews). But it did not take great sophistication to realize that, although Jewishness was nowhere mentioned, the family was indeed Jewish. The play is a valid critique of a financially successful, prosperous, unimaginative middle-class Jewish family impoverished in spirit.

Among the Jewish characters by minor Jewish authors in the 1930s were corrupt newspaper men, thieves, and theater managers. In Louis Weitzenkorn's *Five Star Final* (1930), the unscrupulous Ziggie Feinstein feeds inhumanly on the gullibility of the public in a sensation-mongering newspaper. In this satire of the "yellow press" the Jewish arch-villain is a shrewd, despicable person. In *Whistling in the Dark* (1932) by Laurence Gross and Edward Childs Carpenter the Jew is not very different from others in a criminal gang except that he is cleverer than the rest and called "the Boss' hottest dope peddler." The insensitivity toward Jews in Ben Hecht's *A Jew in Love* (1931) recurs in his play *The Great Magoo*, written with Gene Fowler the next year. Also manifested is crass insensitivity toward Blacks. With Hecht's customary contempt for the common man the play is Menckenesque in the extreme. His critical character, band leader Joe Weber, is described as "one of those Semitic fledglings who seem all beak and ego." He seems a collective stereotype: he has "a Jewish haircut" (what can this be?), "a Lou Holtz mouth, a Jolson twang in his speech, a Durante nose."[122] In a crap game he wins a song that turns out to be a hit. Joseph Wood Krutch said of this play in his *Nation* review that Hecht was "doubtless proud of his success in writing down to a great public that he despises."[123] Hecht's earlier *Front Page* (1928), written with Arthur MacArthur, is less directly insulting to Jews. One of the reporters, Schwartz, is Jewish but in no way different from the other reporters. The process server Pincus is not an obnoxious character. But the authors relentlessly used pejorative epithets about many ethnic groups in their cynical reporters' talk of the period throughout the play.

Quite different was Arthur Kober's fabrication of a dramatic plot out of his famous stories about New York's semi-acculturated Jews. They are on the whole unobjectionable in this new form. Set in a Berkshires summer camp, Karefree, with an all-Jewish clientele, it portrays mostly young people, usually nubile, petty bourgeois seeking mates. Almost all speak in Yiddish-ized sentence structure. The two-dimensional characterizations are never-theless a reasonably accurate pastiche of their originals. On the other hand, Victor Wolfson's *Excursion* (1937) is a serious fantasy of the old Jewish couple on an excursion boat out of Coney Island. The captain persuades the excursionists to go southward to a happier, struggle-free life in some imagined lotus land, but all agree to turn back home with this injunction from the captain: "Take the courage and vision back there, like y' fought for your far away island last night. But men and women armed with love an' wonder, mates, an' make life a glowing theng."[124] Wolfson had been connected with the left wing, but this play reflects his disillusionment with the militant left.

AFTER WORLD WAR II

Following World War II the United States was a profoundly changed place. Unlike much of Europe and Asia, the country was spared the awesome devastation inflicted by total war. The nation was now undisputed leader of the capitalist world by virtue of its unchallenged financial and industrial power in world affairs. And as sole possessor—for a few years, anyway—of the atomic bomb, its power was enhanced. But human morale in the entire world was undermined by the prospect of annihilation by the bomb, which became a weapon in the Cold War that so soon followed the Allied victory. Human credulity was still reeling from the visible proof, universally available in the media, of the unfathomable cruelty and inhumanity shown by the Nazis in the cold-blooded murder of millions, especially in the Hol-ocaust, when about two-thirds of all European Jews were killed, as well as in the spectacle of the incineration of the entire cities of Hiroshima and Nagasaki. The postwar world witnessed the breakup of the British, French, and other European colonial empires and the rapid growth of American influence as a neocolonial power.

During the decades after the war, once the transition to a peacetime economy was achieved, the United States experienced perhaps its most af-fluent period. The middle class expanded rapidly, and large sectors of work-ing people had some share in this affluence, so that the persistence of poverty dropped out of general consciousness until reawakened in the 1960s. In-dustrialization of the society became increasingly dehumanizing in response to the demands on social and technical skills of both management and labor. Conformity on the part of the one and exacerbating specialization on the part of the other increasingly reduced the personality and humanity of the individual. During the 1950s, social critics saw a society bogged down in apathy and social conformity.

The total effect of this confluence of dehumanizing influences made more and more explicit the sense of alienation that they generated. A literature of alienation, which was taking shape in this country during the war itself, emerged into full awareness a few years after the war's end.

Together with everything else, the theater changed. Production costs went up steeply, and the pervading pressures toward conformity made theater producers wary. Caution in the selection of plays for production was accentuated by the risk of high loss. As a result, an off-Broadway movement proliferated by virtue of its much lower cost and lesser pressure toward conformity. Off-Broadway thus became a channel for experiment, innovation, and social criticism in the theater. In addition, regional theaters were subsidized in several parts of the country; these were also hospitable to experiment and innovation. But something seemed to have gone out of the theater. Arthur Miller wrote in 1952 that "even optimists now confess that our theater has struck a seemingly endless low by any standard."[125] The trend toward excessive sexual conflict within the individual removed the drama further from its sustenance in the meaningful connections of the individual with the social. Miller was even more discouraged in the 1960s when he told an interviewer that the theater had "moved to a dangerous extreme of triviality. It is a theater with the blues.... The theater will have to find its way back to the daylight world without its inner life."[126]

This condition of the theater by no means signifies that the number of practicing dramatists had shrunk. On the contrary there were numerous aspiring young playwrights, some important and interesting. But the truth is that in retrospect the period has fewer outstanding figures than had emerged in the decades between the wars. Some of these earlier playwrights continued to create in the post–World War II period, but for the most part they had already done their best work. Of all the playwrights who began to create after the war, only two can be said to be of major stature: Arthur Miller and Tennessee Williams. The latter was not Jewish and never treated the Jew in his work, so that we shall not look at his work because it lacks relevance to our specific purpose. The case is quite otherwise with Arthur Miller.

Arthur Miller

The dramatist was born in Manhattan in 1915 of German-Jewish parents. His father's business declined, and the Millers moved to Harlem, where they lived from Miller's sixth to fourteenth year, and then to Brooklyn in 1932, where he remained until he went to the University of Michigan in 1934. There he studied drama and won the Hapgood Prize for his first play, which demonstrated an almost instinctive talent for drama, since he had by then seen only a single play. He continued to write plays and received instruction in playwriting. After graduation he joined the WPA Federal Theater Project and wrote many radio plays and scripts in obscurity. His *All My Sons* which was successfully produced on Broadway in 1947, won the Drama Critics Award for that year as well as wide recognition. His *Death of a Salesman* in 1949 won the Pulitzer Prize and other awards, ran for many hundreds of performances, and secured Miller's reputation as a leading writer, a reputation that was to be confirmed by subsequent work.

From the beginning Miller exemplified the humanistic dramatist who believed that the drama was framed around the conception of the "whole man" and the conflicts created by the shortcomings of his characters in achieving wholeness. He did not consider himself a "social dramatist" in the sense of the 1930s, which he termed a "tired and narrow" concept. An essential element of "wholeness" is connection with others, and this contributes to its social aspect. Realization of this wholeness demands overcoming the "separateness" in which the psychological absorbs content to the exclusion of "social concepts."[127] This wholeness further requires a democratic approach. Miller rejected for modern drama the exclusion of the common man from tragedy. The tragic situation may face human beings regardless of social class: "the tragic feeling is evoked in us when we are in the presence of a character who is ready to lay down his life, if need be, to secure one thing—his sense of personal dignity."[128] Throughout his plays human dignity becomes realizable if the individual fulfills his "responsibility" whose essence is a relation of integrity to others on the compulsory assumption that any person alone is a truncated human being and not a "whole man." The aim of the theater, says Miller, is to "make man more human, which is to say, less alone."[129] For Miller this responsibility is fulfilled in enlarging circles from the immediate family to society as a whole, as Harold Clurman has shown.[130]

How does the Jewish element enter Miller's work? Because, Joel Shatzky has reported, "Miller knew and spoke fluent Yiddish,"[131] his knowledge of Jewish life was intimate; yet none of his produced plays before *Incident at Vichy* (1964) contained explicitly Jewish characters. That this avoidance was intentional we know from a statement he made after his novel *Focus* (1945), about anti-Semitism, had brought down on Miller's head a torrent of anti-Semitic venom. He explained that he resolved to "give up the Jew as literary material." Even, he said, "an innocent allusion" to "wrong doing of an individual Jew" could be turned against the Jews.[132] While Miller did wait until the atmosphere had changed so that he could handle Jewishness in his plays, he did write several short stories on Jewish themes in the 1950s. By 1951 he could publish "Monte Sant' Angelo" about an American-Jewish soldier, Bernstein, in Italy who accompanies his Italian-American friend to a small village to look up a relative. There Bernstein's eye is caught by the gestures of a peasant who reminded him of his father, and he discovers that this peasant is hurrying to get home before dark for a customary Friday night family dinner and gathering. Although the peasant knows nothing of Jews, Bernstein is moved by the inexorable and even unconscious survival of Jewishness which gives Bernstein—and Miller—historical and ineradicable sense of identification.

In 1959 Miller again reverted to his Jewish boyhood in his short story, "I Don't Need You Any More," a detailed, moving account of a small boy's view of a holiday service in the synagogue, obviously Orthodox and perhaps Hasidic. Miller has evidently realized that his Jewish origin does have bearing on his work. In the *Paris Review* interview in 1966 he was asked about this. He replied that he had not before believed this was so, but "I think now that, while I hadn't taken over an ideology, I did absorb a certain viewpoint. That there is a tragedy in the world but that the world must continue: one is a condition of the other. Jews can't revel too much in the tragic because it might overwhelm them. Consequently in most Jewish writing there's always the caution, 'Don't push it too far toward the abyss, because you're liable to fall in.' "[133] It is extraordinary how close this comes to the approach of two other outstanding contemporaries of Miller, Saul Bellow (at least until *The Dean's December*) and Bernard Malamud. Both renounced current moods of hopelessness and would agree with Miller's concluding remark, "I think it's part of that psychology, and it's part of me, too. I have, so to speak, a psychic investment in the continuity of life. I couldn't ever write a totally nihilistic work." Contrary to many votaries of alienation or nihilism among writers of our time, Miller categorically affirmed, in the Introduction to his *Collected Plays*, that "the assumption— or presumption—behind these plays is that life has meaning."[134]

More specifically, Jewish elements can be found in most of his plays. His unpublished, unproduced play, *They Too Arise* (1938), concerns the Jewish family of a garment manufacturer in the 1930s with some likeness to Odets' Gordon family in *Paradise Lost* (1937) with Yiddishness in the dialogue. Miller is even more specific than Odets in the social and ethical standards demanded of Jews. In *Paradise Lost* Ben Gordon prevents his corrupt partner Sam Katz from using thugs to intimidate his striking workers and dismisses with profound disgust Katz' suggestion that they recoup their losses by collecting insurance through arson of their shop. In *They Too Arise*, Abe Simon speaks out at a manufacturers' meeting against the use of strikebreakers. "Maybe," Abe tells his fellow shop owners, "it's honest for the steel companies to work this way, but I can't see that it's the way for Jewish men to act."[135] It is not exaggeration to regard this awareness of a standard of conduct as a major element in Miller's social outlook that all men are responsible for one another. This is the foundation for Miller's conception of the "social drama," which he tried to exemplify in his plays. In a more restricted sphere it is also rooted in the strong sense of mutual responsibility within the family with which Jewish life is so closely associated. And this is one of the most strongly emphasized features in *All My Sons*. Joe Keller, father of the family who allows defective airplane parts to pass inspection, which results in the death of twenty-one pilots during World War II, perversely uses love and devotion to family as a primary excuse for his action. And it is his son Chris' sense of the offense to his family, as well as the frightful betrayal of social responsibility by his father, that precipitates the crisis in the Keller family. Joe Keller's problem, wrote Miller, is that "his cast of mind cannot admit that he, personally, has any viable connection with his world, his universe, or his society."[136] Although Miller does not say so, the play shows that his "connection" seems to stop with his family and is consequently a perversion of the whole idea of "connection."

Distortion of sense of family is also one of the implications derivable from the multi-meaninged *Death of a Salesman*. Willy Loman pursues the false, spurious values of a commercialized society by which he believes he can advance the position of his family's well-being as he conceives it. And when Willy is confronted by indubitable failure in his vocation and with rejection by his son Biff, who cannot forgive either Willy's night with a woman or the false values that Willy inculcated in him, Willy believes he can recover family solidarity by endowing it with his insurance money through his suicide. The Jewish elements in *Salesman* are more specific as well. We know that the character of Willy was suggested by a salesman Miller had actually known, and the dramatist's attempt to avoid ethnic identification was not altogether successful. To be sure, the American shib-boleths of the salesman are only too well known—"It's contacts, ... I got important contacts!" as Willy says. "It's not what you do, Ben. It's who you know and the smile on your face! It's contacts."[137] But Miller's outlook on this question was specifically framed in the course of his experience with the business environment of his father's garment shop, and he even knew a salesman who had committed suicide. When I saw the play, one scene struck me as typically Jewish and might have been transposed from the Yiddish theater. Bernard, boyhood friend of Biff and now a successful law-yer, comes in to say goodbye to Willy before leaving for Washington to argue a case before the Supreme Court. The Jewish overtones of this scene struck me forcibly as I witnessed it.

More explicitly Jewish, however, was the use of Yiddishized English expressions. The most famous phrase in the play is one such—"Attention must be paid" (*gib achtung*), as Linda admonishes her sons.[138] Most telling of all was the underlying saturation in his Jewish milieu in the first decade or so of his creativity. When *Salesman* was reenacted in Yiddish translation in 1951, George Ross, an actor and director, was struck by the ease with which the play fitted into the Jewish scene. In fact, Ross asserted that "this Yiddish play is really the original, and the Broadway production was merely—Arthur Miller's translation into English." Ross further maintained that the Yiddish Willy was a better realized character than he was in the English version, in which Willy was supposed to be the "American Every-man" and hence lacking in concreteness. Miller seemed to have lost this concreteness in "censoring out the Jewish part" of the milieu he was treating. In the process, wrote Ross, the focus was shifted from a play about an unsuccessful salesman to "a play about a Jewish *family*."[139] If that is indeed the case, then the English version is closer to Miller's intention. It was not lack of success that was central to Miller's aim. If so, Willy would have been accounted merely pathetic. But Miller intended him as a "tragic" figure because, Miller wrote, Willy "was agonized by his awareness of being in a false position, so constantly haunted by the hollowness of all he had placed his faith in."[140] At the stage of development at which he wrote the play, however, the Jewish figurations of Miller's mentality remained sharp, and it would seem true, as Mary McCarthy remarked, that "Willy seemed to be Jewish, to judge by his speech-cadences."[141]

Much happened after *Salesman*, which was an immense success. His plays were performed all over the world and he was recognized as in the front ranks of American dramatists. But Miller was profoundly disturbed by the prevailing McCarthyism and with the "kind of interior mechanism of confession and forgiveness of sins." This meant to him that "conscience was no longer a private matter but one of state administration."[142] The affinity of McCarthyism with the Salem witch hunts was obvious enough, and it provided the occasion for *The Crucible* (1953). But to Miller the play had a larger meaning—assertion of the primacy of the individual conscience as against conformity enforced by state and public sanctions. And Miller looked beyond punishment of guilt to the recognition of guilt itself. Characters *in extremis* like John Proctor and his wife are not without guilt in their relationship to one another, but the same integrity that recognizes guilt in themselves makes them all the more firm in their refusal to surrender to the witch-hunters. Thus, Miller asserted that his "central impulse for writing" the play was "not the social but the interior psychological question" the guilt "merely unleashed" in Salem. The witch-hunt "did not create" it.[143]

This play received a mixed response from the critics on its opening in 1953 when McCarthyism was rampant but won several drama awards. McCarthyism had receded by 1958 when the play was revived, and it became a hit play which has been performed many times since in many parts of the world. It will probably remain in the lively repertory of world drama, for it deals with a problem that is universally relevant and constant. In Miller's words, the play deals with "the conflict between a man's raw deeds and his conception of himself; the question of whether conscience is in fact an organic part of the human being, and what happens when it is handed over not merely to the state or the mores of the time but to one's friend or wife."[144]

Not until the 1960s did Miller feel free to include explicitly Jewish characters in his plays. In the first of these, *After the Fall* (1964), which is palpably autobiographical at least in part, Jewish characters are necessarily included, although without being so designated. Quentin, the central character, obviously represents Miller. His mother appears briefly. Since Miller wished to reduce diversionary ideas from his main purpose to explore responsibility for Hitlerism, he minimized the Jewish element. In early drafts the mother had slipped occasionally into Yiddishized English phrases, but as Leonard Moss shows, Miller excised these in the final draft.[145] Quentin is not in any way identified as a Jew, nor are any of his friends, though a few, like Lou, the ex-Communist lawyer who commits suicide, may be taken as such. Formal structural symbols of the Nazi concentration camp are present as the permanent background of the set throughout the play, and since Jews were such a large part of its inmates, together with dissidents of every kind, the Nazi crimes against Jews inevitably figure essentially in the underlying Nazi evil. It is erroneous, however, to identify the play with an exploration of specifically anti-Jewish inhumanity. The play, wrote the author in the Foreword to the text, "is the trial of a man by his own conscience, his own values, his own deeds."[146] Miller always disclaims the primacy of the topical interest in his plays—betrayal of the nation by fraud in *All My Sons*, McCarthyism in *The Crucible*, or Nazism as such in *After the Fall*. These are always for him the occasion for exploration of responsibility involved in these instances. When *After the Fall* was published and before it was produced, many were repelled by what they believed too intimate a resemblance to events in the dramatist's own life, especially the disastrous marriage with the recently deceased Marilyn Monroe.

But just as Jewishness as such was transcended, so also Miller expected the personal aspects would be, and the perspective would focus on Quentin's degree of responsibility for the violent, repressive events in the world. Quentin concludes that he must acknowledge his own complicity in their happening. He must recognize that he is not innocent—no one is innocent.

What Miller is seeking is the existentialist state of good faith, the stark recognition of the truth about one's self, no matter where it leads. Critical writing on Miller has, I believe, given insufficient attention to the existentialist influence at this time. In the Foreword to the play Miller writes that in order to make a "choice" of a mode of life, "one must know oneself"— the existentialist "good faith"—and this means, "face the murder in him, the sly and everlasting complicity with the forces of destruction."[147] Miller assigns centrality to choice, the existentialist act that betokens freedom. Since Miller is not a systematic thinker, it would be an error to expect from him adherence to the full panoply of the existentialist system. For instance, he asserts that life is not meaningless, a departure from existentialist absurdism. But he has adopted the centrality of choice.

Harold Clurman calls attention to Miller's short story, "The Fitter's Night," published in 1966, which seems existentialist in essence. In this powerful story about a ship's "fitter" during World War II (Miller had worked as a "fitter" at the Brooklyn Navy Yard during World War II), Tony is a crude, soiled, earthy sort of man. On the night shift he is on a winter night called out for an emergency fitting job on a warship due to leave with a convoy the next morning. The job is dangerous and the outcome uncertain, and because of the danger Tony is free to choose to refuse to do it. The same is true for the captain of the ship, who is free to choose to stay or join his convoy. What follows can be said to be Tony's existentialist experience.

Suddenly it was as clear and cold as the air freezing to them, Tony and the captain where they stood—that both were on a par; they were free. . . . For the first time in his life he [Tony] had a kind of space around him in which to move freely, the first time, it seemed, that it was entirely up to him with no punishment if he said no, nor even a reward if he said yes. Gain and loss had suddenly collapsed, and what was left standing was a favor asked that would profit nobody.[148]

In an intense and suspenseful passage the repair is accomplished, with a wordless exchange of understanding between the two men, Tony and the captain. Both had made a "choice" as purely free as can be.

This existentialist influence extends not only into *After the Fall*, but also into the next plays as well. But, like the post–World War II French writer Jean-Paul Sartre, Miller felt tension between the existentialist and his social, sometimes near-Marxist position. Like Sartre, Miller locates the existentialist situation in his plays within a dense social context. While Sartre as a philosopher tried to reconcile his existentialism and Marxism—unsuccessfully, in my view—Miller is untroubled by any inconsistency between his existentialism and his sense of social responsibility. From the start Miller endeavored to advance his conviction of the mutual responsibility of people in both the family and society as a whole. To bring out his human perspective in his plays before the 1960s, he couched his themes in social terms—money-making during World War II even if it meant sending out fatally defective materials, or trivialization and falsification of values in current commercial notions of pecuniary success, or the working out within the individual of betrayal of social care for one another by McCarthyism.

If Miller's focus is on his generalizations about human responsibility, this does not mean that the social theme is not also highly significant to him. The fact is that he is able without tension to project several levels of interest simultaneously even though he believes his basic intention is the universal. In an essay on Miller, the British Marxist cultural critic Raymond Williams gives a Marxist perspective to aspects of Miller's early plays without doing violence to their meaning—only if he will not attribute such meaning as central to Miller's own intention. Williams quotes Miller as writing that "Joe Keller's trouble in *All My Sons* . . . is not that his cast of mind cannot admit that he personally has any viable association with his world, his universe, or his society." Keller, Miller continues, has "become a function of production to the point where his personality becomes divorced from the actions it propels." Williams then comments: this "is the classical Marxist concept of alienation . . . embodied both in action and a personality" with which "Miller is ultimately concerned. The true social reality—the needs and destinies of other persons is meant to break down this alienated consciousness." Of *Salesman*, Williams comments: "In the end it is not Willy Loman as a man but the image of the salesman ... [and] sums up the theme ... [of] alienation, for this is the man who from selling things has passed on to selling himself, and has become, in effect, a commodity."[149] But even these early plays, which lend themselves so easily to Marxist interpretation, also convey universal aspects of humanity as intended by Miller. It is to such complexity of levels of interpretation that one may attribute one of Miller's distinctions as a playwright.

But Miller believed that man is an existentialist being. The first act of humanity, he says in the Foreword to *After the Fall*, in the story of Adam and Eve is the choice before them. "Where choice begins," he wrote, "Paradise ends, Innocence ends, for what is Paradise but the absence of any need to choose this action?" The play is concerned with the same problem as confronted Adam—"the terrifying act of choice." In order to choose, it is necessary to "know oneself." The Nazis succumbed to the human proclivity for destruction; people must judge themselves to the degree to which they resist this avenue of choice, with greater or lesser success, and that is what Quentin did in the play. Miller once told a reviewer that he "always felt that concentration camps were ... a logical conclusion of contemporary life." The essence of the camps is "human separateness," he said.[150] But unlike the existentialists, Miller believed this "separateness" can be reduced by choices to accept that social responsibility that is ever present in his plays. Miller himself was faced with such a choice when he refused to betray others before an "investigative" committee and was cited for contempt; his silence about others was finally upheld by the Supreme Court.

Incident at Vichy (1964) is more pointedly existentialist than any of his plays to that date. Nazi persecution of the Jews is at the play's social center. Over a half-dozen characters in the play are there by virtue of their Jewish identity. Together with a few non-Jews they find themselves in the waiting room of a Nazi office in Vichy in 1942. The Jews are being rounded up, and they are positively identified as Jews by inspection off-stage for circumcision. Among the Jews are an actor, a painter, a bearded old Orthodox man who is speechless throughout, a wealthy businessman whose identity is uncertain and who probably bribes his way to release, a small boy, and an electrician.

In the last minutes of the play the existential issue is joined between the two remaining detainees, the liberal Viennese Prince Von Berg and the Jewish psychiatrist Leduc. "Man," says Leduc, expressing Miller's own viewpoint, has "accepted his own nature, that he is *not* reasonable, that he is full of murder, that his ideas are only the little tax he pays for the right to hate and kill with a clear conscience." Von Berg dissents from this dark view and offers Leduc his friendship. Leduc replies that his psychoanalytic experience with gentiles has demonstrated to him that none of them is free from at least latent "dislike if not hatred of the Jews." Von Berg denies this is true of himself. Leduc then tells Von Berg that his cousin Kessler, who is a Nazi, was a party to dismissal of all Jews from Leduc's medical school. Von Berg admits that he had known this but had forgotten it. To Leduc this demonstrates the truth of his view. He tells Von Berg: "It's not your guilt that I want, it's your responsibility—that might have helped. Yes, if you had understood that Baron Kessler was in part, in some part, in some small and frightful part—doing your will. You might have done something then, with your standing, and your name, and your decency."[151] Von Berg vehemently denies that he is anti-Semitic in any sense. He is then called in for inspection but soon emerges. He suddenly gives Leduc his pass and orders him to leave; Leduc weakly protests, but, feeling guilty at accepting the pass, nevertheless goes out free and Von Berg has made the ultimate existential choice to prove his own faith in humanity.

A quite potent existential element in the play is Leduc's earlier generalization of the idea of the Jew akin to the notion of Jew as symbol of alienation which was widespread in the literature of those years. Indeed, Malamud also used the Jew for universal symbolic purposes, for instance in his short story, "Angel Levine," where the unearthly Black, Angel Levine, effects a miraculous cure of Manischevitz' wife, whereupon the grateful man tells his wife, "Believe me, there are Jews everywhere."[152] The Jew here is in a general sense the agency for redemption through suffering. And since the Jew has been alien for centuries in the Western world, Leduc tells Von Berg, "Jew is only the name we give to that stranger, that agony we cannot feel." The word as well as the concept of the stranger obviously recalls Camus. Leduc expands on this view. The existentialist strives to face his true self, not the aspect he exposes to the world; difficult as this is, it is virtually impossible to penetrate to the real being of another self; hence, the "other" is also a "stranger." "Part of knowing who we are," says Leduc, "is knowing we are not someone else.... Each man has his Jew: it is the other. And the Jews have their Jews." In this present situation in which the Jews face the camps and death, Von Berg "must see that you have yours— the man whose death leaves you relieved that you are not him, despite your decency. And that is why there is nothing and will be nothing—until you face your own complicity with this . . . your own humanity."[153] Even though Von Berg, by giving his pass to Leduc enables him to escape and exercises his power of choice, Leduc is no less the stranger, the other.

But Miller carries these ideas derived from Camus to an extreme by regarding all men as willy-nilly in "complicity" with the Nazis, just as in *After the Fall*, Quentin, like all humanity, must guard forever "against his own complicity with Cain."[154] There is here a moral preciosity which is even more profound in Camus. Looking at the camp towers, Quentin says to the German girl Helga, "Do you ever feel when you come here . . . some strange complicity?" Helga replies, "No one they did not kill can be innocent again."[155] The recognition of the inevitably hurtful potentialities in all human beings does not mean that all share the specific guilt of the person or society that has actually acted them out. As applied to Nazism, the notion that "we are all guilty" of the crimes of Nazism has the effect of mitigating the specific responsibility of the Nazis themselves and of the German people by a universal, indiscriminate distribution of guilt to humanity as a whole. To be sure, this does not mean that individuals who lived at the time are free of any responsibility at all, since they probably did not do enough in their corner of the world to combat the advance of Nazism. But emphasis on the universality of blame, universal "complicity," the concrete, to some extent blunts the immediate guilt of the Nazis themselves. This theory of complicity is an abstract morality whose effect in practice is to diminish guilt of the criminal.

A certain common sense correction is present in *The Price* (1968) in the character of the eighty-nine-year-old Solomon despite the persistence of existential ambiguity in the confrontation of the two brothers, Victor and Walter. They meet for the first time since they parted in anger thirty years earlier during the Depression over the care of their sick and bankrupt father. Victor had chosen to give up college in order to support and care for his father, and had ended up a policeman. Walter went through medical school and became an affluent doctor. They have now met to settle the disposal of the family furniture in the attic of their old house. What then ensues are revelations of bad faith, betrayals, and commitments for dubious reasons on the part of all three, father and two sons, in their relation to one another. The successive disclosures of bad faith and the dubiousness of the moral choices made by each of the brothers, which had determined their futures, is an exercise in what is popularly known as rationalization and in more strictly existential terms, bad faith, or the attempt to justify one's actions by appearing to oneself and to others as motivated in some approved manner rather than by actuality.

The family might easily be regarded as Jewish, though it is nowhere identified as such. But there is no doubt about the eighty-nine-year-old Solomon, whose name is not random; he introduces a note of down-to-earth common sense and the survivor's wisdom of experience in the conflict between the brothers. For a while after he appears he supplies comic relief almost like a comic Jew with Yiddishized English. But after his questions about the furniture elicit further information about the family background, a highly serious personality emerges. The inability of Victor to face the truth about himself and others becomes apparent from Victor's distrust, to which Solomon replies, "Let me give you a piece advice. It's not that you can't believe nothing, that's not so hard—it's that you still got to believe it. That's hard. And if you can't do that, my friend—you're a dead man."[156]

Bargaining in which the brothers participate brings back memories of their past relations and mutual analyses of each other's motives in making their decisions about their futures thirty years before. Walter had chosen to leave the responsibility for support and care of their father to Victor. But so many deceptions on both sides are exposed that one is led to believe that the "price" of their decisions is a lifetime of discontent and self-deception, an ambiguity that makes it difficult to extricate good from bad faith in the situation.

Throughout Solomon serves as a balance wheel in the relations of the brothers, for the bargaining and assignment of money from the sale of the furniture is confused with the mixed-up and ambiguous feelings toward one another after nearly thirty years of resentment and separation. Solomon brings them back to reality from time to time. Walter stamps out angrily in the end, and there is no reconciliation, but Solomon reinforces the inexorability of human clashes by telling how he is haunted by the vision of his own daughter, who had committed suicide many years before, as a sign of his own failure in human relations. Though Solomon has learned to understand, he has paid the price in experience as Victor is now doing. Unlike fiction, life does not issue neat conclusions, but it may increase comprehension.

Thus in the end existential ambiguities remain in the relations of Victor and Walter. But in the end Miller's own common sense also asserts itself in the person of Solomon, to whom life remains meaningful despite its almost inevitable failures. Although Miller goes further than Bellow and Malamud into contemporary ambiguities, like these Jewish writers he too in the end endorses life. It is fitting that the exemplar of this assertion of life should be an old Jew.

Other Postwar Playwrights

"The situation of postwar drama was paradoxical," wrote Ihab Hassan. "It boasted the most challenging experiments while claiming the fewest figures of prominence."[157] These figures are limited to Arthur Miller and Tennessee Williams, while surviving dramatists of the 1920s and 1930s continued to produce. Numerous competent playwrights emerged after the war, and their work appeared in off-Broadway and later off-off-Broadway theaters, as well as regional theaters, all of which proliferated. Perhaps the competition of radio and television and the all-absorbing commercialization of culture somehow diluted dramatic talent. Whatever the reason, it is clear that, unlike the previous decades, high distinction in drama was more rare after the war. For a time Edward Albee raised a great stir, but the question remains if his promise was fulfilled. There were many Jews among the emerging dramatists, as in the other literary areas. The Jewish character also appeared regularly—perhaps more frequently than before, especially, but by no means exclusively, in the work of Jewish dramatists.

There were a number of anti-Nazi plays and some about anti-Semitism during World War II and in the years after. The successful and moving *Tomorrow the World* (1943), by the non-Jewish dramatists James Gow and Arnaud D'Usseau, concerns the twelve-year-old son of a martyred anti-Nazi German philosopher who comes to the United States during the war to live with his father's relative, a scientist. The boy, Emil, is a thoroughly indoctrinated Nazi, kept ignorant of his father's anti-Nazi convictions and mode of death, and manifests vicious anti-Semitism toward his Jewish school principal, who was the fiancée of his guardian. The boy recruits a German janitor into helping him steal his guardian's scientific work for transmission to the Nazis. He is caught, frightened, told the truth about his father's heroic anti-Nazi life and death. These traumatic experiences give promise of changing the boy, and his guardian keeps him to rear him with kindness and understanding. The play was gripping and fast-moving, thus succeeding in conveying the nature of Nazism as exemplified in concrete human relations. It can be imagined how effective it proved to be in the midst of war, and the ugliness of Nazi anti-Semitism was brought out.

Also exposing German anti-Semitism was the musical *Cabaret* (1966), based on the John Van Druten play *I Am a Camera*, by Joe Masteroff with music by John Kandor, which was in turn based on Christopher Isherwood's *Berlin Stories*. A German landlady in Berlin during 1929–1930 and her tenant, Herr Schultz, fall in love and want to marry. But when she discovers that he is Jewish, she refuses marriage for fear of losing her rooming house through this association. *The Diary of Anne Frank* (1955), dramatized by Frances Goodrich and Albert Hackett, spread even more widely the tragic waste of life and talent and unfathomable cruelty of the Nazi regime.

The Jew also figures in several plays about the war itself. *Home of the Brave* (1945), by the Jewish playwright Arthur Laurents, shows the eruption of anti-Semitism under stressful war conditions of engagement with the enemy on a Pacific island. The Jewish soldier, Coney, is profoundly shocked by his non-Jewish friend Finch, who is on the verge of Jew-baiting during a Japanese attack. Finch is then shot, and Coney feels joy at being safe. He then develops pathological guilt feelings because he interprets his joy as retribution when Finch is killed after nearly exposing himself as an anti-Semite. Coney's guilt brings on a hysterical paralysis, which is treated on stage by the use of the confessional drug pentathol that reveals to him the real cause of his joy—at his remaining alive—which he finally is persuaded is a common experience on the battlefield. Significantly, when the play was transposed to the screen a few years later, the victim of prejudice became a Black. By then the mass media were reluctant to broach the "controversial" Jewish problem.

But this caution did not obtain in the case of *The Caine Mutiny Court-Martial* (1954) by Herman Wouk, the author's own dramatization of his best-selling novel. The Jew in this play was a conservative, anti-intellectual lawyer and defender of the military establishment. How could such a figure be "controversial"? In any case the public knew Greenwald well after two years on the best-seller list.

The postwar years also saw the decline of the vaudeville and stage Jew, though not his demise. Vaudeville itself was fading out, and its place in comedy was taken to some extent by the radio sketch. This transition is in a manner symbolized in the extraordinary popularity and durability of Gertrude Berg's radio sketch about the Goldberg family. It played from 1929 to 1946, thanks to the depiction of Molly by Ms. Berg. She translated the matter of this series into a play, *Me and Molly* (1948), in which the trials, troubles, and small happinesses of Molly's family are dramatized: efforts to buy a piano by a marriageable daughter, all climaxed by the Bar Mitzvah of the son. The play is banal and sentimental but avoids individous humor.

Yet the Jewish stereotype did manage to survive in one way or another even though dialect comedy declined in acceptance. Not only were the audiences growing more sophisticated, but sensitivity to ethnic ridicule was heightened. In the theater of the 1940s and 1950s comic exploitation of the Jew continued in less objectionable form than before, and plays set in the Jewish milieu continued to be produced, despite the reluctance of the mass media like the movies to touch the sensitive nerve of the public concerning Jewish issues while awareness of Nazism was still fresh. What also happened was the emergence of the Jewish *shlemiel* as the vehicle for both comedy and symbolic comment on society, a new phenomenon in recent English language social thought and artistic expression.

Interest in the Jewish milieu in the theater continued. Something of a rapidly disappearing Jewish past was recaptured in Hy Kraft's *Cafe Crown* (1942), the name given to the actual East Side Cafe Royale, which closed its doors several years afterward. The cafe was, the author explains, "to the East Side what Sardi's and the Algonquin are to Broadway. It is the meeting and eating place for the Yiddish actors and actresses, the last cultured rendezvous of the cultured Jewish American, the country store of New York's ghetto." The play celebrates the last days of the great Yiddish stage and depicts its decline through the allure of Hollywood and Broadway to the younger generation of Yiddish actors. It exhibits the grandiloquent, flamboyant character of the older Yiddish male and female stars and their children on their way to Hollywood. Typical East Side characters move in and out of the cafe—the beggar (*schnorrer* on the model of Israel Zangwill's creation in "The Schnorrer"), who disdains nickels and dimes for grander largesse. There is the dominating, intimidating Jewish waiter, the unemployed playwright with "hundreds" of unproduced plays. The dramatist cautions, "Since all the characters in the play speak in the same idiom, no accents of dialects are necessary. Some of the people in the play, however, use a characteristic inflection."[158] As might be expected, this well-made play contains an abundance of nostalgia and sentimentality and recalls an important East Side situation.

Several other activities associated with Jews were noticed in the theater of the 1950s. The garment industry was the setting for Sylvia Regan's *The Fifth Season* (1953). She had authored *Morning Star* (1940), a social play under Odets' influence in which a strong Jewish matriarch on the East Side guides her family with awareness of the negative aspects of American life. In *The Fifth Season* she fills her play with stock characters of the garment center—the playboy salesman, the good-hearted tailor, the factory owner, the bright bookkeeper who is a German refugee. The play takes place almost totally in the Jewish milieu of the garment industry, but Jewishness is largely taken for granted. In Arnold Shulman's *A Hole in the Head* (1957), a play is set in a Miami hotel which a recent widower, Sidney, is unable to manage profitably and which is on the verge of bankruptcy. A loving relationship between Sidney and his teenage son is sorely tested when Sidney falls in love with a non-Jewish widow who had inherited a business in a small town in which Sidney and his son are loath to settle. There is reconciliation all around with the probability that Sidney will marry the widow and the son will stay with him. The play is superficial but clever; some of the talk is Yiddish-inflected. An interesting implicit aspect is the latter-day quite natural relationship between the Jew and non-Jew in the play.

The non-Jewish playwright William Inge was too serious about life's problems to treat lightly his Jewish character in *The Dark at the Top of the Stairs* (1957). He gives a searing lesson in the effect of anti-Semitism on a sensitive boy, and he ventures into the dark side of familial relations in a non-Jewish family. Samuel Goldenbaum is the son of a Jewish father and a non-Jewish mother, a divorced Hollywood actress. Samuel has been rejected by his mother and sent away to one military school after another. At one in Oklahoma Sammy gets acquainted with Reenie Flood, whose family's tensions are at the center of the play. Reenie is kind and tolerant and agrees to go with Sammy to a country club dance. At the dance the hostess crudely stops Sammy's dancing with her daughter, saying she "wasn't giving this party for Jews, and she didn't intend her daughter to dance with a Jew; and besides, Jews weren't allowed in the country club anyway."[159] Sammy desperately searches for Reenie but can't find her; he goes to a hotel in town and jumps out a fourteenth-floor window. Because Sammy had established a loving relationship with Reenie's ten-year-old brother Sonny, his death shakes the family. Sonny's deep feeling for Sammy becomes the agency for reconciliation of the family tensions. The play is grim, but showed Inge to be a dramatist of promise.

In a light vein was Leonard Spigelglass' *A Majority of One* (1959), which dealt with the problems of tolerance and intermarriage in the love and courtship of a Jewish widow of fifty-eight, Mrs. Jacoby, and a Japanese businessman, Asano. Mrs. Jacoby is accompanying her daughter and son-in-law on a trip to Japan where he is to serve on a trade negotiating team. They meet Asano on the boat, and he falls in love with Mrs. Jacoby and she with him. He turns out to be the Japanese trade negotiator. At first she rejects his offer of marriage but accepts him months later when he is in New York on United Nations trade matters for Japan. They agree to retain their own values and to respect each other's; they exchange knowledge of their respective cultures in food and other areas. In one passage Mrs. Jacoby and her son-in-law chide a Jewish neighbor for moving away from a neighborhood into which Blacks are moving. "I seem to remember," says the son-in-law, "that in this very neighborhood, years ago, they didn't allow Jews.... The only way you can stop prejudice is in yourself."[160] The play is really a modern middle-class fairy tale of tolerance, for both Mrs. Jacoby and Asano possess saintly understanding and goodness.

Popularity of the Jew in the theater undoubtedly reached a climax of sorts with Fiddler on the Roof (1964), book by Joseph Stein, music by Jerry Bock, and lyrics by Sheldon Harnick. It was based on Sholem Aleichem's fictional character of Tevye the milkman and was an instant, sensational popular success. Critical opinion was divided. Walter Kerr shrewdly remarked in his review of the opening, "It might be an altogether charming musical if only the people of Anatevka did not pause now and then to give their regards to Broadway, with remembrance to Herald Square." Was this musical "a fair approximation of Sholem Aleichem, or have I just heard the voice of 45th Street?"[161] But the public overrode discerning critics, as the public often does, and the musical became one of the longest-running hits in Broadway history. Indeed, its popularity quickly became world-wide so that by 1971 it had played in thirty-two countries in sixteen languages.

A few years earlier a dignified, moving, and generally successful effort had been made in an off-Broadway production of The World of Sholem Aleichem by Arnold Perl, with music by Serge Hovey, which captured something of the spirit of the shtetl with its humor and travail. It was a dramatized adaptation of several Yiddish stories: Sholem Aleichem's "High School," I. L. Pertz' "Bontshe Shweig," and folklore from Chelm. The adaptation was close to the original and inspired by total integrity to the life depicted. It was fortunate in its outstanding, sensitive actors, both Jewish and non-Jewish. The production evoked respect from the critics and the play was successful and has been revived since. The contrast with Fiddler is marked. On the one hand, it was a modest effort to render the subject faithfully without pressure or expectation of large monetary return: the objective was art free of commercial corruption. On the other, it was a sumptuous production at high cost dominated by the idiom of commercial musical theater with the necessity of commercial success to avoid great financial loss. The result in Fiddler was commensurable with these aims: a Yiddishized commercial musical score and wedding dances presented more in the sophisticated musical comedy style than in the traditional Jewish manner. Irving Howe has relevantly remarked, "they dance a *freilachs* as if they were stomping out a tune for *Carousel*."[162]

On occasion Sholem Aleichem does peep out when they use his actual lines. But one is hardly in the mood to appreciate them fully. An example of the approach can be drawn from the hit song, "If I Were a Rich Man." The title and idea is taken from Sholem Aleichem's story, "If I Were Rothschild" from *Tevye's Daughters*. But why did the lyricist choose for the content of this song another story, "The Bubble Burst"? In the latter story Tevye dreams of "a large house with a tin roof, . . . big rooms and little rooms, a yard full of chickens and ducks and geese. . . . Golde had the manners of a rich man's wife with a double chin and a neck hung with pearls. . . . She strutted around like a peacock giving herself airs, and yelling at the servant girls."[163] There is a basis in Sholem Aleichem, then, for the musical's song, but in *Fiddler* Goldie is converted from an arrogant, rich *baliboste* to a vulgar, nouveau riche American pretender to middle-class recognition. Why did the lyricist not choose rather to follow the story under the song's title? In "If I Were Rothschild," Tevye would "take my garbardine out of pawn"; he would buy a house "with three rooms"; he would stop "worrying about making a living"; he would "donate a new roof to the old synagogue"; he would build a hospital in place of the old poor house; he would create an interest-free society for the poor all over; he would "put an end to wars once and for all"; and, finally, he would "do away with money altogether."

Apparently the lyricist believed that a vulgar, unpleasant social climber not unknown in American-Jewish life would be easier to use in a Broadway song than the less blatant *shtetl* climber of more modest pretensions, let alone the humane aspirations represented in the titular story. The preference would appear to have been determined by a theater version of Gresham's Law—the more immediately apprehensible and popular crowds out the quieter, more genuine article. The result in the case of *Fiddler* is a worldwide dispersion of a somewhat factitious view of the *shtetl*. Yet, whatever its shortcoming, *Fiddler* was significant in making more evident the full acceptance of the Jew into the arts of the postwar period and the emergence of an abundance of talented Jewish writers who were no longer regarded as a peripheral manifestation in literature.

Among those who emerged in the theater of the 1950s perhaps the most noted was Paddy Chayevsky, who wrote for television and the movies as well as for the theater. Significantly Chayevsky, stressing a theme we have already observed in Bellow, Malamud, and Arthur Miller, affirmed, "I suppose my primary concern is the preservation of humanity in our increasingly dehumanized world."[164] Each in his way rejected the passive capitulation to the powerful alienating influences of the time which afflicted so many artists of the period. Early in Chayevsky's career this feeling led him to focus on bringing back the problems of working people into the arts. When his *Marty* (1954) appeared as a television play and then as a movie, it was widely hailed as breaking the current barrier to presentation of the working class in the arts, and as a swing from the almost exclusive preoccupation with the middle class. The movie of the working man, Marty, did do much to break what was almost a taboo against depiction of working-class life. However, unlike Odets and Arthur Miller, who in varying ways and degrees were concerned with social issues, Chayevksy dealt with the individual assertion of humanity through love. Yet in his very popular movie, *Network* (1976), he incited an anarchistic, spontaneous, unplanned, unspecified refusal on the part of the people "to take it any more" by verbal protest by the mass of unorganized individuals.

Two of Chayevsky's Broadway plays dealt with Jewish themes, *The Tenth Man* (1959) and *Gideon* (1961). Far more than Odets and Miller, however, he was influenced by the "entertainment" values of the commercial theater; this is evident in his resort, at times, to the humor of the wisecrack. *The Tenth Man* is a modern-day version of Ansky's *The Dybbuk*. At a small *shul*, some of whose worshipers' faith is dubious, one man is lacking for the *minyan* of ten at morning prayers. They drag off the street, as the tenth man, Arthur Carey. The granddaughter of one of the worshipers is schizophrenic, and a Kabbalist among the worshipers arranges for an exorcism by a rabbi. Arthur is himself in need of help, and calls his psychoanalyst for an appointment. He and Evelyn, who has come to submit to the exorcism, fall in love. An example of Chayevsky's occasional descent into triviality is Arthur's remark to Evelyn that "I left the Communist Party when I discovered there were easier ways to seduce girls." He believes Evelyn should undergo exorcism because he regards it as a form of psychotherapy. However when they are ready for the exorcism, it is Arthur, not Evelyn, who screams and falls to the floor. Thus he is exorcised of his despair and finds in Evelyn his hope for love. A final irrational note of social hopelessness is sounded in Arthur's final observation that "these are forlorn times.... The suicidal and the insane [that is, the types of Arthur and Evelyn] are all that is left to make a better life."[165] The only recourse for the individual, according to Chayevsky, is love in an individual enclosure. Considering the inexorable penetration of the social into individual life, the untenability, even superficiality, of such a view becomes evident. The dramatist cannot found this view on a solid reality, and the human relations in the play are contrived, with correlative injury to the play as serious drama.

In an attempt to adapt the biblical story of Gideon and his conquests to modern terms, Chayevsky again succeeds in trivializing the issues involved. Gideon is depicted as a very ordinary man and his victories as solely God's doing. Gideon is throughout ambivalent about his feelings toward God. At first, he believes in God; he then fears more than loves him; and in the end it is questionable if he loves God at all. Gideon is silly, especially at the beginning, particularly in his conversations with God, which are sometimes even ludicrous. At the end, he tells God, "I do not love you, God, and it is unreasonable to persist with each other when there is no love." In the course of the play the scholar and scientist Hezekiah questions the existence of Yahweh because only Gideon has seen or heard him. Hezekiah concludes that Gideon has invented God "to inspirit the troops." The Midianites, he maintains, were driven to war by "economic conditions, ... drought in the desert." For their part, he goes on, Gideon and his army went to wage war over "the need to protect our growing cities," to "increase the caravan trade." Gideon is influenced by this rational approach and finally tells his relatives there was nothing "mysterious" about the war with the Midianites. It was, he says, "the inevitable outgrowth of historico-economic, socio-psychological cultural forces prevailing in these regimes" which one takes to be a spoof of Marxist theory.[166] However, as an object-lesson in the decline of faith the play does not inspire confidence. It tries too hard to achieve "modern" effects. By the time Chayevsky died in 1981, he had become an enormously successful playwright commercially.

Most new plays were then being produced off-Broadway and in little theaters everywhere, while a lesser number were produced by regional theaters and on Broadway. But there were several new elements in the postwar theater. A number of new Black and female playwrights emerged in the wake of the civil rights and women's liberation movements. Both Blacks and women had brought out plays since the end of World War I but never before in such numbers and with such consistency of militance for their respective causes. Some Black playwrights like James Baldwin, Amiri Baraka (LeRoi Jones), Ed Bullins, and others showed how the postwar assertion of civil rights had brought out impressive talents. The same is true for the women who articulated the militancy of equality for women. Some Black women like Ntozake Shange vigorously presented the situation of Black women under the dual oppression of racism and male supremacism.

In addition to the usual fare of classical revivals, musicals, and conventional comedies, most of the serious plays of younger dramatists expressed the dark outlook of the troubled postwar world threatened by atomic annihilation and cruel wars for national economic purposes from which the superpowers sought economic and strategic advantage in the Third World. For the rest, individual plays by younger writers flashed across the scene, made a temporary impress, but seemed unable to sustain that achievement over the period that bespeaks the major playwright. Thus Jack Gelber, author of *The Connection* (1959), the extraordinary play about drug addiction which includes one well-sketched Jewish figure, has done nothing comparable since.

Many of the newer playwrights were Jewish, and Jewish characters appeared steadily on the stage. In the 1960s it became apparent that the traditional *shlemiel* figure of Yiddish literature, transposed into the novels of both Jewish and non-Jewish leading American writers, was also translated onto the stage. But in many of the run-of-the-mill plays, which comprised the greatest part of theater fare, this character takes the place of traditional stereotypes. What had happened in effect was a fusion of the Jewish vaudeville comedian with the traditional *shlemiel* to supply comic relief on the stage. Yet this is only one type of Jewish "comic image." Sig Altman's study of the "comic image of the Jew" found among all the Broadway plays from the seasons 1964–1965 to 1969–1970 that, of forty-five plays that contained Jewish characters, only five were not comic, and the characters of three of these were not American Jews. "The Jew," Altman concludes from this survey, "is increasingly a comic figure in the theaters often less than benignly conceived."[167] He dates this tradition in the American theater from the Potash and Perlmutter plays in 1913. While the crudely hostile stage Jew of past centuries is rarely met today, the tradition dies hard, and is replaced with a less blatant, less hostile "comic Jew" of the late twentieth-century drama. The devolution of the stage Jew is a fascinating subject that still demands analysis in detail and is still taking place. But as we have seen, since the 1920s the American theater has also offered many serious representations of Jews.

Altman seems to overstate his case when he includes *The Price* among those with the "comic image." True, as he says, the octogenarian Solomon "has all the laugh lines," while the brothers, not named as Jews though they could easily have been, "have all the drama." Altman suggests that "Jewish characters cannot be avowedly Jewish if they are intended to make a 'universal' serious point."[168] Aside from the fact that this is contradicted in recent theater history, with respect to *The Price* he misses the crucial role of Solomon, whose function in the play is precisely that. He represents the healthy, life-embracing opposition to the confusions and existential despair of the brothers. Nevertheless, Altman's thesis does apply to some aspects of the most recent American theater.

The comic mode of writing about Jews, whose results may be comic but not necessarily hostile, is often called "writing Jewish," and its modern master is Neil Simon, who emerged in the 1960s. Not all his plays have had specifically Jewish characters, but nearly all have been urban and New Yorkish. Martin Godfried has written that Neil Simon "is the most popular playwright in the history of the American theater"—if popularity is judged in terms of consistent size of the contemporary audience for his quick succession of plays. From 1961 to 1972 he produced nine hugely successful plays and musicals, and Godfried observes that Simon's "writing is closer to advertising copy than literature." Simon, he says, "can be extremely funny" and has a genuine folk sense, but this is submerged in his suburban middle-class themes. The content of his plays is "a homogenized world of middle class materialists. A real reason Simon has been so successful is that his plays reflect and support the life of their white, middle class audience," reinforced by his comic talent.[169] Perhaps the most successful play, *The Odd*

Couple (1964), does not specifically refer to Jewishness, but its ethnic over-tones in speech and mores is clear. The pair of divorced husbands who try to create a viable household has convulsed audiences and made a deep impression on the public. It abundantly confirms Simon's success in giving "entertainment." The durability of a play like this remains to be seen.

In the period after World War II the number of Jewish dramatists in-creased but the Jew as character received varied treatment, and there was a certain timidity about including the Jew in plays. However, when the conformist McCarthyite era ended and the almost paralyzing effect of the Holocaust had thawed, the Jew was presented on the stage with frequency by all sorts of dramatists, from the most serious like Arthur Miller to the most popular writers of comedy like Neil Simon. While the stage Jew vir-tually disappeared, the effect of anti-Semitism on the theater lingered in the much diluted and less ill-intentioned but nevertheless invidious image of the Jew as inherently comic. In one respect the Jew as *shlemiel*, as he appeared in the writing of important Jewish novelists as the vehicle for universal criticism of the state of society, or of a somber view of life in a comic version, is a valid image. But when the Jew was invoked on the stage merely to produce laughter, it was a survival of the bad old days.

Since the 1960s, however, the Jewish character has increasingly appeared in plays as a Jewish sense of ethnicity has spread more widely and penetrated more deeply into the new generations. This may in part account for the fact that Neil Simon resorted to several autobiographical plays during the 1980s, which also had more significant impact than his previous works and contain explicit assertions of Jewishness. *Brighton Beach Memoirs* (1984) is a patent treatment of his own early family life in which he represents himself as a growing youth with its tribulations. The play was treated with considerable respect by the critics who gave the New York Drama Critics Award for 1982–1983 to this heretofore enormously successful commercial play-wright. This play was followed in 1985 by *Biloxi Blues*, dealing with the young Eugene Jerome (Neil Simon) in an army camp as he meets challenges as a Jew from his fellow soldiers. The final play of the trilogy, *Broadway Bound* (1986), was a great hit and carries Simon's story to his emergence as a playwright. These plays have an underlying seriousness lacking in his others.

Simon was born in 1927 and arrived at this point rather late in his career. Perhaps one reason why he did so was the invisible atmospheric pressure from the work of many younger dramatists he must inevitably have felt from their preoccupation with the Jewish theme. Many of these younger writers were born around the time of World War II or even later. In fact the past few decades have seen the production of an accelerating number of plays, most often by Jewish dramatists, with Jewish characters and some pursuing Jewish themes. As Ellen Schiff has shown, "Jewish theater is a more vibrant and versatile force in our society than anybody had reckoned."[170] The frequency and volume of Jewish theater production has had a natural sequel in organization to further the tendency. American-Jewish theaters have sprung up in various parts of the country from New York to Los Angeles, leading to the formation of the Jewish Theater Association in 1979. In June 1980 a Jewish Theater Festival was held in New York, attended by several thousand. It showed without cavil that something new was happening in American theater, and more specifically in Jewish theater. In 1983 a conference on Jewish playwriting was held. That this movement is not confined to the United States but is international is indicated by the holding of the First International Conference and Festival of Jewish Theatre in Tel Aviv in 1982.

The basis for this fever of organization was fully justified by the fulfillment of the first requirement for drama—the emergence of a number of talented Jewish writers for the theater. Some of the older generation, born in the 1920s and 1930s, responded to the receptivity of the audience, a general and not only specific Jewish audience for writing about Jews and on Jewish themes. Not only Neil Simon (born 1927), joined the trend, but Arthur Kopit, born 1937; Woody Allen, born 1935; and Larry Gelbart, born 1928 are among this earlier generation who have written on Jewish characters and Jewish themes. Among those talented writers of a younger generation born in the 1940s and even later are Mark Medoff, born in 1940; David Mamet, born in 1947; Wendy Wasserstein, born in 1950; and Harvey Fierstein, born in 1954. Among these well-known playwrights are many who have won numerous drama awards. There is also a flock of perhaps lesser-known young playwrights. As a whole these dramatists are serious and too knowledgeable to produce stereotyped figures in their plays. They deal for the most part with personal conflicts in our troubled world. For them the Jewish stereotype is a matter of past history. One frequent theme, as in the American theater in general, is frustration in love.

Yet, to one who has lived through witnessing theater since the 1920s, it seems that something of basic value has been lost. Talented as these playwrights may be, none seems to have attained the stature of an Odets, or Hellman, or Miller, let alone an O'Neill. Will a longer perspective cause one to alter such a judgment?

Conclusion

As we end our study of the Jew in the country's literature in our century, we have witnessed a remarkable phenomenon. From a peripheral position in the country's literature at the end of the last century, we have seen Jewish writers grow in maturity, in talent, and in numbers, about mid-century to assume a leading position among the nation's writers. In time this became true not only of fiction but also of drama and poetry. Accompanying these developments also was the gradual erosion of the centuries-old invidious Jewish stereotypes.

In the course of the century there was also a flowering of vigorous, militant Black creative writing in all the genres. When this happened, it became apparent that a special literary relationship existed between Blacks and Jews as in society itself. The reasons are fairly obvious. The two groups have been paired objects of denigration by Christian whites. American history has shown how individual Jews have been among the allies of the Blacks and also occasional Black indulgence in Jew-baiting. For their part Jews have also been guilty of anti-Black prejudice. Yet, throughout, they have had a common interest in repelling discrimination that overhangs both groups (although immeasurably more oppressively over Blacks), and this moves the more far-sighted of both groups to perceive the persisting need for alliance. Since Richard Wright's *Native Son* (1940) and in some Black fiction for the next few decades this positive relationship was exemplified in a succession of novels of writers like John Killens, Paule Marshall, and others as well as some Jewish writers. By the 1970s, however, deep influence exerted by the social reality on literature was nakedly exposed. Estrangement ensued between many in the two groups when deep disagreements arose over such relatively new and more complex issues as affirmative action, wholesale removal of whites from leadership positions in the civil rights movement, and exacerbation of crime, all of which affected Jews. This temporary hostility was accordingly reflected in literature by the respective groups, as is amply demonstrated in the literature itself.

A connection can also be established between social life and humor, for in some respects humor is a ruthless expression of attitudes toward social status of the person or group aimed at by the humorist. There is much hidden history in humor in the United States in the changing forms targeted at the Jews. Traditionally Jews have long served as stereotyped comic figures. When Jews immigrated in large numbers, they joined other immigrant groups—the Irish, the Germans, and foreigners, generally—as comic figures by the self-designated "superior" American population. Such humor was often contemptuous and demeaning in the first few decades of the century, as "humor" magazines like *Life* and *Puck* only too fully illustrated.

The Jew was often caricatured by dialect humor. But with the virtual end of immigration in the mid–1920s and the growing acculturation of the second generation this type of humor tended to diminish until it was replaced by often benignly intended though condescending versions of Yiddishized or ungrammatical English in the writing of such writers as Arthur Kober and Leo Rosten in the 1930s. It should be noted that Yiddishized or ungrammatical English used in serious contexts does not necessarily detract from the dignity of the user. Following World War II the crisis in human affairs, when the world was in a state of shock at the barbarities of the war, the Holocaust, the multi-million war dead of many nations and, overhanging all, the threat of annihilation by the nuclear bomb, accompanied by infatuation with superficial, egotistical values of a new numerous middle class, led to a mood in which "black humor" could flourish.

Finally, the last chapter of this volume surveys the drama since 1900. As it developed, the drama grew in sophistication with the economic and cultural maturation of society, with an access of skill and technical competence as well and, at times, exhibited the decadence of a spiritually exhausted value system. New fresh currents came to expression during the second decade of the century and reached fruition in the 1920s. The stereotyped "comic Jew" or "stage Jew" which had been conventional on the Continental and British stage, was also taken over by the American theater during the nineteenth and twentieth century as the model for the depiction of the Jew. At the same time, in the second decade, one can witness the beginnings of breakdown of the stereotype with the dawning realization that the image of the Jew had been abused on the stage for centuries and that it was time to stop. The Jew began to be treated as an individual within the limits of the dramatist's talent and knowledge. However, the use of the Jew for "comic relief," benignly intended though it may at times have been, could hardly be said to have ceased.

Together with this gradual change toward rendering the Jew as a rounded human being came also an increase in the number and quality of Jewish playwrights. By the 1920s and 1930s Jews were numbered increasingly among the leading dramatists of the day. Many participated in the radical and labor theaters of the Depression 1930s in which Jews were characters more often than not. Of these playwrights, Clifford Odets was outstanding for his projection of lower-middle-class Jewish life. Eugene O'Neill, who had emerged at the very beginning of the modern American theater in the 1920s and was himself the prime example of it, was the towering figure of American drama and remains so. But of the many noteworthy playwrights other than O'Neill, the entire period following World War I and the early years of the modern American theater, many were Jewish. Harold Clurman once named four playwrights—Arthur Miller, Tennessee Williams, Lillian Hellman, and Clifford Odets—as the best since O'Neill, and I agree. (Williams never touched on the Jew in any of his plays.) Williams was the only non-Jew of the four.

Of the generation of dramatists born after World War II, it is too early to form any but the most tentative judgments. Yet it is true that a large number of unusually talented men and women have emerged, of whom a considerable number are Jewish. But to my knowledge none has as yet made the impact which the others named succeeded in doing. In recent decades Jews have appeared as characters in large numbers. The younger generation of Jewish playwrights participate in varying degrees in the swelling assertion of Jewish ethnicity. At the same time their acculturation becomes ever more complete without being converted to full assimilation and obliteration of Jewish ethnicity. This ethnic assertion has even led to the creation of specifically Jewish theaters in English in several metropolitan centers which encourage creation of plays with specific Jewish content. The weakening of the Jewish ethnic sense among the second generation evident in the first decades of the century has by now been reversed irrevocably, one may believe for the foreseeable future, and dramatization of intra-Jewish matters is becoming common. The present outlook for an ethnically oriented Jewish drama now seems favorable for the indefinite future.

Notes

1. SPECIAL BLACK-JEWISH LITERARY RELATIONS

1. Morris U. Schappes, *A Documentary History of the Jews in the United States, 1654–1875* (New York, 1950), pp. 18, 154.

2. Ibid., pp. 118, 597.

3. Ibid., pp. 327, 667.

4. Kate E. R. Packard, *The Kidnapped and the Ransomed* (New York, 1941 [c1856]).

5. Schappes, *Documentary History*, pp. 352 ff., 355.

6. Ibid., pp. 444 ff.

7. Yuri Suhl, *Ernestine Rose and the Battle for Human Rights* (New York, 1959).

8. Schappes, *Documentary History*, pp. 699–700.

9. Langston Hughes, *Fight for Freedom: The Story of the NAACP* (New York, 1962), pp. 23–27.

10. Nathan Hurvitz, "Blacks and Jews in American Folklore," *Western Folklore*, Vol. 23, No. 4 (October 1974), 303.

11. Ibid., p. 304.

12. Ibid., p. 307.

13. Ibid., p. 322.

14. Ralph Ellison, "The World and the Jug," *Shadow and Act* (New York, 1964), p. 117.

15. Richard Wright, *Black Boy* (New York, 1945), pp. 53, 54.

16. James Baldwin, "The Harlem Ghetto, Winter, 1948," *Commentary*, Vol. 5, no. 2 (February 1948), 168, 169, 170.

17. Richard Wright, "How Bigger Was Born," *Native Son* (New York, 1966 [c1940]) (paperback), p. 364.

18. Ibid., p. xviii.

19. Richard Wright, *Native Son* (New York, 1940), p. 163.

20. Ibid., p. 295.

21. Dudley Randall, ed., *The Black Poets* (New York, 1971), pp. 79–80.

22. Willard Motley, *We Fished All Night* (New York, 1951), p. 399.

23. Lorraine Hansberry, *To Be Young, Gifted and Black: Lorraine Hansberry on Her Own Work*, adapted by Robert Nemeroff with an introduction by James Baldwin (Englewood Cliffs, N.J., 1969), p. 177.

24. Ibid.

25. Ibid., p. 200.

26. Lorraine Hansberry, *The Sign in Sidney Brustein's Window* (New York, 1975), pp. 82, 96.

27. Ibid., Act II, Scene III.

28. Paule Marshall, *Brown Girl, Brownstone* (New York, 1959), pp. 253, 252, 253.

29. Ibid., pp. 194, 251, 254.

30. Paule Marshall, "Brooklyn," *Soul Clap Hands and Sing* (New York, 1961), p. 38.

31. Ibid., p. 61.

32. Paule Marshall, *The Chosen Place, The Timeless People* (New York, 1969), p. 142.

33. Ibid., p. 164.

34. Ibid., p. 262.

35. John Oliver Killens, *And Then They Heard the Thunder* (New York, 1963), pp. 173.

36. Ibid., p. 471.

37. John A. Williams, *The Man Who Cried I Am* (Boston, 1967), pp. 39, 203.

38. Ibid., p. 203.

39. Quoted, Robert E. Weisbord and Arthur Stein, "Negro Perceptions of Jews Between World Wars," *Judaism*, Vol. 18, No. 4 (Fall 1969), 437. This informative article is densely documented.

40. Ibid., p. 444.

41. Ibid., p. 447.

42. Claude Brown, *Manchild in the Promised Land* (New York, 1965), p. 92.

43. Ibid., pp. 284, 286, 288, 289.

44. Ibid., p. 326, 336.

45. Herbert J. Gans, "Negro-Jewish Conflict in New York," *Midstream*, Vol. 25, No. 3 (March 1969).

46. Louis Harap, "Anti-Negroism Among Jews," *Negro Quarterly*, Vol. 1, No. 2 (1941), 106.

47. Alvin H. Rosenfeld, "What to Do About Literary Anti-Semitism," *Midstream*, Vol. 24, No. 6 (December 1978), 46.

48. Nikki Giovanni, *Black Telling, Black Talk, Black Judgment* (New York, 1979), pp. 19, 38.

49. LeRoi Jones, "Black Art," *Black Fire: An Anthology of Afro-American Writing*, ed. LeRoi Jones and Larry Neil (New York, 1968), pp. 302–303.

50. Quoted by Rosenfeld, "What to Do About Literary Anti-Semitism," p. 46.

51. Werner Sollers, *Amiri Baraka/LeRoi Jones: The Quest for a Populist Modernism* (New York, 1978), p. 199.

52. Henry Dumas, "cuttin' down to size," *Black Fire*, pp. 661, 349–350.

53. Norman Podhoretz, "My Negro Problem—and Ours," *Doings and Undoings* (New York, 1964), pp. 364, 366, 370.

54. Irving Howe, "Black Boys and Native Sons," *A World More Attractive* (New York, 1963), pp. 98, 113, 112, 115.

55. Ralph Ellison, "The World and the Jug," *Shadow and Act* (New York, 1964), pp. 107, 112.

56. Ralph Ellison, *The Invisible Man* (New York, 1953) (paperback), p. 503.

57. Ellison, "The World and the Jug," p. 126.

58. Ralph Ellison, "A Very Stern Discipline," *Harper's*, March 1967, pp. 78, 79.

59. Bruce Jay Friedman, *Scuba Duba* (New York, 1967).

60. Stanley Schatt, "The Faceless Face of Hatred: The Negro and Jew in Recent American Literature," *Western Review*, Vol. 70 (1970), 50–51.

61. Jay Neugeboren, *Corky's Brother* (New York, 1969), p. 195.

62. Jay Neugeboren, *Big Man* (Boston, 1966), pp. 90, 165.

63. Saul Bellow, *Mr. Sammler's Planet* (New York, 1970) (paperback), pp. 9, 17.

64. Saul Bellow, *The Dean's December* (New York, 1982), pp. 193, 201, 207.

65. Evelyn Gross Avery, *Rebels and Victims: The Fiction of Richard Wright and Bernard Malamud* (Port Washington, N.Y., 1979), pp. 4, 93, 97.

66. Bernard Malamud, "Angel Levine," *The Magic Barrel* (New York, 1958), pp. 54, 56.

67. Bernard Malamud, "Black Is My Favorite Color," *Idiots First* (New York, 1963), p. 22.

68. Bernard Malamud, *The Tenants* (New York, 1971), pp. 229–230.

69. Israel Shenker, "For Malamud...," *New York Times Book Review*, October 3, 1971; Addison Gayle, Jr., "Controlling Black Images," New York *Amsterdam News*, January 1, 1972, p. D5.

70. Jerome Greenfield, "Without Hope," *The American Zionist*, January 1972, pp. 42, 44.

2. FROM DIALECT HUMOR TO BLACK HUMOR

1. Harry L. Newton and A. S. Hoffman, *Glicksman, the Glazier* (Chicago, 1904), p. 3.

2. *Puck*, Vol. 51, No. 1311 (1902), 6, cited by Rudolf Glanz, *The Jew in Early American Wit and Humor* (New York, 1973), p. 65.

3. "Stage Character of the Jew," *American Israelite*, vol. 47, No. 40 (April 4, 1901), reprinted from the *Indianapolis News*.

4. James Oppenheim, review of *Potash and Perlmutter*, *The Bookman*, Vol. 31 (March-August 1910), 631.

5. Sigmund Freud, *Jokes and Their Relation to the Unconscious*, trans. James Strachey (New York, 1960), p. 111.

6. Peter Gay, *Freud, Jews and Other Germans* (New York, 1978), p. 209.

7. *Isaac Asimov's Treasury of Humor* (Boston, 1971), pp. 211–212.

8. Anne Nichols, *Abie's Irish Rose*, in *S.R.O.: The Most Successful Plays in the History of the American Stage*, comp. Bennett Cerf and V. H. Cartmell (New York, 1946), p. 624.

9. Max Eastman, *The Enjoyment of Laughter* (New York, 1936), p. 132.

10. Leo Rosten, *O, Kaplan! My Kaplan!* (New York, 1976), p. xv.

11. Ibid.

12. Ibid., pp. 145, 147.

13. Ibid., p. 181.

14. Ibid., p. xvii.

15. Freud, *Jokes*, p. 90.

16. Ibid., p. 168.

17. Henry Popkin, "The Vanishing Jew of the Popular Culture," *Commentary*, Vol. 14 (1952), 46.

18. Ibid., p. 47.

19. Ibid., p. 48.

20. Ibid., p. 49.

21. Yuri Suhl, *One Foot in America* (New York, 1950), pp. 136, 31.

22. Anzia Yezierska, review of Yuri Suhl, *Cowboy on a Wooden Horse*, *New York Times Book Review*, October 25, 1953.

23. Freud, *Jokes*, p. 11.

24. Sig Altman, *The Comic Image of the Jew: Exploration of a Pop Culture Phenomenon* (Rutherford, N.J., 1971), p. 31.

25. Ibid., p. 13.

26. Ibid., p. 17.

27. Ibid., p. 119.

28. Ibid., p. 120.

29. Ibid., p. 107.

30. Freud, *Jokes*, p. 229.

31. Thomas Pynchon, *V* (Philadelphia, 1963), pp. 383, 384.

32. Postcards from Joseph Heller to Louis Harap, June 22, 1980, and July 24, 1979. In the chapter on Jewish writers in the *Harvard Guide to Contemporary American Literature* (1979), Mark Shechner wrote, "Yossarian (who in an early draft of Heller's *Catch–22* is Jewish...)" (p. 214). Shechner has written me that his source for this erroneous statement was Stephen Whitfield's "Laughter in the Dark: Notes on American Jewish Humor," *Midstream*, Vol. 24, No. 2 (February 1978), 5, whose original source was in turn James Nagel. "Two Brief Manuscript Sketches: Heller's *Catch–22*," *Modern Fiction Studies*, Vol. 20 (Summer 1974), 221–224.

33. Bruce Jay Friedman, "Black Humor," *Sense of the Sixties*, ed. Edward Quinn and Paul J. Dolan (New York, 1968), pp. 435, 436, 437–438, 438, 439, reprinted from Bruce Jay Friedman, *Black Humor* (New York, 1965).

34. Burt Blechman, *How Much?* (New York, 1961), p. 171.

35. Burt Blechman, *Camp Omango* (New York, 1963), pp. 182, 210.

36. Jeremy Larner, *Drive, He Said* (New York, 1964), pp. 75–76.

37. Ibid., p. 135.

38. Ibid., p. 190.

39. S. J. Perelman, *The Last Laugh* (New York, 1981), p. 158.

40. S. J. Perelman, *Crazy Like a Fox* (New York, 1944), p. 92.

41. Ibid., p. 202.

42. *The Most of S. J. Perelman* (New York, 1958), p. 599.

3. JEWS AS POETS

1. For a sketch of Emma Lazarus' life and work, see my *Image of the Jew in American Literature: From Early Republican to Mass Immigration*, (Philadelphia, 1974; 2d ed., 1978), pp. 284–299; and for other nineteenth-century Jewish versifiers, see pp. 261–262, 271–272.

2. Robert Alter, "Varieties of Jewish Verse," *Commentary*, Vol. 72, No. 1 (July 1978), 54, 50.

3. George F. Whicher, "Poetry After the Civil War," *American Writers on American Literature*, ed. John Macy (New York, 1934), p. 382.

4. F. O. Matthiessen, "Poetry," *Literary History of the United States*, 3d ed., 1-Vol., ed., rev., ed. Robert E. Spiller et al. (New York, 1963), p. 1335.

5. Louis Untermeyer, ed., *Modern American Poetry: A Critical Anthology*, 3d ed., rev. (New York, 1925), p. iv.

6. William Harmon, ed., *The Oxford Book of American Light Verse* (New York, 1979), p. xx.

7. Philip M. Raskin, comp. *Anthology of Modern Jewish Poetry* (New York, 1927), p. 9.

8. Kenneth F. Fearing, review of Raskin, *Menorah Journal*, Vol. 14, No. 4 (April 1928), 109.

9. Louis Untermeyer, "The Jewish Spirit in Modern American Poetry," *Menorah Journal*, Vol. 7, No. 3 (August 1921), 121–122.

10. Fearing, review of Raskin, p. 110.

11. Florence Kiper Frank, "The Jew as Jewish Artist," *Poetry*, Vol. 22, pp. 209–210.

12. Irving Malin and Irwin Stark, eds., *Breakthrough: A Treasury of Contemporary American-Jewish Literature* (New York, 1964), p. 3.

13. Ibid., p. 233.

14. Abraham Chapman, ed., *Jewish-American Literature: An Anthology of Fiction, Poetry, Autobiography, and Criticism* (New York, 1974), pp. xxiii, lxii.

15. Abraham Segal, "Foreword," *A Time to Seek: An Anthology of Jewish American Poetry*, ed. Samuel Hart Joseloff (New York, 1975), p. xi.

16. Ibid., p. xii.

17. Samuel Hart Joseloff, "Introduction," *A Time to Seek: An Anthology of Jewish American Poetry* (New York, 1975), p. xx.

18. Howard Schwartz and Anthony Rudolf, eds., *Voices Within the Ark: The Modern Jewish Poets, An International Anthology* (New York, 1980), pp. xxxiii, xxxi.

19. Ibid., pp. xxxi, xxxii, xxxvi.

20. The first published collection of Greenberg's poetry is *Poems by Samuel Greenberg*, ed. Harold Holden and Jack McManus, Preface by Allen Tate (Westport, Conn., 1971 [originally published in 1947]).

21. Philip Horton, "Identity of S. B. Greenberg," *The Southern Review*, Vol. 2, No. 2 (1937–1938), 423. (Horton tells the story of his discovery of Greenberg in "The Greenberg Manuscript and Hart Crane's Poetry," *The Southern Review*, Vol. 2, No. 1 [1936–1937], 148–159).

22. See, for instance, Marc Simon, "Samuel Greenberg and Hart Crane: A Study of the Lost Manuscripts," Dissertation, New York University, 1968.

23. *Poems by Samuel Greenberg*, p. xiv, also in text, p. 44. "The Glass Bubbles" was included, along with two other Greenberg poems, in *The New Pocket Anthology of American Verse*, ed. Oscar Williams (New York, 1955), pp. 219–220.

24. Samuel Greenberg, *Poems from the Greenberg Manuscripts*, ed. with a commentary, James Laughlin (Norfolk, Conn., 1939), p. 363.

25. *Poems by Samuel Greenberg*, pp. 11, 49, 112. For more on Greenberg, see

my article, "Mute Inglorious Miltons: Maimie Pinzer and Samuel Greenberg," *Studies in American Jewish Literature*, Annual II (1982), 11–14.

26. See Harold Bloom, "The Sorrows of American-Jewish Poetry," *Commentary*, Vol. 53, No. 3 (March 1973), 68–74.

27. Charles Reznikoff, "Kaddish," *By the Waters of Manhattan, Selected Verse* (New Directions/San Francisco Review, 1962), pp. 52–53.

28. Charles Reznikoff, "Hanukkah," *The Complete Poems of Charles Reznikoff, 1918–1936*, Vol. 1 (Santa Barbara, Calif., 1976), pp. 68–69.

29. Charles Reznikoff, *Holocaust* (Los Angeles, 1976), pamphlet.

30. Charles Reznikoff, *The Complete Poems of Charles Reznikoff, 1937–1975*, Vol. 2 (Santa Barbara, Calif., 1977), pp. 65–69.

31. Reznikoff, "The Hebrew of Your Poets, Zion," *Poems*, Vol. 1, p. 107.

32. Karl Shapiro, "The Jewish Writer and the English Literary Tradition," Part II, *Commentary*, Vol. 8 (1949), 370.

33. Karl Shapiro, "The Jewish Writer in America," *In Defense of Ignorance* (New York, 1960), pp. 207, 211, 212, 219.

34. Karl Sharpiro, "The 151st Psalm," *Voices Within the Ark*, p. 652.

35. Karl Shapiro, *Poems of a Jew* (New York, 1958), pp. ix, xi.

36. Ibid., "The Synagogue," p. 8; "Jew," p. 50; "The Alphabet," p. 76.

37. Ibid., "The First Time," p. 4.

38. Ibid., "Israel," p. 9.

39. Shapiro, "The Jewish Writer in America," p. 213.

40. Ibid., p. 212.

41. Irving Feldman, *Works and Days and Other Poems* (Boston, 1961), p. 101.

42. Ibid., "The Gates of Gaza," p. 94.

43. Ibid., "The Face of God," p. 95.

44. Ibid., "The Wailing Wall," pp. 96–97.

45. Ibid., "Assimilation," pp. 98–99.

46. Irving Feldman, *The Pripet Marshes and Other Poems* (New York, 1965), p. 35.

47. Irving Feldman, *Magic Papers* (New York, 1970), p. 14.

48. James Oppenheim, "Hebrews," *Modern American Poetry*, 3d rev. ed., ed. Louis Untermeyer (New York, 1925), pp. 303, 304.

49. Alter Brody, "Ghetto Twilight," *Modern American Poetry*, p. 428.

50. Ibid., "The Lost Leader (for C. E. R.)," *A Family Album and Other Poems* (New York, 1918), p. 128.

51. Ibid., "To Russia—1917," p. 128.

52. Kenneth Fearing, "Afternoon of a Pawnbroker," *New and Selected Poems* (Bloomington, Ind., 1956), pp. 111–112.

53. *The Collected Poems of Muriel Rukeyser* (New York, 1978), p. 3.

54. Ibid., "Chapman," p. 195.

55. Ibid., "Bubble of Air," p. 228.

56. Ibid., "Letter to the Front," p. 239; this is the title of the long poem from which the epigraph is drawn.

57. Ibid., "The Soul and Body of John Brown," p. 245.

58. Ibid., "Akiba," p. 425n.

59. Allen Guttmann, *The Jewish Writer in America: The Crisis of Identity* (New York, 1971), p. 128.

60. Louis Zukofsky, "Autobiography," *All the Collected Short Poems, 1923–1964* (New York, 1971), pp. 18–20.

61. Stanley Kunitz quoted in Chapman, ed., *Jewish-American Literature*, p. 325.

62. Stanley Kunitz, "Father and Son," *Selected Poems, 1928–1978* (Boston, 1979), pp. 157–158.

63. Ibid., "Journal for My Daughter," pp. 42–43.

64. Ibid., "Reflections by a Mailbox," p. 151.

65. Hyam Plutzik, "For T.S.E. Only," *Jewish-American Literature*, p. 338.

66. Hyam Plutzik, "The King of Ai," *Voices Within the Ark*, pp. 588–589.

67. Ibid., "On the Photograph of a Man I Never Saw," pp. 589–590.

68. Plutzik, "Portrait," *Breakthrough*, p. 232.

69. David Ignatov, "Noah," *Poems, 1934–69* (Middletown, Conn., 1970), p. 143.

70. Ibid., "Job's Anger," pp. 144–145.

71. Ibid., "Europe and America," p. 49.

72. Ibid., "1905," *A Time to Seek*, p. 111.

73. Ibid., "Kaddish," *Voices Within the Ark*, pp. 491, 492.

74. Howard Nemerov, "Lot's Wife," *The Collected Poems* (Chicago, 1977), p. 41.

75. Ibid., "Lot Later," pp. 263–264.

76. Ibid., "Moses, the Finding of the Ark," p. 165.

77. Ibid., "The Icehouse in Summer," pp. 232–233.

78. Ibid., "Boom," p. 222, 369–370.

79. Ibid., "Money," pp. 369–371.

80. Ibid., "Debate with a Rabbi," pp. 270–271.

81. Louis Simpson, *North of Jamaica* (New York, 1972), p. 87.

82. Louis Simpson, "Night in Odessa," *Adventures of the Letter I* (London, 1971), p. 16.

83. Ibid., "Meyer," p. 8.

84. Ibid., "Isadore," p. 11.

85. Ibid., "Adam Yankov," p. 12.

86. Adrienne Rich, *Jewish-American Literature*, p. 413.

87. Adrienne Rich, "Prospective Immigrants Please Note." *Adrienne Rich's Poetry*, ed. Barbara Charlesworth Gelpi and A. Gelpi (New York, 1975), p. 21.

88. Denise Levertov, *Contemporary Authors*, vols. 41–44 (Detroit, 1974), p. 563.

89. Denise Levertov, "Illustrious Ancestors," *Jewish-American Literature*, pp. 362–63.

90. Harvey Shapiro, "The Prophet Announces," *Battle Report* (Middletown, Conn., 1966), p. 46.

91. Ibid., "Death of a Grandmother," p. 55.

92. Harvey Shaprio, "The Synagogue on Kane Street," *This World* (Middletown, Conn., 1971), p. 50.

93. Robert Alter, review in *Commentary*, September 1975, p. 96.

94. John Hollander, "Graven Image," *Jewish-American Literature*, p. 430.

95. John Hollander, "Ninth of Ab," *Visions from the Ramble* (New York, 1965), pp. 19–21.

96. John Hollander, "At the New Year," *Night Mirror* (New York, 1971), pp. 38–39.

97. Ibid., "Letter to Jorge Luis Borges: Apropas of the Golem," p. 37.

98. Robert Mezey, *Voices Within the Ark*, pp. 544, 545.

99. Robert Mezey, "The Wandering Jew," *Door Wide Open: New and Selected Poems, 1954–69* (Boston, 1970), pp. 9, 10, 11.

100. Ibid., "The Great Sad One," pp. 47, 57–58.

101. Ibid., "Theresienstadt Poem," pp. 57–58.

102. Harold Bloom, "The Heavy Burden of the Past," review of *Voices Within the Ark*, *New York Times Book Review*, January 4, 1981, p. 5.

103. Bloom, "The Sorrows of American-Jewish Poetry," p. 69.

4. THE JEW IN DRAMA

1. M. J. Landa, *The Jew in Drama* (Port Washington, N.Y., 1968 [c1926]), p. 207. For a discussion of four early American-Jewish dramatists, see Louis Harap, *The Image of the Jew in American Literature: From Early Republic to Mass Immigration* (Philadelphia, 1974; 2d ed., 1978), pp. 261–269, and a sketch of the Jew as author and subject in United States dramatic literature in the nineteenth century, see also Chapter 9, "The Drama," pp. 200–239.

2. Arthur Hobson Quinn, *A History of the American Drama from the Beginning to the Civil War*, 2d ed. (New York, 1943), p. 156.

3. "Stage Character of the Jews," *The American Israelite*, Vol. 47, No. 40 (April 4, 1901), 1, reprinted from the *Indianapolis News*.

4. David Bloom, *Pictorial History of the American Theatre, 1860–1980*, new 5th ed., enlarged by John Willis (New York, 1981), p. 55.

5. Edward D. Coleman, comp., *The Jew in English Drama: An Annotated Bibliography*, with a Preface by Joshua Bloch, and "The Jew in Western Drama, An Essay and a Checklist" (1968) by Edgar Rosenberg (New York, 1968), pp. 147–150.

6. Ibid., pp. 160–163.

7. Douglas Gilbert, *American Vaudeville: Its Life and Times* (New York, 1940), p. 288.

8. Joe Laurie, Jr., *Vaudeville: From the Honky-Tonk to the Palace* (New York, 1953), p. 177.

9. Montefiore Bienstock, "The Hebrew Comedian," *The American Citizen*, Vol. 1 (1912), 314–317. Reprinted from *Reform Advocate* (Chicago), Vol. 44 (1912), 107–108.

10. Elmer Rice, *Minority Report: An Autobiography* (New York, 1963), pp. 73, 416.

11. Ibid., p. 416.

12. C. W. Hancock, *Down on the Farm* (New York, 1906), p. 53.

13. "Next Great Play on American Jew," *New York Telegraph*, May 9, 1908.

14. *Chicago Tribune*, January 10, 1909.

15. *Chicago Record*, January 10, 1909.

16. Unidentified Chicago paper, May 31, 1908.

17. Charles W. Collins, "The Drama of the Jew," *Theater Magazine*, Vol. 9, No. 96 (February 1909).

18. *American Hebrew*, Vol. 84, No. 18 (March 5, 1909), 475.

19. Augustus Thomas, *As a Man Thinks* (New York, 1911), p. 112.

20. Louis Lipsky, review of *As a Man Thinks*, *American Hebrew*, Vol. 89, No. 1 (May 5, 1911).

21. Review, *Current Literature*, May 1911.

22. Clayton Hamilton, review, *The Bookman*, January 1911.

23. "H.T.P.," review, *Boston Transcript*, February 27, 1912.

24. Edna Ferber, *A Peculiar Treasure* (New York, 1939), p. 218.

25. John Corbin, *Husband* (Boston, 1910), pp. 58, 216.

26. Theodore Dreiser, *The Hand of the Potter* (New York, 1918), pp. 196, 199.

27. Ludwig Lewisohn, review, *The Nation*, Vol. 113 (October 28, 1921), 762–763.

28. Edgar Selwyn, *The Country Boy* (New York, 1917 [c1910]), p. 58.

29. Arthur Hobson Quinn, *A History of the American Drama from the Civil War to the Present Day*, rev. ed. (New York, 1964), p. 104.

30. Joseph Wood Krutch, "Introduction," Eugene O'Neill, *Nine Plays* (New York, 1936), p. xi.

31. Arthur Gelb and Barbara Gelb, *O'Neill* (New York, 1962), pp. 854.

32. Ibid., p. 454.

33. Ibid., p. 360.

34. Ibid., pp. 448–449.

35. Ibid., pp. 550, 552.

36. Ibid., p. 548.

37. Ibid., p. 599.

38. Eugene O'Neill, "Lazarus Laughed," *Nine Plays*, pp. 388.

39. Ibid., p. 393.

40. Ibid., p. 479.

41. Ibid., pp. 480, 481.

42. Ibid., p. 382.

43. Ibid., p. 383.

44. Ibid., p. 393.

45. Ibid., pp. 401, 420.

46. Ibid., p. 468.

47. John Gassner, "Introduction," *Twenty-Five Best Plays of the Modern American Theater, Early Series* (New York, 1967), p. x.

48. Burns Mantle, ed., *Best Plays of 1925–1926* (New York, 1926), p. 160.

49. Rice, *Minority Report*, p. 104.

50. Ibid., p. 165.

51. Ibid., p. 200.

52. Elmer Rice, "The Adding Machine," *Representative Modern Drama, National and Local*, ed. Montrose J. Moses (Boston, 1925), p. 591.

53. Elmer Rice, "Street Scene," *Twenty-Five Best Plays of the Modern American Theater, Early Series*, p. 597; Rice, *Minority Report*, p. 416.

54. Scott Meredith, *George S. Kaufman and His Friends* (New York, 1974), p. 14.

55. Ibid., pp. 36–37. In her *Modern American Playwrights* (1966), Lois Gould gives a different reason for Kaufman's departure from the *Washington Times*. Munsey, she writes, "did not appreciate Kaufman's [columns'] quality of broad exaggeration, of brash, unadulterated attack on stupidity and narrowness. After a slight disagreement with the publisher over one of his verbal assaults, the future playwright

walked out of the Washington office, never to return" (p. 155). Considering the extensive nature of Meredith's research, his account is more likely to be correct.

56. Meredith, *George S. Kaufman*, p. 396.

57. Edna Ferber and George S. Kaufman, "Stage Door," *Best Plays of 1936–1937* (New York, 1937), p. 205.

58. Ibid., pp. 206, 210.

59. Meredith, *George S. Kaufman*, p. 198.

60. George S. Kaufman, "The Butter and Egg Man," *Best Plays of 1925–1926* (New York, 1926), p. 340.

61. George S. Kaufman and Edna Ferber, "The Royal Family," *Best Plays of 1927–1928* (New York, 1928), p. 83.

62. Ibid., pp. 112, 113.

63. Ring Lardner and George S. Kaufman, "June Moon," *Best Plays of 1929–1930* (New York, 1930), p. 252.

64. Moss Hart and George S. Kaufman, "Once in a Lifetime," *Best Plays of 1930–1931* (New York, 1931), p. 121.

65. Ibid., p. 122.

66. George S. Kaufman and Edna Ferber, "Dinner at Eight," *Best Plays of 1932–1933* (New York, 1933), p. 97.

67. Quoted, Meredith, *George S. Kaufman*, p. 439.

68. George S. Kaufman and Morris Ryskind, *Of Thee I Sing* (New York, 1932), pp. 4, 5.

69. George S. Kaufman and Morris Ryskind, *Let 'Em Eat Cake*, with lyrics by Ira Gershwin (New York, 1933), pp. 73–74.

70. Ibid., p. 208.

71. Meredith, *George S. Kaufman*, p. 464.

72. Harold Clurman, "A Reckless Preface," *Two Plays*, by John Howard Lawson (New York, 1934), p. xxiv.

73. John Howard Lawson, *Processional: A Jazz Symphony of American Life* (New York, 1925), pp. 182, 193, 2, 4, 6, 7.

74. Harold Clurman, *The Fervent Years* (New York, 1975), p. 100.

75. Rice, *Minority Report*, p. 394.

76. S. N. Behrman, *Serena Blandish* (New York, 1934), pp. 19, 38.

77. S. N. Behrman, "Rain from Heaven," *Theater Guild Anthology*, pp. 954, 913.

78. Malcolm Goldstein, *The Political Stage: American Drama and the Theater of the Great Depression* (New York, 1970), p. 118.

79. Arthur Hobson Quinn, *History of the American Theater*, 4:293.

80. S. N. Behrman, *The Cold Wind and the Warm* (New York, 1958), p. 165.

81. Quoted, Jean Gould, *Modern American Playwrights*, pp. 175–176.

82. Sidney Kingsley, *Men in White* (New York, 1933), p. 65.

83. Clurman, *The Fervent Years*, pp. 67, 150.

84. Ibid., p. 150.

85. Clifford Odets, "Waiting for Lefty," *Six Plays* (New York, 1939), pp. 27, 28.

86. Harold Clurman, "Introduction," "Awake and Sing," in Clifford Odets, *Six Plays*, p. 421.

87. Odets, "Awake and Sing," p. 57.

88. Ibid., pp. 100–101.

89. R. Baird Sherman, *Clifford Odets* (New York, 1962), p. 73.

90. Clifford Odets, "Paradise Lost," *Six Plays*, p. 174.

91. Ibid., pp. 127–128.

92. Clifford Odets, "Golden Boy," *Six Plays*, p. 249.

93. Clifford Odets, "Rocket to the Moon," *Six Plays*, pp. 416–417, 417.

94. Clifford Odets, "The Flowering Peach," *Best Plays of 1954–1955* (New York, 1956), p. 203.

95. Maxwell Anderson and Harold Hickerson, "Gods of the Lightning," *Twenty-Five Best Plays of the Modern American Theater, Early Series*, p. 539.

96. Sidney Howard, *Half Gods* (New York, 1930), p. 58.

97. Sidney Howard, "The Late Christopher Bean," *Best Plays of 1932–1933* (New York, 1933), p. 251.

98. Sidney Howard, "Dodsworth," *Best Plays of 1933–1934* (New York, 1934), pp. 122, 136.

99. Sidney Howard and Paul de Kruif, "Yellow Jack," *Best American Plays, 1918–1958*, ed. John Gassner (New York, 1961), pp. 462, 463, 464, 470.

100. Robert E. Sherwood, *This Is New York* (New York, 1931), p. 74.

101. Philip Barry, "Hotel Universe," *The Theater Guild Anthology* (New York, 1936), pp. 705, 704, 714, 717, 738.

102. Clurman, *The Fervent Years*, p. 314.

103. Michael Gold, "Money," *The American Scene*, ed. Barrett H. Clark and Kenyon Nicholson (New York, 1930), pp. 140, 143, 145, 149.

104. John Dos Passos, "Airways, Inc.," *Three Plays* (New York, 1934), p. 105.

105. John Wexley, "They Shall Not Die," *Best Plays of 1933–1934* (New York, 1934), pp. 252, 247.

106. Irwin Shaw, "Bury the Dead," *Twenty Best Plays of the Modern American Theater* (New York, 1939), pp. 746, 742.

107. Paul Green, "Johnny Johnson," *Twenty Best Plays*, p. 157.

108. Elias Lieberman, review of *The Unwritten Chapter* by Samuel Shipman and Victor Victor, *American Hebrew*, Vol. 107, No. 25 (November 5, 1920), 740.

109. William H. Spiegelman, "The Jew on Stage and Screen," *B'nai B'rith Magazine*, Vol. 43 (January 1929), 143.

110. Ibid.

111. Lenore Coffee and Joyce Cowen, "Family Portrait," *Best Plays of 1938–1939* (New York, 1939), p. 321.

112. Owen Davis, "The Detour," *Representative American Drama, National and Local*, ed. Montrose J. Moses (Boston, 1925), pp. 505, 504.

113. Martin Flavin, *Lady of the Rose* (New York, 1925), pp. 505, 504.

114. Dana Burnet and George Abbott, *Four Walls* (New York, 1928), p. 101.

115. Review in *Jewish Forum* (New York), Vol. 3, No. 10 (December 1920), 632.

116. Samson Raphaelson, *The Jazz Singer* (New York, 1925), p. 9.

117. Ibid., pp. 10, 60, 79. The jazz singer says, in discussing his singing style with the girl, that he feels like an "ostrich." "I feel like him with this black on," he tells her. "It covers your face and hides everything" (p. 110). Raphaelson here enunciates a theory about Jewish singers in blackface of that period that still has currency today and has reappeared in Irving Howe's *The World of Our Fathers*

(1976), who notes that, "Ronald Sanders, in a fine study, has suggested that blackface provided 'a kind of Jewish musical fulfillment' through a strain of 'ethnic pastiche.' When they took over the conventions of ethnic mimicry, the Jewish performers transferred it into something emotionally richer and more humane. Black became a mask for Jewish expressiveness, with one woe speaking through the voice of another.... Put Yiddish and Black together," Howe wrote, and in Isaac Goldberg's words, "they spell 'Al Jolson' " (Howe, *World of Our Fathers*, p. 563). To regard the "Mammy" singing style as "emotionally richer" than, say, the blues, is to mistake sentimentality for deep emotion.

118. Ludwig Lewisohn, *Adam* (New York, 1929), p. 8.

119. Howard Lindsay, *She Loves Me Not* (New York, 1935), p. 107.

120. Clare Boothe (Luce), "The Women," *Twenty Best Plays*, pp. 448, 450.

121. John L. Balderston and J. E. Hoare, *Red Planet* (New York, 1933), pp. 6, 44.

122. Ben Hecht and Gene Fowler, *The Great Magoo* (New York, 1933), pp. 26, 27.

123. Joseph Wood Krutch, review, *The Nation*, Vol. 135 (December 21, 1932).

124. Victor Wolfson, "Excursion," *Best Plays of 1936–1937* (New York, 1937), p. 355.

125. *The Theater Essays of Arthur Miller*, ed. with an introduction by Robert A. Martin (New York, 1978), p. 22.

126. Ibid., p. 232.

127. Ibid., pp. 53, 57, 62.

128. Ibid., p. 4.

129. Ibid., p. 123.

130. Harold Clurman, "Introduction," *The Portable Arthur Miller*, ed. Harold Clurman (New York, 1971), pp. xii–xiv.

131. Joel Shatzky, "Arthur Miller's Jewish 'Salesman,' " *Studies in American Literature*, Vol. 2, No. 2 (Winter 1976), 1.

132. Arthur Miller in *This Land, This People*, ed. Harold U. Ribalow (New York, 1950), p. 4.

133. *The Theater Essays of Arthur Miller*, p. 292.

134. Ibid., p. 119.

135. Arthur Miller, "They Too Arise," typescript, The Theater Collection, New York Public Library, quoted by Joel Shatzky, pp. 2–3.

136. *The Theater Essays of Arthur Miller*, pp. 130–131.

137. "Death of a Salesman," *The Portable Arthur Miller*, pp. 43, 79.

138. Ibid., p. 51.

139. George Ross, " 'Death of a Salesman' in the Original," *Commentary*, Vol. 11, No. 2 (February 1951), 184, 195.

140. *The Theater Essays of Arthur Miller*, p. 148.

141. Mary McCarthy, *Sights and Sounds, 1937–1956* (New York, 1956), p. xv.

142. *The Theater Essays of Arthur Miller*, pp. 154–155.

143. Ibid., pp. 156, 156–157.

144. Ibid., p. 173.

145. Leonard Moss, *Arthur Miller* (New York, 1967), p. 90.

146. Arthur Miller, Foreword to "After the Fall," *Saturday Evening Post*, February 1, 1964, p. 32.

147. Ibid.

148. Arthur Miller, "The Fitter's Night," *The Portable Arthur Miller*, p. 537.

149. Raymond Williams, "The Realism of Arthur Miller," *Arthur Miller: A Collection of Critical Essays*, ed. Robert Corrigan (Englewood Cliffs, N.J., 1969), pp. 72–73, 75.

150. Arthur Miller, Foreword to "After the Fall," *The Theater Essays of Arthur Miller*, pp. 255, 256, 257, 289. Critics have pointed out clear parallels of the material in *Incident at Vichy* to the fiction of Albert Camus, a leading existentialist of the period who enjoyed great vogue at the time. Cf. Leonard Moss, *Arthur Miller* (New York, 1967), pp. 94–96.

151. Arthur Miller, "Incident at Vichy," *The Portable Arthur Miller*, pp. 138–139, 289, 338–339, 340.

152. Bernard Malamud, "Angel Levine," *The Magic Barrel* (New York, 1958), p. 5.

153. Miller, "Incident at Vichy," *The Portable Arthur Miller*, p. 339.

154. *The Theater Essays of Arthur Miller*, p. 257.

155. Miller, "After the Fall," *Saturday Evening Post*, p. 40.

156. Arthur Miller, "The Price," *The Portable Arthur Miller*, p. 375.

157. *Literary History of the United States*, ed. Robert E. Spiller, et al., 3d ed., rev., 1-vol. ed. (New York, 1963), p. 1435.

158. Hy Kraft, *Cafe Crown* (New York, 1952), pp. 5, 4.

159. William Inge, "The Dark at the Top of the Stairs," *Best Plays of 1957–1958* (New York, 1958), p. 178.

160. Leonard Spigelglass, *A Majority of One* (New York, 1959), pp. 8–9.

161. Walter Kerr, *New York Herald-Tribune*, September 24 and October 11, 1964.

162. Irving Howe, "Tevye on Broadway," *Commentary*, November 1964, p. 73.

163. The passage from Sholem Aleichem's "The Bubble Bursts" is quoted from Henry Goodman, letter, *Jewish Currents*, Vol. 19, No. 5 (May 1965), 44–45. So far as I know, Goodman is the only one to point out that the contents of the song derive from this story.

164. Paddy Chayevsky, quoted, *Contemporary Dramatists*, ed. James Vinson (New York, 1973), p. 148.

165. Paddy Chayevsky, "The Tenth Man," *Best Plays of 1959–1960* (New York, 1959), pp. 65, 74.

166. Paddy Chayevsky, *Gideon* (New York, 1961), pp. 127, 122, 137.

167. Sig Altman, *The Comic Image of the Jew* (New York, 1971), p. 66.

168. Ibid., pp. 52, 53.

169. *Contemporary Dramatists*, p. 703.

170. Ellen Schiff, "The Greening of American-Jewish Drama," in *Handbook of American-Jewish Literature*, ed. Lewis Fried, forthcoming in 1988 from Greenwood Press. Professor Schiff's extensive work on recent American-Jewish drama, which she has studied exhaustively, provided the stimulus for these final observations on contemporary theater in these final paragraphs in my study. I wish to thank her for sharing her research with me while the responsibility for my observations is entirely my own.

Bibliographical Note

Once again I would urge, as I did in some detail in the Preface to *Creative Awakening*, the first volume of this series, the advisability for a genuine understanding of the course of the several genres sketched here, that an acquaintance not only with the literary history, but also the socioeconomic development of the period be studied as well as the history of the Jews in general and specifically also in the United States. How essential such awareness outside the immediate literary confines is for full grasp is patently evident in the first chapter of this book, in which we analyze the special literary relations of Blacks and Jews. A large number of studies of both Black and Jewish history during the period are available. Careful perusal of the issues which arose between the two groups in the late 1960s which temporarily impaired the long-standing alliance between the two groups and the whole train of events which preceded and followed will enlarge the view of the reader on contemporary writing.

In considering the Jews and humor, one is impressed with the extent to which personal taste colors one's conception. The best course is to become acquainted with as many approaches to the problem as feasible and thus to discover where one's own tastes lead. Sources for some of these notions of humor can be found in the notes to the chapter on humor. Perspective on humor in our own country can be found in Constance Rourke's classic *American Humor* (1931).

For aid in surveying the Jew as poet, the obvious need is to acquaint oneself as completely as possible with the history of American poetry. A useful compendium of work of Jewish poets in this century is the large anthology, *Voices Within the Ark: The Modern Jewish Poets*, edited by Howard Schwartz and Anthony Rudolph (New York, 1980), which contains nearly one hundred American-Jewish poets, as well as those from many other countries in English translation. A highly selective group of poems appears in the landmark volume, *Breakthrough: A Treasury of Contemporary American-Jewish Literature*, edited by Irving Malin and Irwin Stark (New York, 1964). Essays about some thirteen Jewish poets among the forty-one treated in Richard Howard's *Alone with America: Essays on the Art of Poetry Since 1950* (New York, 1969) could be helpful. The reader is cautioned that the number of Jewish poets is large and increasing rapidly, and the total number of American poets since World War II is very large. What specifically constitutes the Jewishness of a poem is even more elusive than this question in other genres because of its intrinsic relation to the word more intimately than in any other genre. This makes the question of what constitutes the Jewishness of poetry all the more controversial.

For any study of the Jew in drama in the United States the indispensable bibliography is Edward D. Coleman, comp., *The Jew in English* (that is, both British and American) *Drama: An Annotated Bibliography*, with a Preface by Joshua Bloch (original book publication by the New York Public Library, 1943); with "The Jew in Western Drama: A Checklist (1968)," by Edgar Rosenberg, and "Addenda to The Jew in English Drama (1968)," by Fola L. Shepard, with indices (New York, 1970). This work includes not only a bibliography of British and American plays but also references to critical articles and reviews of plays. For a sketch of four American-Jewish dramatists in the first third of the nineteenth century, see my *The Image of the Jew in American Literature*, pp. 261–269, and pp. 200–239. For a history of the stage Jew in English and American literature, the standard work is J. M. Landa, *The Jew in Drama* (New York, 1969) [c1926]). Especially useful for the Jew in recent drama is Ellen Schiff's *From Stereotype to Metaphor: The Jew in Contemporary Drama* (Albany, 1982). In addition to the extensive bibliography of recent plays themselves in the Schiff work is Edward D. Cohen, ed., *Catalogue of Plays of Jewish Interest*, 2d ed. (New York, 1981).

As has been the case for the entire series, the detailed bibliographical information in the footnotes serves as an aid to the primary materials, in addition to many secondary studies.

Index

Brown Girl, Brownstone (Marshall, 1959), 8–9
Brown, John, 2
Buber, Martin, Karl Shapiro follows on his idea of indistinguishable sacred and profane, 59
Bullins, Ed, 16–17, 138
Burnet, Dana, and George Abbott, *Four Walls* (1927), 115–16; ex-convict attains moral freedom, 116
Bury the Dead (Shaw, 1936), 112

Cabaret (Joe Masteroff, 1966), anti-Nazi musical, 132
Caine Mutiny Court Martial, The (Wouk, 1954), 132–33
Cafe Crown (Kraft, 1942), 133
Call It Sleep (Henry Roth), 111
Camus, Albert, and Arthur Miller, 129–30
Carmichael, Stokely, 14
Carruthers, Hayden, 68
Catch–22 (Heller, 1961), 41
Cather, Willa, comments on *Potash and Perlmutter*, 31
Chaney, James, 4
Chapman, Abraham, analysis of Jewish writing, 53–54; ed. *Jewish-American Literature: An Anthology of Fiction, Poetry, Autobiography, and Criticism* (1974), 53–54
Chayevsky, Paddy, 136–38; concerned about current mood of despair, 138; not concerned with topical social issues, 137; *Gideon* (1961), 137–38; his modern *Dybbuk*, 137; influenced by "entertainment" values, 137; *Marty* (1954, movie), 137; *The Tenth Man* (1959), 137
Cheating Cheaters (Marcin, 1916), 80
Chesnutt, Charles Waddell, 20
Chosen Place, The Timeless People, The (Marshall, 1969), 9
Clurman, Harold, on four leading dramatists since O'Neill, 84; and Arthur Miller, 122, 126; and John Howard Lawson, 94, 95; and Odets,

94; says, by 1935 Odets central left dramatist, 100, 101
Coffee, Lenore, and Joyce Cowen, *Family Portrait* (1939), Jesus and his family in modern dress, 115
Cold Wind and the Warm, The (Behrman, 1958), 98
Cominsky, Mrs. Lena, sister of Emma Goldman, 82; motherly comfort to O'Neill, 82
Commentary, 36
Conference on Jewish Playwrights (1983), 141
Congress of Racial Equality (CORE), 14; and "Black Power," 14
Corbin, John, *Husband* (1910), "advanced" Jewish woman on the stage, 78
Cormack, Bartlett, *The Rocket* (1927), 116
Crane, Hart, and Samuel Greenberg, 56–57; uses Greenberg material in "Voyages," "White Buildings," 57
Crothers, Rachel, *A Little Journey* (1918), friendly picture of Jewish man, 78
Crucible, The (Miller, 1953), 125
Current Literature (1909), interest in question of intermarriage, 76

Dark at the Top of the Stairs, The (Inge, 1957), 134
Davis, Allen, *The Promised Land* (1908), play about Herzl and Zionism, 75
Davis, Owen, *The Detour* (1921), 115
Day, Dorothy, and Eugene O'Neill, 82
Dean's December, The (Bellow, 1982), 24–25, 123
Death of a Salesman (Miller, 1949), 122, 124
Deutsch, Babette, 51
Diary of Anne Frank, The, dramatized by Frances Goodrich and Albert Hackett (1955), 132
Dinner at Eight (Kaufman, with Ferber, 1932), 92
Dodsworth (Howard, 1934), 107

The Modern Jewish Poets, An International Anthology (1980), 54; Orthodox orientation, 55

Schwerner, Michael, 4

Selwyn, Edgar, The Country Boy (1917), not a stereotyped Jew, 80

Sforim, Mendele Mocher, concept of shlemiel, 40

Shange, Ntozake, Black women and male supremacism, 138

Shapiro, Harvey, 53; Battle Report (1966), 68; "Death of a Grandmother," 68–69; influenced by Objectivism, 68; many poems with Jewish themes, 68; "The Prophet Announces," 68; "The Synagogue on Kane Street," 69; translates poem from Yiddish, 66

Shapiro, Karl, 49, 50; "The Alphabet," 60; Bollingen Prize for Poetry, 1969, 50, 53, 54, 58, 79; and Buber, 59; editor, Poetry Magazine, 52; and Ezra Pound's anti-Semitism, 59; "The First Time," 60; Israel," 60; "The Jewish Writer in America" (essay), 59; Poems of a Jew (1958), 59; Poetry Consultant for Library of Congress, 50; receives Pulitzer Prize for Poetry, 1945, 50; rejects "sociological Judaism," 60; "The Synagogue," 60; and T. S. Eliot's anti-Semitism, 59; votes to reject Bollingen Prize for Pound, 59; "151st Psalm," 59

Shaw, Irwin, Bury the Dead (1936), anti-fascist play, 112; The Gentle People (1939), resistance to U.S. fascists, 112–13

Sherwood, Robert E., 87, 108–9; This Is New York, 109

Shipman, Samuel, and Victor Victor, The Unwritten Chapter (1920), erroneous view of Haym Solomon in Revolution, 113

Shlemiel, examples of: in Bellow, Don Quixote, Malamud ("The Last Mohican"), Mendele, Peretz, Sholem Al-

eichem, 40; in "black humor," 40–41; in Bruce Jay Friedman's Stern (1962), 43; in A Mother's Kisses (Friedman, 1964), 43; shlemiel figure dominates 1960s fiction, 138, 139, 140

Shulman, Arnold, A Hole in the Head (1957), play about failing Miami hotel owner, 134

Sign in Sidney Brustein's Window, The (Hansberry, 1964), 7–8

Simon, Neil, 139–41; more substance in Brighton Beach trilogy, 140; most popular playwright, 139; The Odd Couple (1964), 139–40; suburban middle-class themes of, 139

Simpson, Louis, 50; "Adam Yankov," 68; decided he was a Jew, 67, 68; late realization he was half-Jewish, 67; "Meyer," 67–68; "A Night in Odessa," 67; Pulitzer Prize for Poetry, 1964, 50

Sondheim, Stephen, 50

Spewack, Samuel, and Bella Cohen, Poppa (1928), comic distortion of East Side life, 114

Spigelglass, Leonard, A Majority of One (1959), fairy-tale play about Jewish middle-class tolerance, 134

Stage Jew, protests against, 72; fantasy protest against, 73; stage directions of "Jew's" costume, 74

Stern (Bruce Jay Friedman, 1962), 43

Stevens, Wallace, 57

Stoller, Werner, 16

Street Scene (Rice, 1926), 79, 88

Student Non-Violent Coordinating Committee (SNCC), and "Black Power," 14

Suhl, Yuri, benign immigrant Jewish humor by, 37; Anzia Yezierska on, in review, 37–38; Cowboy on a Wooden Horse (1953), 37; One Foot in America (1950), 37

Tate, Allen, writes Preface to Samuel Greenberg's poems, 1944, 57

Tenants, The (Malamud, 1984), 25, 26, 27
Tenth Man, The (Chayevsky, 1959), 137
Theater Guild, 82
Theater Magazine, 76
They Shall Not Die (Wexley, 1934), 112
Thomas, Augustus, starts discussion of great play with an American Jew (1908), 75; *As a Man Thinks* (1911), 77; describes this type of character, 75–76; his own play (1911) fails to confront issues, 77; repeats call in Chicago, 76; warnings against flattery of Jew, 76; widely discussed in press, 76
Time to Seek: An Anthology of Contemporary Jewish American Poetry, A (Joseloff, ed., 1975), 54
Traubel, Horace, 48, 49
Treasury of Yiddish Poets, A (Howe, with Greenberg), 66

Union of American Hebrew Congregations (Reform), sponsor Jewish poetry anthology, 54
Untermeyer, Jean Starr, 51, 61
Untermeyer, Louis: edits *Modern American Poetry: A Critical Anthology* (1919), 49; Fearing critique of his conception of Jewish poetry, 51; a founding editor of *The Masses* (1911), 62; *Leviathan* (1923), 61; many editions, 49, 51; poem in *The Lyric Year*, 49

Van Druten, John, *I Am a Camera*, anti-Nazi play, 132
Voices Within the Ark: The Modern Jewish Poets, An International Anthology (Schwartz and Rudolf, eds., 1980), 54

Waiting for Lefty (Odets, 1935), 101, 102
Wasserstein, Wendy, 141

Watch on the Rhine (Hellman, 1941), 99
West, Nathanael: anticipations of "black humor," 40; *The Day of the Locust* (1939), 40; *Miss Lonelyhearts* (1933), 40
Wexley, John, *They Shall Not Die* (1934), accurate portrayal of Sacco-Vanzetti trial, 112; Jews in legal defense, 112
What Price Glory? (Anderson with Stallings, 1924), 106
Whicher, George, on Emma Lazarus, 48
Weitzenkorn, Louis, *Five Star Final* (1930), about unscrupulous Jew, 119
Williams, John A., 11–12; *The Man Who Cried I Am* (novel, 1967), 11–12
Williams, Raymond, gives Marxist perspective on Arthur Miller, 127–28
Williams, Tennessee, no Jews in his plays, 84, 86, 131
Williams, William Carlos, 57
Winterset (Anderson, 1935), 106–7
Wise, Rabbi Isaac M., 47
Wise, Rabbi Stephen S., 2
Wolfson, Victor, *Excursion* (1937), 120
World of Sholem Aleichem, The, by Arnold Perl (book) and Serge Hovey (music): based on several Yiddish stories, 135; favorably contrasted with *Fiddler on the Roof*, 135
World War II: changes in U.S. after, 120–21; Off-Broadway movement, 121; theater production more costly after, 121
Wouk, Herman, *The Caine Mutiny Court Martial* (1954), anti-war play, 132–33
Wright, Richard, 13; and Bigger Thomas' motive for murder, 5; model for "protest" novel, 13, 25; *Native Son* (1940), 5–6, 7, 18

About the Author

LOUIS HARAP received his A.B. and Ph.D. from Harvard University. He is the former editor of *Jewish Life* and is currently on the editorial board of *Jewish Currents*. He is the author of *Creative Awakening: The Jewish Presence in Twentieth-Century American Literature, 1900–1940s* and *In the Mainstream: The Jewish Presence in Twentieth-Century American Literature, 1950s–1980s* (both published by Greenwood Press, 1987), *Social Roots of the Arts*, and *The Image of the Jew in American Literature: From Early Republic to Mass Immigration* (1974). His articles have appeared in *Journal of Ethnic Studies, Science and Society, Jewish Currents*, and numerous other journals.